Pop Culture
and the Everyday
in Japan

JAPANESE SOCIETY SERIES
General Editor: Yoshio Sugimoto

Lives of Young Koreans in Japan
Yasunori Fukuoka

Globalization and Social Change in Contemporary Japan
J.S. Eades, Tom Gill and Harumi Befu

Coming Out in Japan: The Story of Satoru and Ryuta
Satoru Ito and Ryuta Yanase

Japan and Its Others:
Globalization, Difference and the Critique of Modernity
John Clammer

Hegemony of Homogeneity: An Anthropological Analysis of Nihonjinron
Harumi Befu

Foreign Migrants in Contemporary Japan
Hiroshi Komai

A Social History of Science and Technology in Contempory Japan, Volume 1
Shigeru Nakayama

Farewell to Nippon: Japanese Lifestyle Migrants in Australia
Machiko Sato

The Peripheral Centre:
Essays on Japanese History and Civilization
Johann P. Arnason

A Genealogy of 'Japanese' Self-images
Eiji Oguma

Class Structure in Contemporary Japan
Kenji Hashimoto

An Ecological View of History
Tadao Umesao

Nationalism and Gender
Chizuko Ueno

Native Anthropology: The Japanese Challenge to Western Academic Hegemony
Takami Kuwayama

Youth Deviance in Japan: Class Reproduction of Non-Conformity
Robert Stuart Yoder

Japanese Companies: Theories and Realities
Masami Nomura and Yoshihiko Kamii

From Salvation to Spirituality: Popular Religious Movements in Modern Japan
Susumu Shimazono

The 'Big Bang' in Japanese Higher Education:
The 2004 Reforms and the Dynamics of Change
J.S. Eades, Roger Goodman and Yumiko Hada

Japanese Politics: An Introduction
Takashi Inoguchi

A Social History of Science and Technology in Contempory Japan, Volume 2
Shigeru Nakayama

Gender and Japanese Management
Kimiko Kimoto

Philosophy of Agricultural Science: A Japanese Perspective
Osamu Soda

A Social History of Science and Technology in Contempory Japan, Volume 3
Shigeru Nakayama and Kunio Goto

Japan's Underclass: Day Laborers and the Homeless
Hideo Aoki

A Social History of Science and Technology in Contemporary Japan, Volume 4
Shigeru Nakayama and Hitoshi Yoshioka

Scams and Sweeteners: A Sociology of Fraud
Masahiro Ogino

Toyota's Assembly Line: A View from the Factory Floor
Ryoji Ihara

Village Life in Modern Japan: An Environmental Perspective
Akira Furukawa

Social Welfare in Japan: Principles and Applications
Kojun Furukawa

Escape from Work: Freelancing Youth and the Challenge to Corporate Japan
Reiko Kosugi

Japan's Whaling: The Politics of Culture in Historical Perspective
Hiroyuki Watanabe

Gender Gymnastics: Performing and Consuming Japan's Takarazuka Revue
Leonie R. Stickland

Poverty and Social Welfare in Japan
Masami Iwata and Akihiko Nishizawa

The Modern Japanese Family: Its Rise and Fall
Chizuko Ueno

Widows of Japan: An Anthropological Perspective
Deborah McDowell Aoki

In Pursuit of the Seikatsusha:
A Genealogy of the Autonomous Citizen in Japan
Masako Amano

Demographic Change and Inequality in Japan
Sawako Shirahase

The Origins of Japanese Credentialism
Ikuo Amano

Pop Culture and the Everyday in Japan: Sociological Perspectives
Katsuya Minamida and Izumi Tsuji

Social Stratification and Inequality Series

Inequality amid Affluence: Social Stratification in Japan
Junsuke Hara and Kazuo Seiyama

Intentional Social Change: A Rational Choice Theory
Yoshimichi Sato

Constructing Civil Society in Japan: Voices of Environmental Movements
Koichi Hasegawa

Deciphering Stratification and Inequality: Japan and beyond
Yoshimichi Sato

Social Justice in Japan: Concepts, Theories and Paradigms
Ken-ichi Ohbuchi

Gender and Career in Japan
Atsuko Suzuki

Status and Stratification: Cultural Forms in East and Southeast Asia
Mutsuhiko Shima

Globalization, Minorities and Civil Society:
Perspectives from Asian and Western Cities
Koichi Hasegawa and Naoki Yoshihara

Fluidity of Place: Globalization and the Transformation of Urban Space
Naoki Yoshihara

Advanced Social Research Series

A Sociology of Happiness
Kenji Kosaka

Frontiers of Social Research: Japan and beyond
Akira Furukawa

A Quest for Alternative Sociology
Kenji Kosaka and Masahiro Ogino

MODERNITY AND IDENTITY IN ASIA SERIES

Globalization, Culture and Inequality in Asia
Timothy S. Scrase, Todd Miles, Joseph Holden and Scott Baum

Looking for Money:
Capitalism and Modernity in an Orang Asli Village
Alberto Gomes

Governance and Democracy in Asia
Takashi Inoguchi and Matthew Carlson

Liberalism: Its Achievements and Failures
Kazuo Seiyama

Health Inequalities in Japan: An Empirical Study of Older People
Katsunori Kondo

Pop Culture and the Everyday in Japan
Sociological Perspectives

Edited by

Katsuya Minamida
and
Izumi Tsuji

Translated by
Leonie R. Stickland

Trans Pacific Press
Melbourne

First published in Japanese in 2008 by Minerva Shobō as *Bunka Shakaigaku No Shiza – Nomerikomu Media Bunka to Soko ni Aru Nichijo No Bunka*. Copyright © 2008 by Katsuya Minamida, Izumi Tsuji. English translation rights arranged with Minerva Shobō through Japan UNI Agency, Inc., Tokyo.

First published in English in 2012 by:
Trans Pacific Press, PO Box 164, Balwyn North, Victoria 3104, Australia
Telephone: +61 (0)3 9859 1112 Fax: +61 (0)3 8611 7989
Email: tpp.mail@gmail.com
Web: http://www.transpacificpress.com

Copyright © Trans Pacific Press 2012

Designed and set by Digital Environs, Melbourne, Australia. www.digitalenvirons.com

Printed by BPA Print Group, Burwood, Victoria, Australia

Distributors

Australia and New Zealand
DA Information Services/Central Book Services
648 Whitehorse Road
Mitcham, Victoria 3132
Australia
Telephone: +61-(0)3-9210-7777
Fax: + 61-(0)3-9210-7788
Email: books@dadirect.com
Web: www.dadirect.com

USA and Canada
International Specialized Book Services (ISBS)
920 NE 58th Avenue, Suite 300
Portland, Oregon 97213-3786
USA
Telephone: 1-800-944-6190
Fax: 1-503-280-8832
Email: orders@isbs.com
Web: http://www.isbs.com

Asia and the Pacific
Kinokuniya Company Ltd.
Head office:
3-7-10 Shimomeguro
Meguro-ku
Tokyo 153-8504
Japan
Telephone: +81-(0)3-6910-0531
Fax: +81-(0)3-6420-1362
Email: bkimp@kinokuniya.co.jp
Web: www.kinokuniya.co.jp
Asia-Pacific office:
Kinokuniya Book Stores of Singapore Pte., Ltd.
391B Orchard Road #13-06/07/08
Ngee Ann City Tower B
Singapore 238874
Telephone: +65-6276-5558
Fax: +65-6276-5570
Email: SSO@kinokuniya.co.jp

All rights reserved. No reproduction of any part of this book may take place without the written permission of Trans Pacific Press.

ISSN   1443–9670 (Japanese Society Series)
ISBN   978–1–920901–45–5

Cover illustration: Vocaloid 2 characters Rin and Len Kagamine, © Crypton Future Media, Inc., illustrated by Mathurin Julphuthiphong.

Contents

Figures	ix
Tables	xi
Contributors	xii
Acknowledgments	xvi
Preface: what is the appeal of the sociology of culture? *Katsuya Minamida and Izumi Tsuji*	xviii

Part I: Approaches to Culture

1 Introduction: the scope of the sociology of culture *Katsuya Minamida and Izumi Tsuji* — 3

2 Perspectives on media-and-group culture: from an empirical/critical approach to a multi-method approach *Izumi Tsuji* — 14

3 Perspectives on expressive culture: what do cultural works give people, and how do they link people together? *Katsuya Minamida* — 36

4 Perspectives on the culture of generations and life-phases: the quantitative approach and qualitative approach *Daisuke Tsuji* — 61

Part II: Addictive Media Culture — 81

5 Why do people become addicted to mobile phones?: the sociology of email communication *Kensuke Suzuki* — 83

6 How has the style of television viewing changed?: the active receiver and the transformation of the subversive riposte *Keiichi Nabe* — 105

7 Where is differentiated communication heading?: through analysis of the readers' column in the fashion magazine, *CUTiE* *Sōichirō Matsutani* — 122

8 Why make e-*moe*-tional attachments to fictional characters?: the cultural sociology of the post-modern *Yoshimasa Kijima* — 149

9 Why do people gather at rock festivals?: communication mediated by music *Jun'ichi Nagai* — 171

Part III: Immediate Everyday Life   193

10 What are contemporary aspects of the parent/child relationship?: mother/daughter friendship and its social context *Yasuko Nakanishi*   195

11 Is 'poverty' or 'affluence' the reality?: towards consideration of 'living in the regions' *Hisashi Fujii*   218

12 What is at question in youth labour issues?: the two phases of specialisation, 'manual-based' and 'qualified' *Masahiro Abe*   247

13 What does it mean to be a 'Japanese'?: the current state of 'national identity' in Japan, based on ISSP 2003 *Shunsuke Tanabe*   260

Bibliography   282
Index   297

Figures

2.1:	Fans of male idols gathered at a concert venue	15
2.2:	Kazumasa Oda's 'Rabu sutōrī wa totsuzen ni (A love story, suddenly)'	21
2.3:	Schematic diagram of the multi-method approach	30
2.4:	Examples of multi-method approach analysis	30
2.5:	Visual-*kei* rock band fans gathered at Jingu Bridge (Jingū-bashi) in front of Harajuku Station	33
3.1:	A) The 'person–work' relationship	39
3.2:	B) The 'person–work–person' relationship	39
3.3:	Patrilineal/matrilineal kinship structures	49
3.4:	Burgess' concentric zone model	50
3.5:	Relationship model of cultural taste groups, exemplified by Japanese rock music	51
5.1:	Number of mail messages sent and received per day	97
5.2:	I reply promptly to mail from friends	97
5.5:	Mobile dependence and mail usage frequency	98
5.6:	Frequent checking for incoming mail and fear of loneliness	99
5.7:	Anxiety over signal condition and fear of loneliness	100
5.8:	Immediate reply to mail and fear of loneliness	100
6.1:	Street television in the early 1950s	113
6.2:	The three types of television viewing	119
7.1:	*CUTiE*, March 2008	130
7.2:	*Popteen*, October 2007 issue	132
7.3:	Matrix of fashion magazines as of Spring 2008	135
7.4:	Targets of conformity for *CUTiE* girls	145
8.1:	A signboard bearing Minabe Town's mascot character, Binchō-tan	151
8.2:	The single, 'Hoshizora no pasupōto (Starlight passport)'	152
8.3:	'Binchō-tan' inside an electric rice cooker	154

8.4:	Transformations in the '*bishōjo* (beautiful girl)' in *otaku* culture	155
8.5:	Tōru Honda and his 'family'	166
9.1:	Magazines and free newspapers reporting festival scenes	172
9.2:	Shifts in CD sales and audience mobilisation numbers at the four major rock festivals, 2006–2007 financial year	174
10.1:	*Manga* scenes of parent/child relationships	199
11.1:	[Scene A] *Fragments I* (Yamamoto 1997, p. 14)	229
11.2:	[Scene B] *Fragments I* (Yamamoto 1997, p. 75)	229
11.3:	[Scene C] *Fragments I* (Yamamoto 1997, p. 90)	231
11.4:	[Scene D] *Fragments I* (Yamamoto 1997, p. 209)	232
11.5:	[Scene E] *YOUNG & FINE* (Yamamoto [1992] 1997, p. 105)	234
11.6:	[Scene F] *YOUNG & FINE* (Yamamoto [1992] 1997, p. 98)	235
11.7:	[Scene G] *YOUNG & FINE* (Yamamoto [1992] 1997, p. 110)	237
11.8:	[Scene H] *YOUNG & FINE* (Yamamoto [1992] 1997, p. 186)	238
11.9:	[Scene I] *YOUNG & FINE* (Yamamoto [1992] 1997, p. 218)	240
11.10:	The structure of 'an existence lived in the regions'	256
12.1:	The two phases of specialisation	256
12.2:	'Job choice' simulation	259
13.1:	Distribution of opinions on conditions for membership of the nation	267
13.2:	Distribution of opinions on national pride	270
13.3:	Distribution of anti-foreign views	274

Tables

4.1: Awareness vis-à-vis views on romantic love/
marriage and love rings — 66
8.1: Differences in ways of enjoyment in the second
and third stages — 165
10.1: Combinations of daughters' ideal life-course and
mother's life-course (% of total) — 209
10.2: Determining factors in synchronous action and
emotional intimacy — 210
10.3: Summary of results of analysis — 211
13.1: Results of factor analysis of conditions for
membership of the nation — 268
13.2: Results of factor analysis of national pride — 271
13.3: Results of factor analysis of anti-foreign sentiment — 275
13.4: Mean values of subordinate concept scores and
respective properties in each cluster — 276

Contributors

Katsuya MINAMIDA （南田勝也）
Katsuya Minamida is a professor in the Department of Sociology, Musashi University. His main area of investigation is the sociology of music, and he has related popular music with Pierre Bourdieu's 'field' theory, and discussed it. In recent years, he has been undertaking social research on digital audio players, and so on. His main publication is *Rokku myūjikku no shakaigaku* (Sociology of rock music) (2001, Seikyūsha).

Izumi TSUJI （辻泉）
Izumi Tsuji is a sociologist specialising in the sociology of culture. He has conducted extensive research on Japanese fan culture, including a study of fans of young idol musicians and railway fans. He is coeditor of *Fandom Unbound: Otaku Culture in a Connected Age* (2012, Yale University Press), a book on Japanese and American fan culture. He works as an associate professor at Chuo University in Japan.

Daisuke TSUJI （辻大介）
Daisuke Tsuji is an associate professor of sociology at the Graduate School of Human Sciences, Osaka University. His main areas of research are media and communication studies, with particular interest in ICT use by youth. His publications include 'Defending the Anonymity of Existence against "Ex Deus Machina" in the Information Era,' in Hiroki Azuma and Satoshi Hamano (eds), *ISED: Interdisciplinary Studies on Ethics and Design of Information Society* (2010, Kawade shobō shinsha publishers); and 'A Discourse Transformation of TV Advertising in Japan, 1950s–1960s,' in Kōhei Kōno and Kōji Nanba (eds), *Archaeology of TV Commercials* (2010, Sekaishisōsha).

Kensuke SUZUKI （鈴木謙介）
Kensuke Suzuki is an associate professor at Kwansei Gakuin University and a research fellow at Center for Global Communications, International University of Japan. His single-authored books deal with globalisation, the social and psychological aspects of network society, the sociology of cyberspace, and sociological theories. His best-known work is *Kānibaruka suru shakai* (Carnivalising society) (2005, Kōdansha gendai shinsho). He has published five co-authored books, and four book chapters.

Keiichi NABE （名部圭一）
Keiichi Nabe is an associate professor of sociology at St. Andrew's University in Japan. His main concern is the study of social and cultural transformation in late modernity from a theoretical perspective. His books include *Guidebook to Social and Cultural Theory*, (2005, Nakanishiya shuppan), and *Introduction to the Sociology of Modern Culture* (2007, Minerva shobō).

Sōichirō MATSUTANI （松谷創一郎）
Sōichirō Matsutani, a writer for magazines and a marketer, has written on the culture of diverse genres, including films, *manga*, novels, music and fashion. His main publication is *Gyaru to Fushigi-chan* (Gals and Miss Mysterious) (2011, Hara shobō), which sketches the thirty-year history of Japanese *shōjo* (girls).

Yoshimasa KIJIMA （木島由晶）
Yoshimasa Kijima is a sociologist who has been studying video game culture and people's hobbies. He has conducted several qualitative research projects on Japanese '*otaku*,' people who have an interest in activities that can be exercised at home, such as watching *anime*, reading *manga*, and playing video games. His methods of analysis are mainly ethnographic surveys. He is the co-author of *Today's Video Game Culture in Japan* (2007, Yūhikaku) and the co-author of *A New Sense of Masculinity in Japanese Clubs which Provide Male Companions* (2009, Keisō shobō). He works as an assistant professor at St. Andrew's University in Japan.

Jun'ichi NAGAI （永井純一）
Jun'ichi Nagai is a lecturer at the University of Kobe Yamate. He has been majoring in sociology and popular music studies, and studying

the consumption of popular culture and live performance. His papers include 'The Active Audience in Rock Festivals: The Case of the Fuji Rock Festival,' *Popular Music Studies* (2007, The Japanese Association for the Study of Popular Music), and 'The Active Audience of Home-grown Comics—The Alternative Reading of Media,' *Soshioroji* (Sociology) (2002, Shakaigaku kenkyūkai).

Yasuko NAKANISHI （中西泰子）

Yasuko Nakanishi is a sociologist interested in family studies, especially parent–adult child relationships She is an author of *Wakamono no kaigo ishiki* (Young people's awareness of care) (2008, Keisō shobō), a book on young people's attitudes of filial responsibility toward ageing parents, viewed in terms of gender. She works as a lecturer at Sagami Women's University in Japan.

Hisashi FUJII （藤井尚）

Hisashi Fujii is an abbot at a Buddhist temple. At the same time as researching and preaching on Buddhist thought focused upon Shinran, he also studies Japanese subcultures such as *manga*. Moreover, as he has long resided in a region far from Tokyo, he also harbours an interest in how living in a regional area of contemporary Japan differs from living in the capital. He is co-author of *Bunka shakaigaku no shiza* (Perspectives on the sociology of culture) (2008, Minerva shobō).

Masahiro ABE （阿部真大）

Masahiro Abe is a sociologist who has been studying the problems facing young people about to join the workforce. He has conducted several pieces of qualitative research on Japanese youth. His method of analysis is mainly participant observation, and he is the author of *Ethnography of Motorcycle Messengers* (2006, Shūeisha) and *Sociology on Ibasho* (2011, Nikkei Publishing). He works as a lecturer at Konan University in Japan.

Shunsuke TANABE （田辺俊介）

Shunsuke Tanabe is a sociologist who has been studying national identity and people's perceptions of foreign countries. He has conducted several pieces of quantitative research on Japanese cognition of foreign people and their nationalism. His method of analysis is mainly advanced social statistics. He is the author of *National Identities in a Comparative Perspective* (2010, Keio University Press) and the editor and co-author of *Perceptions on Foreigners and Political Attitudes: Analysis on Japanese Nationalism by Social Survey Data* (2011, Keisō shobō). He works as an associate professor at the University of Tokyo in Japan.

Acknowledgments

In publishing this book, we received permission to use several figures, and greatly appreciate the consideration of the rights holders. The figure numbers and associated copyright details are as listed below.

Chapter 2
- Figure 2.2: Kazumasa Oda's 'Rabu sutōrī wa totsuzen ni (A love story, suddenly)' © Ariola Japan Inc.
- Figure 2.5: Visual-*kei* rock band fans gathered at Jingu Bridge (Jingū-bashi) in front of Harajuku Station © Sōichirō Matsutani

Chapter 6
- Figure 6.1: Street television in the early 1950s © Sankei Shinbun-sha

Chapter 7
- Figure 7.1: *CUTiE*, March 2008 © Takarajimasha
- Figure 7.2: *Popteen*, October 2007 issue © Kadokawa Haruki Jimusho

Chapter 8
- Figure 8.1: A signboard bearing Minabe Town's mascot character, Binchō-tan © Alchemist; © Minabe Town
- Figure 8.2: The single, 'Hoshizora no pasupōto (Starlight passport)' © Sony Music Entertainment (Japan), Inc.
- Figure 8.3: 'Binchō-tan' inside an electric rice cooker © Alchemist
- Figure 8.5: Tōru Honda and his 'family' © Sansai Books

Chapter 10
- Figures 10.1–10.2: *Manga* scenes of parent–child relationships (Scene 1 © Nanae Haruno; Scene 2 © Satoru Makimura)

Chapter 11
- Figures 11.1–11.4: [Scene A]–[Scene D] *Fragments I* © Naoki Yamamoto
- Figures 11.5–11.9: [Scene E]–[Scene I] *YOUNG & FINE* © Naoki Yamamoto

Preface: what is the appeal of the sociology of culture?

Katsuya Minamida and Izumi Tsuji

Knowing culture, knowing society

If one were asked, 'What is the appeal of the sociology of culture?,' one's answer could probably be divided into two main elements: one being the dynamism of its gaze, which surveys the whole of society in a broad manner from the standpoint of things that could be regarded as quite familiar and trivial; and the other being one's fresh astonishment at the realisation of how profoundly connected such familiar things are to society in its entirety. Getting to know a culture means getting to know oneself, as it were, and getting to know society means finding out how deeply they are interconnected, does it not? We believe that readers will be able to savour such appeal to their hearts' content in any of the chapters contained in this book.

What is presently being sought from the sociology of culture is a way of approaching culture that involves taking an 'objective view.' A grasp of culture that involves exhaustively delving into the depths of one's target while dispassionately reappraising it at arm's length – one that manipulates the viewpoint at will – is being pursued.

Culture is something found extremely close at hand, and it is difficult to try to push it away as if it were something situated in another place. It is probably due to this characteristic that any excessively positive or excessively negative way of discussing some kind of culture will be felt to have missed the mark, or to lack persuasiveness. This is because, in the sociology of culture, both a way of understanding that is 'too familiar,' so to speak, and one that is 'too distant,' are lacking some vital element.

Culture is indeed a target that is difficult to approach 'objectively.' In Japanese society nowadays, along with the slogan 'COOL

JAPAN,' there has also been a focus upon the so-called content industry, and the place is awash with debate relating to culture. On the other hand, though, it must be admitted there is a quite surprising dearth of analysis that has attempted to come to grips with it in an 'objective' manner. Much is 'too familiar' or 'too aloof,' and an overwhelming proportion of ways of understanding is biased towards one or the other.

Another thing peculiar to Japanese society is that the very ways of understanding employed in discussing culture have been imported from external societies at various times, and there has also been a cycle of their being used and discarded on the whims of fashion without having undergone sufficient scrutiny.

Could it not be argued that this present kind of situation is proof that we in Japanese society have not sufficiently reappraised ourselves – in other words, that we have not completely understood what kind of society Japan has?

For that reason, we have placed weight on approaching culture in contemporary Japanese society both positively and empirically in this volume. Moreover, while taking up the challenge of grasping the present state of culture from that broad objective, we simultaneously have added detailed examination from multiple viewpoints in regard to that approach. Our focus upon discussing what approach would be suited to the circumstances of culture in contemporary Japanese society, especially in relation to that way of understanding, is a feature of this book. We hope that readers in societies other than Japan's will gain knowledge of how Japanese society really is, through the actual condition of its culture.

How does it differ from other sociologies?

Admittedly, the attraction we mentioned previously – knowing oneself, finding out about society, and getting to know the connection between these – is something that also broadly applies to sociology as a whole. We suggest, however, that one could call sociology of culture a discipline in which that appeal makes itself felt with particular intensity. The reason for this, as will also be described in detail in the Introduction to follow, is expressed in the fact that the word 'culture' has two meanings, one in the broad sense, and one in the narrow sense. Based on this point, let us compare it with other sociologies.

In the first place, there are numerous types of sociology, some called '*Bindestrich-Soziologie* (hyphenated sociology),' as in 'XX-sociology,' 'ZZ-sociology' and the like, and these, as it were, have become disciplines which sociologically analyse their respective fields within society. Compared to those 'hyphenated sociologies,' the sociology of culture occupies something of a special position, however. In short, the sociology of culture does not merely approach culture in a sociological manner, but rather is a discipline which grasps society through culture.

Here, the two senses of culture become important. Frankly speaking, culture in the broad sense means social lifestyles in general, while culture in the narrow sense means culture (in approximately the same sense as we use it ordinarily) as distinguished from other domains such as politics or economics. Accordingly, when we mention the sociology of culture, if we understand culture simply to be culture in the broad sense, this will be the 'sociology of society' and take on almost the same meaning as the whole of sociology. Here, in this situation, it will not be well understood what the sociology of culture comprises. As it is now, the answer is half right; but if, alternatively, we speak in terms of the two senses of the word, then the aims of the sociology of culture will be precisely getting to know culture in the broad sense through culture in the narrow sense, getting a grip on the overall picture of the former by making concrete phenomena relating to the latter its avenue of entry, and finding out how deeply they are interconnected.

In answer to the question why the sociology of culture has the kind of aims that overstep boundaries, it is merely because culture in the narrow sense and culture in the broad sense are not separate phenomena, but have profound connections and are seamlessly tied to one other.

To cite a common example in Japanese society, supposing there were a young woman who was engrossed in animation – she would not be living her life solely within *anime*. She might be a 'good daughter' in the family with whom she lived her daily life; in her relationships with her pals, she might be 'a leader-class presence, with some sensitivity to fashion,' while otherwise belonging to a variety of communities such as a school, workplace, area of residence, and could be expected 'also' to be a young person engrossed in *anime*. Accordingly, in pondering why that individual was so absorbed in *anime*, it would become vital not only to think within the parameters of *anime*, but rather to find out how other social situations were affecting it, and, turning that perspective on its head, getting to know what kind of state the society was in.

To reiterate, the gaining of a broad, unobstructed view of society as a whole in this manner, from things that could be seen as extremely familiar and trivial; the realisation of how deeply such familiar things have been connected with society in its entirety; and being able to feel – more strongly than in the case of other sociologies – a sense of dynamism and fresh surprise when finding out these things, probably comprise the attraction of the sociology of culture.

Yet this perspective belonging to the sociology of culture is both a late development in comparison with the history of the whole of sociology, and an ambitious and provocative endeavour. To that extent, it is probably also true that some parts of it remain insufficiently refined. For that very reason, the refinement of its way of understanding could be said to be its urgent business, while simultaneously continuing its attempts to improve its grasp of the state of culture in contemporary society.

On this point, learning the sociology of culture could be said to entail not the indulgence in 'passive reception' of knowledge constituting some kind of complete system, but rather the repetition of operations where one continually reappraises oneself, and continually reappraises society. We urge all of our readers to expand their own particular mode of the 'sociology of culture' from here on.

It is a delight beyond expectation that this volume has been translated into English, and that many readers outside Japan will be reading it. We imagine that through perusal of this book, perhaps comparisons relating to cultural differences between Japanese society and their own society will cross readers' minds; or it will be perceived that unexpected influences from their own society's culture are present in Japanese culture, or that the reverse impact also may exist. We are strongly convinced that, in such a manner, the perspective of comparative sociology, which seeks a deeper understanding of one's own culture through comparison with other cultures, will continue to drive great advances in the sociology of culture.

We wish to express our sincere gratitude to the General Editor of Trans Pacific Press, Emeritus Professor Yoshio Sugimoto of La Trobe University, who extended us such an opportunity; to Mrs

Machiko Sugimoto, who always gave us unerring advice at our briefing sessions; and to the translator, Dr Leonie Stickland, who produced an English version of extremely high quality. We thank them all very much.

Part I: Approaches to Culture

1 Introduction: the scope of the sociology of culture

Katsuya Minamida and Izumi Tsuji

On thinking about culture

This book is compiled as a guide to the sociology of culture. Its special features are its introduction of several themes and methodologies relating to culture and its development of concrete and empirical analysis of broad targets. In the various chapters, cultural forms are sketched from their respective viewpoints, but first, we wish to ponder the word 'culture' with which we are likely to be intimately involved on a quotidian basis. In any case, this is because the word is presently employed on such a broad scale, and also because its definition is no simple matter (Yanabu 1995). After coming to grips with its image here, we will launch into a discussion of each chapter.

Culture in the broad sense

When Japanese people hear the word '*bunka* (culture),' what might it bring to their minds? Many would probably think of something pertaining to historically- or geographically-fostered lifestyles, such as cultural assets, multinational culture, climate and culture, or things that expressed those things symbolically. There would also be no lack of people who would think of high culture or subculture as deriving from the creation of artworks, such as artistic culture, high culture and popular culture, culture schools, and the like. Some Japanese might even bring to mind terms spawned in the Taishō (1912–26) era, such as *bunka jūtaku* ('cultural dwelling' = a new type of apartment house) or *bunka bōchō* ('cultural cleaver' = a multi-purpose kitchen knife).

Whatever the case, these expressions are likely to contain the shared implication of the world opening up and advancing, and lifestyle content improving, or else new values being generated through the workings of the human spirit. Certainly, if one were to replace the 'cultural' portion of the phrase 'cultural life' with another expression, one such as 'abundant' or 'human' would fit snugly. It means, in short, that it is 'not animal-like,' and not 'rude nature.'

What do we mean by 'things that only human beings can do?' We mean people's putting their heads together, sharing the same concepts, and leaving material and non-material symbols for later generations. We indicate such pursuits by the name 'culture.'

In a manner of speaking, though, this applies to every facet of human lifestyle, does it not? Mutually communicating through language would be one example, and it would also apply to improving one's lifestyle by efficiently utilising fire and water, or jointly offering up prayers to a deity. Clothing, cooking and housing, and their associated human behaviour; the vaguely shared consciousness that generations or localities hold; gatherings of people with emotional attachments for specific targets; actions that preserve and pass on works of art and poetic language – even as to animal desires such as sleep and courtship, some unique manners and modalities have developed in every corner of the world, and it could be permissible to call these 'culture,' too.

This word 'culture' (*bunka*) can be used in any number of ways if one widens one's interpretation. It could be said to be the inclusive consolidation of human thinking, but it is also true that this definition is too broad and ambiguous. Perhaps for that reason, in the context of social science, culture has tended to receive secondary treatment (Miyajima 2000, p. 2).

That indeed is also plausible. In examining human behaviour scientifically, fields such as economics, law and politics, which are accustomed to stating things clearly in a readily-quantifiable manner, have developed as systematic sciences where it is easy to control the thinking. By comparison, there would be too many unclear points to treat the field of culture in a similar manner. Furthermore, it is not only that it is easy for scientists to conduct conceptual manipulation in the spheres of economics, law, politics and the like, but these have also been regarded as constituting the principles for human activity, the foundations of the social structure, and the things which bring about order.

Karl Marx, for example, thought that economic activity provided the base structure of society ([1859] 1912) (here, 'base' does not mean 'lower-ranking,' but is used in the 'fundamental' or 'basic' sense). By contrast, Marx deemed cultural practices that determine the breadth of human values and behaviour to belong to the superstructure, and to be activities that would change only when there was arrangement and variation of the base structure.

Talcott Parsons, moreover, posited that the four social processes expressed in the AGIL (an acronym of 'adaptation,' 'goal-attainment,' 'integration,' and 'latency' or 'latency pattern maintenance') Paradigm which he devised respectively corresponded to economics, politics, law and culture in social systems. This way of thinking, which interprets culture as a mechanism for maintaining latent order, is at odds with that of Marx in the sense of having controlling force over the economic system as well, but both treat culture as an object which is not economics, nor politics, nor a legal norm, but one that is difficult to survey in its entirety (Parsons 1961).

At a glance, the approach of such social scientists could be read as dealing with culture as a residual sphere that has spilled over (stated only in negative terms) from more important social activity, though I suggest it could be said rather that they imagined culture as something akin to the atmosphere that envelops the core.

Supposing that a certain firm were to succeed in developing a new product by means of innovative technology, and made an enormous profit: what is important in such an instance is, of course, the product, the technology that pertains to it, and its economic effect, but the question of how the development of that product got the go-ahead and this led to its actual sales will relate to the firm's company spirit, namely a factor called 'corporate culture' (even if economic conditions had spawned that firm's corporate culture in the first place.) Alternatively, supposing there were a novel which had become a best-seller on its reputation for having captured the times, then quality would undoubtedly have been central in terms of grounds for the work's acceptance, but there would be a need to take into account the 'generational culture' that supported its popularity. Core conditions give rise to culture in the form of people's value-consciousness, beliefs and attitudes, while culture conversely becomes the world-picture which underpins that core. That kind of atmosphere-like role is played by culture as sociologists apprehend it.

In his work, *Structures of Thinking*, Karl Mannheim states as follows:

If one is attuned to an artwork in the original way, there is only the insular, self-enclosed work. The attitude towards it disappears, as does the functionality of the sphere. Sociological consideration of culture is a kind of non-immanent consideration, which seeks out the functionality of every cultural formation ([1922] 1982, p. 64).

The 'functionality' in this context refers, in short, to 'connections.' What must be understood is the semantic content of culture in terms of a connection that binds people to their objects. In this manner, the sociology of culture has accepted that there is a cultural aspect to every part of concrete social life, and has made its underlying principle the adoption of the aspects of the meaning and value of actions that cling to individual objects as its research target.

Culture in the narrow sense

If, however, we take the stance of using the term 'culture' in the sense of a word indicating the collective representation for many human activities, such as generational culture, religious culture, regional culture, and so on, and of discussing them in a non-immanent manner, then it would be no different from what is called the 'sociology of knowledge.' On the other hand, it could even be considered non-problematic to call it simply 'sociology.'

Diana Crane directs a critical eye at the way leading sociologists have handled culture in the abovementioned sense, that is, 'as an "implicit feature of social life"'(Crane 1994, p. 2, citing Wuthnow and Witten 1998, pp. 50–51). If culture is interpreted in the broad sense of people's collective values and beliefs when the sociology of culture focuses on its object, this can be confusing and misleading. Nevertheless, such a situation did continue until recent years.

> [I]n contemporary societies, this emphasis on implicit culture is incomplete. Culture today is expressed and negotiated almost entirely through culture as explicit social constructions or products, in other words, through *recorded culture*, culture that is recorded in either print, film, artifacts or, most recently, electronic media...Without analysing the content and effects of recorded cultures as well as the factors that affect the content of recorded cultures, we cannot understand the role of culture in modern society (Crane 1994, pp. 2–3).

Introduction: the scope of the sociology of culture 7

In this manner, Crane is advocating 'new sociologies of culture' that deal with 'various types of recorded culture such as information, entertainment, science, technology, law, education and art.'

Wendy Griswold, in turn, advocates a structural model consisting of four elements at four points (with six links) which she calls a 'cultural diamond,' and displays a cultural-sociological approach applicable to broad-ranging targets. Her four elements are 'cultural objects (meanings embodied in symbols),' 'creators (people who produce cultural objects, including the institutions and systems that diffuse them),' 'receivers (people who experience culture and substantial cultural objects),' and the 'social world (the situation in which culture is produced and experienced),' and her definition of 'cultural objects' as things that are accompanied by a substantive form is a special feature. Moreover, she takes the quest to understand the circumstances in which these elements affect each other to be the task of the sociology of culture (Griswold 2008, pp. 14–17).

Objects created by human hands (recorded culture; cultural objects), the media that transmit them, the receivers associated with these, and the space made ready by the people that are the receivers: these, it was begun to be argued in recent years, constitute the range of the sociology of culture.

Speaking from the viewpoint of doctrinal history, humanities fields that dealt with the above-mentioned objects, from literature and the arts to discourses on mass society, had existed in large numbers even prior to that time; and in Japan, too, *Shisō no kagaku* (Science of thought), the journal with which Shunsuke Tsurumi, Masao Maruyama and the like were involved, had success in studies aimed at everyday culture and mass culture from soon after the end of the Second World War.

Behind culture in the narrow sense having attracted attention as a trend in recent years, and Crane and Griswold having tried to give that research field a clear-cut definition, there lay the growth of British-born cultural studies as a global school of thought. As there is commentary from Chapter Two onwards about that same school, which had taken up the social meaning of mass culture as an academic topic from the 1960s, we refer readers there for details, but there was great significance in its having adopted pop culture, which had hitherto been treated as a trivial target, as an object of academic research (especially in the context of social science).

In addition, the informational environment changed enormously through media diversification and the growth of computers, and the increase in importance of the content culture provided therein could also be counted as a factor in the way culture in the narrow sense came to notice. What is more, the progress of globalisation not only drove the distribution of goods and the exchange of services on a world scale, but also turned people's eyes towards the management of cultural works as intellectual property. Now, media and cultural works are attracting interest across all fields.

The structure of this book

As mentioned above, when we think about culture, there is a need to give consideration to culture in the broad sense, and culture in the narrow sense. This book has taken care to make its contents cover both of these. This is because eclectic though it may be, a treatment that lacked one or the other would seem insufficient, seeing also that they have brought the nuance of a sociology-of-culture textbook to this work. Specifically, we have called culture in the narrow sense 'addictive media culture,' and made culture in the broad sense the 'everyday culture that is right there.' By establishing a demarcation close to our everyday sentiment, we hope that readers will feel cultural analysis to be something more familiar.

Part I

In Part I, which comprises Chapters Two to Four, general remarks are expanded before concrete analysis is begun. As well as giving an outline of pioneering studies in the sociology of culture, this part explains about the themes and methodology adopted when analysing culture, and makes proposals as to the analytical viewing angles that can be considered most effective at the present point in time. Furthermore, by venturing to discuss them by embedding the systems from prior research in a dichotomy, Part I makes efforts to highlight the vital points in the assertions of each of those systems.

Chapter Two: 'Perspectives on media-and-group culture,' focuses on communities of people that gather on the fringes of groups of artworks mediated by the media, that is, on so-called fan culture. It examines the characteristics and differences, and the merits and demerits, of the empirical approach represented, for example, by uses and gratifications studies (in mass-communications research) which measure the psychological aspects of media recipients, and of the critical approach which emphasises the social context of subcultures and endeavours to discuss their audiences by such means as ethnography.

Chapter Three: 'Perspectives on expressive culture,' thinks about possible methodology for making cultural works themselves into the target of research. Two approaches are applied to the 'person–work' relationship versus the 'person–work–person' relationship model which the author has conceived – an internal reading, which incorporates the literary and aesthetic currents that attempt to close in upon the essence of works; and a sociological external reading, which attempts to appeal to that which, for the work itself, is an external explanation and principle of interpretation. Discussion is carried out on a theoretical level; and, finally, suggestions are made as to a new approach.

Chapter Four: 'Perspectives on the culture of generations and life-phases,' offers guidance on the two representative techniques for social surveys – qualitative and quantitative. This chapter will be especially useful for analysis of culture in the broad sense. With the generational culture of 'love rings' as its topic, it conducts a comparative examination of how to grasp its reality from the two aspects of interview surveys and questionnaire surveys. As this fourth chapter also provides a commentary on survey procedure, as well as clarifying the mutual merits and demerits of both survey techniques, it should become a practical guide for people who would like hereafter to start social surveys.

Part II

Parts II and III, from Chapter Five onwards, point to several specific examples of cultural analysis. These each have been written independently, and can be read as individual papers, but consideration has been given to linking them with the methodology shown in Part I.

Chapters Five to Nine constitute the part that addresses 'addictive media culture.'

Chapter Five: 'Why do people become addicted to mobile phones?' analyses the state of media communication centred on young people, approaching from the angle of mobile-phone mail usage. Mainly by employing the technique of questionnaire surveys, it sheds light on the issues of the modes into which the emotional expression unique to young people has transformed through the progress of technology, and the state of affairs indicated by mobile-phone dependency.

Chapter Six: 'How has the style of television viewing changed?' is a discussion of the act of becoming absorbed in television viewing. In any age, television occupies central place among our sources of information, and the chapter gives a deep reading of how television viewing styles have changed with the times, pivoting around the generational consciousness in Japanese society since the 1960s. The transformation in extremely personal '*tsukkomi* (subversive ripostes)' towards television programmes reflects a dynamism relating to the way distance is maintained between sender and receiver.

Chapter Seven: 'Where is differentiated communication heading?' takes up fashion as its raw material for understanding the phenomenon of trends. Women's fashions, especially, undergo dramatic ups and downs, and the people involved also have a strong consciousness of differentiation from others. Accordingly, by employing rhetorical analysis, one of the methods in constructionism, the chapter will give a close reading to comments that have appeared in the readers' column of a fashion magazine along with the changing times. Young people who make a commitment to fashion culture engage in unlimited differentiated communication with neighbours close at hand. Through reflecting their image, the chapter will foretell the course of fashion in contemporary society.

In contrast to the preceding chapters, which tended to focus rather upon media analysis, Chapters Eight and Nine mainly deal with the communication of cultural works.

Chapter Eight: 'Why make e-*moe*-tional attachments to fictional characters?' closes in on the reality of *otaku* culture, which has often been a hot topic in recent years. If one considers the popularity of stars and idols, the experience of having emotional attachment to people with whom one has never had face-to-face contact and of becoming absorbed in that attachment could be called a general phenomenon. Recently, however, changes have come to those aspects, too, it having become possible to indulge in emotional attachment behaviour (*moe*) towards people who do not actually

Introduction: the scope of the sociology of culture   11

exist, or towards two-dimensional characters. It is this chapter that, by using the life-history method, affords a reading of the sensitivity of subjects who have this 'e-*moe*-tional' attachment to *anime* characters.

Chapter Nine: 'Why do people gather at rock festivals?' by contrast depicts the form of personal networks mediated by musical works, using rock festivals which have now become regular summer events as its theme. At music fests nowadays, patrons gather because they seek elements apart from music, such as 'making friends' or 'taking it easy,' rather than because they are attracted by the music itself, or the artists. The chapter discusses the state of such reception from participant observation at rock fests.

Part III

Chapters Ten to Thirteen make up a part which responds to 'immediate, everyday culture,' and discuss family- and regional culture, fashion, and occupational- and national consciousness, which exemplify culture in the broad sense.

Chapter Ten: 'What are contemporary aspects of the parent/child relationship?' analyses the situation in late modern society where family role-consciousness is in transition. At present, far from human relationships becoming rarefied, a new 'intimacy' is becoming conspicuous in a particular aspect of these relationships, and a tendency for the parent-and-child relationship to become 'friendship-like' reportedly can be seen, mainly among females. While taking up the discourse which appears in *manga* expression in relation to such new 'intimacy,' the chapter analyses its social background, based on quantitative data.

Chapter Eleven: 'Is "poverty" or "affluence" the reality?' deals with the culture of 'the regions (*chihō*),' which is hardly ever directly discussed, though the culture of cities and their suburbs has attracted attention thus far. In this process, it takes up works by *manga* artist Naoki Yamamoto, including *YOUNG & FINE*, as its thematic material, finding the characteristics of 'provincial' culture in the seriousness of having to live 'the endless everyday' (Shinji Miyadai) and a certain 'something akin to affluence' that such seriousness spawns, which are depicted therein.

Chapter Twelve, 'What is at question in youth labour issues?' discusses the reality of labour problems among the youth of today.

On the one hand, some young people try to find work that fits their preferences, but there is a trap lurking in 'making what they like into their occupation.' Others, meanwhile, try to find stable work, but it often happens these days that the stability is only an illusion. The chapter examines the potential of specialisation as a measure to counter such issues, while touching upon their social background, namely the 'Japanese-style welfare society.'

Chapter Thirteen, 'What does it mean to be a "Japanese"?' is one which considers the issue of patriotism in Japan from analysis of quantitative surveys. In the midst of advancing globalisation, the question of what a nation-state means is now being posed anew. In our everyday life, how might we be conscious of this country of Japan? This chapter does not employ a critical approach to the emergence of patriotism, but consistently analyses it empirically, based on quantitative data. In describing the analytical process, it incorporates explanation as how to read data, in what kind of settings to use multivariate analysis, and so on. It is also one of the aims of this book to have readers discover the fascination of statistical methods, which tend to be regarded as difficult.

An invitation to the sociology of culture

As outlined above, in this book we have discovered culture in a variety of objects, and analysed these by multi-faceted means. In addition, the concrete examples in the respective analyses deal with circumstances and affairs arising in contemporary Japanese society. This is because we wished to emphasise how important it is for culture to be contiguous with the everyday, and, in that sense, for us to gaze at what is at our own feet. Moreover, this volume is characterised by the incorporation of a more empirical approach in comparison with similar publications, which tend to take a critical approach. Our basic stance is that even something that started off as a single idea will have its logic fortified by following an empirical process.

More than anything else, though, what all of the chapters have in common is their inquiring stance of wanting somehow to actualise the image of ambiguous culture which, if left alone, would be overlooked, and to bring out into the open. They 1) discover points of uncertainty and problems within quotidian culture; 2) confirm what kinds of things have been debated about those aspects or targets;

Introduction: the scope of the sociology of culture

and 3) mobilising their own knowledge, attempt empirical analysis. As well, they 4) present new insights and views of things. That is the process of thought that we researchers routinely employ, and each of the chapters is structured according to those four sections in order to follow that process.

In other words, apprehending the flow in which the above sections one to four are connected as a process of 1) →2)→ 3)→ 4) will also constitute a technique for understanding 'what is going on in our heads' in relation to our interest in and conception of our own culture. We hope that you will find this book interesting reading, but we would be even more delighted if it is one that stimulates readers' intellectual curiosity and spirit of inquiry.

2 Perspectives on media-and-group culture: from an empirical/critical approach to a multi-method approach

Izumi Tsuji

On a daily basis, rather than being alone, we tend to be surrounded by 'people,' that is, friends, family and peers. At those times, we chat about the content of the television programmes we saw the previous day, contact each other on our mobile telephones, and so on. In this way, 'media-and-group culture' has become a truly indispensable, deeply-embedded aspect of our everyday lives, just like us ourselves and the people around us, as well as the media connecting them all.

In this chapter, I make a comparative investigation of various approaches to such 'media-and-group culture.' In substantive terms, I submit a new approach that should now be required, not taking the approaches that have been called the empirical school and critical school and pitting them simplistically against each other in a contest for supremacy, but rather having first firmly probed their respective merits and demerits.

Hitherto, an 'aloof' interpretation has been effected vis-à-vis 'media-and-group culture,' as if something odd were happening somewhere else, as it were. What is now needed instead is a kind of in-depth way of understanding that will reflect upon it as 'our own business.'

Ways of understanding 'media-and-group culture'

Objectives of this chapter

We live lives that are surrounded daily by the media. People who at times take a strong interest in the information the media convey, and who are like-minded in their interest, also tend to gather together.

Perspectives on media-and-group culture 15

Figure 2.1: Fans of male idols gathered at a concert venue

Without doubt, such 'media-and-group culture' has become an indispensable part of our days.

This will be easy to appreciate if I cite a typical example: the existence of people dubbed 'fans' or '*otaku*.' Frequently-observed phenomena include the convergence upon concert venues of fans and *otaku* of the idols and so-called 'talents (*tarento*)' who appear on television and in magazines, arranged through mutual contact by e-mail on their mobile phones, or the exchange of opinions on internet message boards.

If we think hard about this, however, how should we interpret such phenomena? In terms of the example above, why do those people come to like that particular idol or 'talent,' rather than someone else; and even though it seems just as well for each person simply to be using media individually, why do fans deliberately assemble and all do the same thing? Perhaps because such phenomena are all too familiar, full apprehension of them still seems to elude us. If so, then it is necessary, is it not, to begin our consideration from different approaches to those phenomena?

As such, the goal of this chapter is to consider how such various types of media and the communication which collects on the basis of its information have been perceived hitherto, introducing several contrasting views and examining their merits and demerits, while considering the approaches that should now be pursued.

Are fans a 'ridiculous, pathetic bunch'?

Even prior to this, such 'media-and-group culture' has constituted an important topic of research. Till now, however, it seems that the majority of approaches have contained some bias. In other words, many appear to have endeavoured to view these phenomena a little excessively as 'bad things/good things,' or else to specialise in searching for some cause.

This is also expressed by the terms 'fan' and '*otaku,*' used as examples above. It is probably readily understood that the word *otaku* generally is employed in a discriminatory sense, if anything, but actually the term 'fan' originally had a discriminatory implication, also. 'Fan' being an abbreviation of 'fanatic,' it is a word which has the meaning of anyone belonging to a 'laughable and pitiable bunch.' As evident from the sense of such a term, it is no exaggeration to suggest that 'media-and-group culture' has been perceived as something engaged in by a 'ridiculous, pathetic bunch.' Its cause has been sought and understood to lie, as it were, in a specific psychological tendency, social class or position; or in the persuasive power of media messages; or in the existence of various powers behind the scenes.

Research into 'media-and-group culture' harks back as far as the end of the nineteenth century in Europe, becoming prolific in the United States after the Second World War, but what is very interesting is the question of what manner of concept these studies used to refer to such a phenomenon. Of old, in Europe, Gustave Le Bon ([1895] 1968) called it '*la foule* (the crowd),' while Gabriel de Tarde ([1901] 1989) used '*le public* (the public),' the former tending to be a concept with an 'unfavourable' image, the latter with a 'favourable' one.

Around the Second World War, the concept of 'mass' became established, but this was used in the adjectival sense of 'mass-' or 'large-scale-,' when referring to such things as radio and television as the 'mass media.' This was a concept that could be used with either a "favourable' or 'unfavourable' image according to what was under discussion, but it was comparatively common for it to indicate a uniform, monolithic and large-scale phenomenon.

Though uniform, monolithic and large-scale phenomena are not being seen to the same extent as before, along with the spread in recent years of such new media as the Internet and mobile phones, in addition to pre-existing mass media, concepts such as 'carnival (*matsuri*)' (Suzuki 2005) and 'smart mobs' (Rheingold 2002) are coming into use.

Now, when we look back at such past research from a contemporary perspective, do those kinds of approaches not feel a little aloof? Of course, there is no doubt that those studies were ones that achieved important results.

As already mentioned, however, 'media-and-group culture' has become something that is already indispensable nowadays. In this chapter, what I seek is a way of apprehending 'media-and-group culture' as something inseparable from our everyday lives, one that delves deeply into it from a broad perspective.

Past perceptions of 'media-and-group culture'

Here, I would like to reflect broadly on prior studies relating to 'media-and-group culture,' in regard to the so-called mass-media research which developed before and after the Second World War. Let me look back mainly at the two streams called the empirical school and the critical school.

There were reasons for 'mass media research' having originally developed in this period, principally in the West. It was because radio had become widely diffused in the 1920s as the first of the full-fledged mass media. Moreover, in the 1930s, Nazism came to prominence in Germany, and, as exemplified by its propaganda, a war had begun in which emphasis was placed upon 'inciting' the 'mass.'

According to social psychologist Takeshi Satō (1990), the empirical school has a tendency to study the direct effect of media messages, without much attention to the broad-ranging social context. It mainly developed in the United States after the Second World War, and is the approach which later went on to become the mainstream in mass media research. It was also introduced to Japan after that war, and came to form the main current in so-called social psychological 'mass media research.'

The critical school, on the other hand, had an interest rather in the broad-ranging social context of communication, and mainly (though not in every case) was an approach with a Marxist tendency. Part of it derives from the Frankfurt School in Germany around the time of the Second World War, but, due also to the rise of a series of studies called cultural studies from the 1990s onwards, it is drawing attention once more. This probably also involves the issue that the 'empirical school' has failed fully to apprehend the greatly changing social context.

Yet if we focus upon research relating to those respective schools, especially those from the early period, then commonalities to do with historical background also become visible, even more clearly than such differences.

Typical examples from the early empirical school include research targeting the panic stirred by the broadcast, during a radio drama, of a news bulletin telling of an attack by Martians (this, too, actually constituted part of the drama) (Cantril [1940] 1971), and the phenomenon of radio stars having advertised war bonds over a marathon eighteen hours, bringing about huge sales (Merton 1946). These were studies that focused upon the persuasive power of the very information that could be conveyed via the medium called radio, and because the studies highly estimated that persuasive power, they were called the 'powerful effects model.' Furthermore, the kind of approach which measured that effect empirically through questionnaires and the like was later promoted.[1]

In the early period of the critical school, on the other hand, there were studies undertaken which claimed that the 'culture industry,' typified by the film industry, were manipulating 'mass' consciousness (Horkheimer and Adorno [1947] 1979). There, qualitative analysis to bring to light the 'ideology' lurking in such media messages was carried out.

Though admittedly such concrete differences in survey methods did exist, one can also begin to see points of similarity in the approaches of the empirical and critical schools. In the early days of the empirical school, the 'mass,' so to speak, was an easily-agitated presence, and the school sought the cause for that in the persuasive power of media messages. Conversely, the critical school endeavoured to expose the existence of politico-economic power behind the scenes of the media, as thus trying to incite the 'mass.' In other words, both approaches could be said to have a common tendency to try to apprehend 'media-and-group culture' as something in which a 'ridiculous, pathetic bunch' – to reiterate the aforementioned phrase – engages, by concentrating their explanation on some sort of easily-understood cause.

Moreover, another similarity is the way both approaches focus only upon the side that sends and conveys the information, paying scant attention to the people who receive it and gather together. Regardless of whether the approaches perceive the 'mass' in a 'bad' image, as something that is easily 'incited,' or as something that is being made to 'agitate' by authority, it will be noted that each is premised on an understanding that the 'mass' is something uniform and monolithic.

As a result of the exposure of early studies to such criticism, attention vis-à-vis 'media-and-group culture' began to be directed at the actual communication of the people grouping together. This means that focus began to be concentrated upon research not on the 'sender,' so to speak, but on the 'receiver,' so while making a distinction between the 'empirical school' and 'critical school,' let us delve into the characteristics of each approach.

The 'empirical school' perspective: focusing on uses and gratifications studies

The emergence of uses and gratifications studies

The empirical school arguably was the earlier to have adopted an approach focusing upon the 'receiver,' but it was only from the 1970s that this was conducted in earnest.

Well-known as representative of these are uses and gratifications studies. Their main point lies in investigating how the 'receivers' of media messages utilise them, and what kind of gratifications they draw from those messages. Unlike a uniform, monolithic and 'easily excitable' presence such as the so-called 'mass,' 'receivers' were understood as subjective and active beings who obtained gratifications from media messages according to their respective concerns and interests. In concrete terms, this was deemed variously to be for 'diversion,' the maintenance of 'personal relationships,' or for 'personal identity' and 'surveillance' of the entire society that surrounded the self (McQuail 1972, p. 60).

Examples of uses and gratifications studies

A little later, such uses and gratifications studies were also introduced into Japan. Examples include studies from the late 1970s through to 1980, such as those targeting female readers of fashion magazines (Takeshita et. al 1978, for one); and those in the early 1990s, which targeted the fans of different kinds of artists (Matsui (ed.) 1994, among others). Here, let me take up examples from the latter of uses and gratifications studies relating to fans of Kazumasa Oda.

Kazumasa Oda is a representative singer/songwriter in Japan, who was active as the vocalist and leader of a band called Off Course in the 1970s and 1980s. After the disbanding of Off Course in 1989, Oda began solo performing in earnest, and even today produces numerous theme songs for television dramas, advertising jingles, and the like. In 1991, in the very thick of a boom in so-called trendy dramas, his Compact Disc (CD) single, 'Rabu sutōrī wa totsuzen ni (A love story suddenly),' the theme song from the mega-hit drama, 'Tokyo Love Story,' smashed the then-current Japanese CD single sales record of 270 million units. The research whose results I will take up here also was conducted at that time, but why might fans have developed a liking for Kazumasa Oda, or become his fans? And how can this be understood?

Basically, uses and gratifications studies begin by first specifying the type of gratification of the 'receiver.' In terms of Kazumasa Oda fans, several gratification types were discovered in fan letters submitted to the fan club's monthly letterzine. Next, a questionnaire was compiled based on these, a survey[2] targeting people such as members of the 'Kazumasa Oda Appreciation Society' at a certain university was implemented; and, through quantitative analysis, the gratification types were sorted into three broad categories. As a result, it was found that these could be organised broadly into three gratification types, as follows: 'supporting one's feelings with the song' (applicable items included, for example: wanting to be loved by someone of the opposite sex, as in Oda's songs; wanting to experience the kind of love found in Oda's songs); 'worshipping Oda' (similarly: I respect Kazumasa Oda; I think Kazumasa Oda is cool; et cetera); and, 'being attracted by the tenderness of the voice or melody' (similarly: I think the melody in Oda's songs is tender; I think Oda's singing voice is gentle, et cetera). (For further details, see Matsui (ed.) 1994, p. 42).

Furthermore, the study also asked questions of the same targets to elucidate properties of their character, and conducted quantitative analysis of the link between the characteristics of such fans' character and the above-mentioned gratification types.

In this process, if fans are divided into males and females, several deeply interesting outcomes can be obtained. As a conspicuous result, it became clear that in female fans, there was a link between

Perspectives on media-and-group culture

Figure 2.2: Kazumasa Oda's 'Rabu sutōrī wa totsuzen ni (A love story, suddenly)' © *Ariola Japan Inc.*

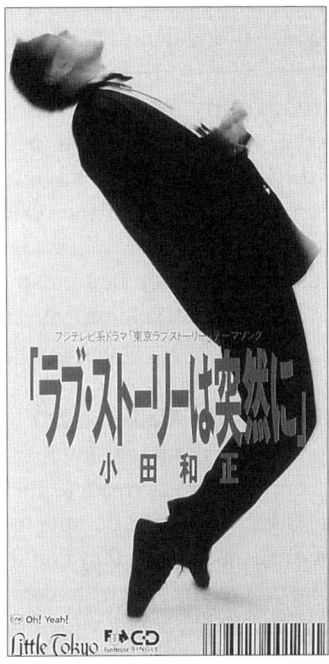

the 'supporting one's feelings with the song' gratification type and the 'interest in the opposite sex' character property; while in male fans, the 'supporting one's feelings with the song' gratification type was linked with a 'need for care.'

Moreover, as a result of content analysis of the lyrics of fifteen songs especially favoured by fans, it became clear that the adjective '*setsunai* (heart-rending/painful)' and the pronouns 'you and I/me' were frequently used; and that Kazumasa Oda's songs had the kind of content that says: 'The present, when everything easily moves with the times, is heart-breaking. But still I want to keep on loving you' (Matsui (ed.) 1994, p. 49).

Accordingly, it came to light that Oda fandom (the 'media-and-group culture' relating to Kazumasa Oda) was a phenomenon in which 'women wanting to be loved, and gentle men' (Matsui (ed.) 1994, p. 44) felt gratification towards melodies and the content of lyrics that expressed love between men and women, and its pain.

Merits and demerits of uses and gratifications studies

In our attempt to understand 'media-and-group culture,' we need to understand what the merits and demerits of uses and gratifications studies would be.

As for their merits, firstly one could cite their attention to communication on the 'receiver's' end. In the case of Kazumasa Oda's fans, for instance, the studies have not merely looked for causes in the persuasive power of the lyrics and in the sales strategies of the music industry, but, while analysing the content of the lyrics, have also gained a detailed grasp of the users of that communication, that is, what gratification type of 'receiver' they are, with what character. The employment of quantitative and empirical methods constitutes the merit here.

On the other hand, one could also point out such demerits of uses and gratifications studies as the following: while they parallel the empirical school approach in as much as they take a systematic and empirical view, their analytical perspective cannot escape a tendency to be limited. To that extent, they could invite the criticism that the broader social context has been abandoned. In other words, this means that even though their focus upon the communication of the 'receiver' deserves credit, it is suggested that, before seeing it in a comparatively 'favourable' light as subjective and active behaviour, these studies have not given sufficient consideration to the social context from the start.

Further demerits one could raise include the point that – while this is something brought about by changes in the social context rather than something inherent in the perspective itself – the more precise the result from limitation of the perspective, the less clear-cut the answer to what it really means becomes, as in the outcome of analysis of Kazumasa Oda fans.

These days, when uniform, monolithic and large-scale phenomena have vanished, one might say, and there exists a diversely segmented 'media-and-group culture,' if one were solely to throw light on Oda fans, exactly what that elucidated about this society would not be readily understood.

By way of example, it would probably be necessary to supply an appropriate social context which would make that phenomenon easier to apprehend, such as how those fans differed from other fans, or how they diverged in comparison to past points in time. Otherwise, uses and gratifications studies would turn into quite a stale, tiresome chore of checking, even if correct in terms of results, as in: 'People who seek "painfulness" feel gratification from "painful" lyrics.'

Uses and gratifications studies vis-à-vis 'media-and-group culture' are both a systematic and empirical way of understanding, and one that it is considered ought to be greatly utilised, but improvements might be needed in relation to such points.

The 'critical school' perspective: focusing on cultural studies

The critical school aspiring to social contextualisation

The empirical school approach, which occupied the mainstream, went on to be criticised over the demerits such as pointed out just now. Strictly speaking, this was probably due to an increase in social contexts that deserved consideration, along with ever more complex changes in the mechanisms of society, rather than problems inherent in the approach itself. In these circumstances, the critical school approach called cultural studies began to draw attention. Cultural studies originally achieved research results with working-class culture in Britain as its object (such as Hoggart 1957; Williams 1958; Willis 1977), while in Japan, since being introduced as one sort of qualitative research on the 'receiver' (Morley 1980, and so on), it started to attract much attention, especially in the 1990s.

What is important here, however, is that this was not merely detailed qualitative research.[3] Research on the 'receiver' in cultural studies, as evidenced by its being called 'audience ethnography,' does not only regard the 'receiver' as a simple 'receiver' of media. It is work that carries out detailed description of 'media-and-group culture,' apprehending the 'receiver' of media as simultaneously being an entity (= audience) that lives everyday life while being impacted by a variety of social contexts, and incorporating consideration of such broad-ranging social contexts and their influence.

Such a perspective flourished in the West from the 1980s onwards, but in that midst, research focusing upon fans – arguably a typical example of an audience – came to occupy a position as an important genre. As such, here I would like to introduce a theoretical model which had enormous influence upon the way of understanding such an audience, namely, Stuart Hall's 'encoding/decoding model' (Hall 1980).

The 'encoding/decoding model'[4]

The characteristic of the 'encoding/decoding model' lies in its having endeavoured also to understand the persuasive power of media messages and the existence of influences behind the scenes, while being swayed by the perception that 'receivers' use media messages for their own gratification, as in uses and gratifications studies.

This point, in particular, emerged when the 'decodings' which the audience can conduct vis-à-vis media messages were arranged into three patterns, namely the 'dominant-hegemonic position,' the 'oppositional position' and 'negotiated position' (Hall 1980, pp. 136–7).

The 'dominant-hegemonic position' is the kind of 'reading' that is influenced by media messages just as the 'sender' intended; the 'oppositional position' is the sort of 'decoding' in which the audience conversely discovers meaning in a subjective and active manner; and the 'negotiated position' is a complex 'reading' that is just as if the others were mixed together. The kind of 'reading' the audience conducts is influenced by the broader social context, but, this point included, let us investigate in more detail among concrete research results.

Examples of fan culture studies

There is a genre called fan culture studies, constituting a typical example of audience ethnography in cultural studies based on such a theoretical model. Let us take up a study by a representative proponent, John Fiske (1991), on the culture of fans of the singer, Madonna.

Madonna is an American-born, world-renowned singing star, and on the impetus of her sixth single, 'Like a Virgin,' becoming a hit in October 1984, she gained popularity not only in the United States, of course, but also world-wide, including Japan; and with her image strategy that skilfully utilised her extreme performances and music videos, she established a position as the sex symbol for a new age. At that time, especially in America, she enjoyed huge popularity among teenage girls, and 'wanna-bes' (what in Japan are called 'cos-players,' who clad themselves in clothes that mimicked Madonna's costumes) grabbed attention, and continue to do so today.

With such fan culture as his object, Fiske first conducted qualitative analysis of the content of Madonna's song lyrics and music videos, and, moreover, implemented an approach involving comparison of fans' reactions to them through analysis of letters to her fanzine.

As a result, he understood Madonna's fan culture to be something stemming from the pleasure derived by girls placed in an inferior position in an androcentric society from making 'oppositional readings' and 'negotiated readings' vis-à-vis the messages that the media conveys.

According to Fiske's analysis, Madonna's sexy image was certainly something created by the so-called 'culture industry,' and one that gave people the image of a subordinate woman. Yet, on the other hand, Fiske says that there is also room left in such an image to make an 'oppositional' or 'negotiated' reading, and fans are by no means manipulated at the whim of the 'culture industry,' but rather feel pleasure in the very act of such 'readings.'

Claiming, for example, that this is manifest in the fact of their 'reading' into the almost excessive audacity of Madonna's sexiness not so much an image of submissiveness as one of independence, Fiske cites fans' words from *Time* magazine, as follows: 'She's sexy but she doesn't need men...she's kind of there all by herself,' and: 'She kind of gives us ideas. It's really women's lib, not being afraid of what guys think' (27 May 1985: 47, cited in Fiske 1991, p. 99).

In other words, for the girls who are her fans, as they 'read' (media messages about) Madonna, this becomes a site (impetus) for opposition to the things that oppress them, and so even for the 'wanna-bes,' who at first glance seem to 'lack the imagination to devise their own styles of dress and merely follow her like sheep,' adopting her style means 'aligning themselves with a source of power.' In a male-oriented society, 'control over the look is not just a superficial playing with appearances, it is a means of constructing and controlling social relations and thus social identity' (Fiske 1991, pp. 100–1).

The merits and demerits of fan culture research (merits and demerits of audience ethnography)

When this is compared with the outcomes of the above uses and gratifications studies, a number of merits and demerits will surface. One merit could be said to lie in its consideration of broad-ranging social contexts. It does not explain 'media-and-group culture' only by the psychological properties of the 'receiver,' nor only by the persuasive power of media messages; rather, in conducting its analysis, it takes into consideration such things as the hidden ando-centrism in society. This could also be said to be a merit of using qualitative analysis, and for that reason, it is possible to delve into the impact of various social contexts, in a problem-finding manner.

On the other hand, however, there might also be the issue of what kinds of social context should be considered. Even in the case of the examples just raised, it feels as if they regard 'media-and-group culture' too much as being a simple 'counter-culture,' and there might be other social contexts that ought to be pondered.

In actuality, 'cultural studies' encompasses a diversity of positions according to different scholars, and there are cases, too, in which their assertions are subtly dissimilar. Recently, there have also been studies that critically reinterpret research which had viewed the above as being unsophisticated 'counter-culture,' and attempt to focus on the behaviour of the sort of people who airily cross between multiple 'cultures of media and groups,' based more on ad hoc tastes and interests. Examples include ones which use terms such as 'urban tribes' (Ueno 2005) or 'post-subcultures' (Muggleton and Weinzierl 2003) to describe such new 'cultures of media and groups' in their quest for understanding. In terms of the example of Madonna fans, the girls are switching among a variety of positions within the social context, at different times being daughters, elder- or younger sisters, friends or other entities.[5] Consequently, they do not always remain in an oppressed position, and the non-entrenchment of their position in this manner is a characteristic of the new perspective.

Nevertheless, there are probably still some definitive differences among uses and gratifications studies. This is because though they may not see the positions as being entrenched, they do not regard them as being totally free, either, and do not abandon a 'dominant–subordinate' interpretation. This is clear also from Toshiya Ueno's emphasising that a 'positive, open, or "disordering" aspect' lurks within 'urban tribes,' and, whatever form they might ultimately take, the locating of 'cultures of media and groups' in social contexts as 'counter-cultures' could be called a major characteristic of cultural studies.

Such an orientation itself is not something that would instantly become a demerit, and it is arguably an approach that shows its full strength according to the society it is in. Nonetheless, could it be really said to be appropriate for understanding 'media-and-group culture' in present-day Japan? How would it be if we were to recall the aforementioned example of Kazumasa Oda fans? When considering the social context, is there perhaps no alternative to a 'dominant–subordinate' way of understanding?

From an empirical/critical approach to a multi-method approach

Comparing the empirical and critical approaches

Having reflected thus upon conventional ways of apprehending 'media-and-group culture,' one could argue that there were two major points.

The first is the question of which one to focus upon: the 'sender' or the 'receiver'? Roughly speaking, attention once used to be upon the side of the 'sender,' but it could be said that as the present day grew nearer, focus began to be directed at the 'receiver's' end – at the very communication by people who actually group together, so to speak. This is likely to be related also to the marked segmentation of 'media-and-group culture.'

The second point is that there were differences in approach between the empirical school and critical school. To reiterate, the critical school's approach was to view 'media-and-group culture' as some sort of 'counter-culture,' without letting go of a 'dominant–subordinate' perspective, while the empirical school's approach, on the other hand, was to strive to elucidate empirically the real state of the actual communication within 'media-and-group culture,' rather than on such background contexts.

Of course, this is not to say that either of these approaches was absolutely correct. As far as they each have their own merits and demerits, they should probably be used as different occasions demand. For that very reason, the critical school's perspective applies a little uncomfortably to 'media-and-group culture' in present-day Japan, and I take the view that it would be more appropriate to reconstitute the empirical school's way of understanding.

Naturally, as already mentioned, though uses and gratifications studies might have been empirical in terms of their survey method, there was a problem in that if there were insufficient consideration of the social context, it would be unclear as to what aspect of the society their outcomes really expressed. On this point, cultural studies' qualitative analysis was thought to give more consideration to a broad-ranging social context. However, if one assumes that Japan is less of a class-bound society than those in the West, where cultural studies flourishes, then the issue seems likely to arise of it being relatively difficult to uphold a 'dominant–subordinate' perspective.

Of course, in future, Japan has the potential to change into such a society, but I suggest that, as is also apparent at least nowadays in such phenomena as 'self-searching,' there will be seen, mainly among young people, the kind of phenomenon where no distinct position that would establish a 'counter-culture' even exists, or, more likely, a phenomenon in which they feel huge confusion at the uncertainty of their position.

If so, then it is probably necessary to think in future about the sort of approach which, while giving credit to cultural studies' qualitative analysis, with its ability to consider the social context, would consider yet other social contexts.

Towards a multi-method approach

Here, therefore, what I wish to advocate is a 'multi-method approach.' This is not, so to speak, a perspective that specifies the explanation of some particular cause in an easily-comprehensible manner. Unlike such an 'aloof' way of understanding, the multi-method approach is a way of understanding that aims to delve both broadly and deeply into 'media-and-group culture,' and one which strives for a comprehensive grasp of multiple targets while employing multiple methods of analysis. Let me explain by means of figures.

Figure 2.3 diagrammatically illustrates the main points of the 'multi-method approach,' while taking the perspectives discussed thus far into account; and Figure 2.4 shows two concrete analytical examples.

To touch first upon Figure 2.3, approaches which once focused on the 'sender,' for instance, were ones that analysed the '(1) Media message patterns' in the figure, and could be said to have concentrated on which patterns had media messages with strong persuasive power, or on how 'External factor 1: All background influences' exerted its impact.

The later approaches, which directed attention at the 'receiver,' focused instead on '(2) Agent's patterns.' These ones could be said to have developed their analysis as to what kind of people used and drew gratification from media messages belonging to what sort of pattern, and, especially in the case of cultural studies, they took a broad-ranging social context into consideration at the same time.

Moreover, though not given detailed treatment in this chapter, in a psychological perspective, there are probably occasions where the aim is to apprehend '(2) Agent's patterns' based on 'External factor 2: Sudden emergence of unique psychological characteristics' (such as that being wildly enthusiastic over an idol as a pseudo-romantic object is a psychological characteristic of adolescence).

Moreover, though not touched upon much in research thus far, when '(3) Grouping patterns' are incorporated into the field of scrutiny, it will be obvious that there could be a comprehensive interpretation consisting of at least three viewpoints vis-à-vis 'media-and-group culture,' namely: what kind of '(2) Agents' receive what manner of '(1) Media messages' while making what sort of '(3) Groupings' (and, though it is my position as author not to place much importance upon it in sociologically understanding 'media-and-group culture' in present-day Japan, still, in certain cases, the necessity may arise to focus on 'External factor 1: All background influences,' as in the critical school approach; or on 'External factor 2: Sudden emergence of unique psychological characteristics,' as does psychology).

For example, using such a 'multi-method approach,' I have conducted analyses between the late 1990s and the early 2000s in Japan on fans of 'Johnny's-type' male idols,[6] and fans of 'visual-*kei*' rock bands,[7] mainly targeting female upper-secondary students in their teens. On those occasions, I selected a concrete survey method

Figure 2.3: Schematic diagram of the multi-method approach

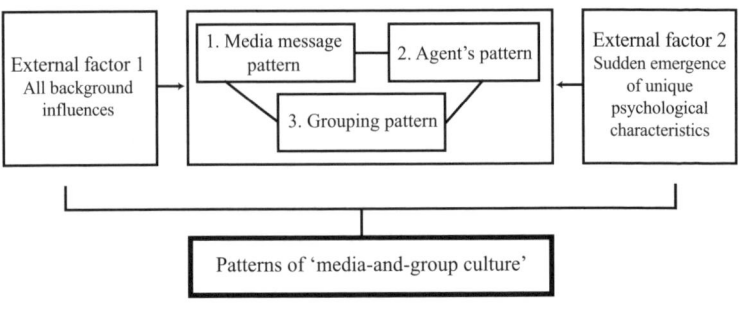

Figure 2.4: Examples of multi-method approach analysis

Analytical example 1

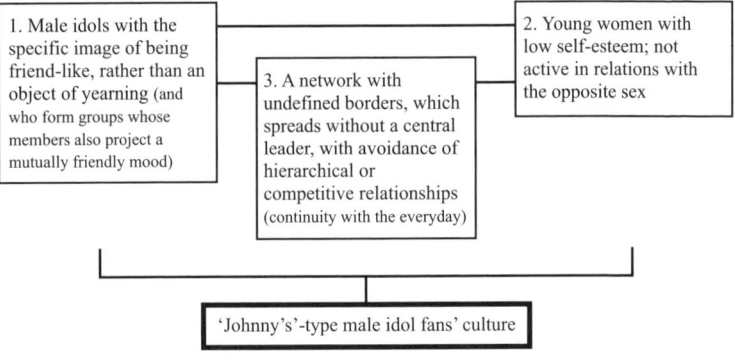

Analytical example 2

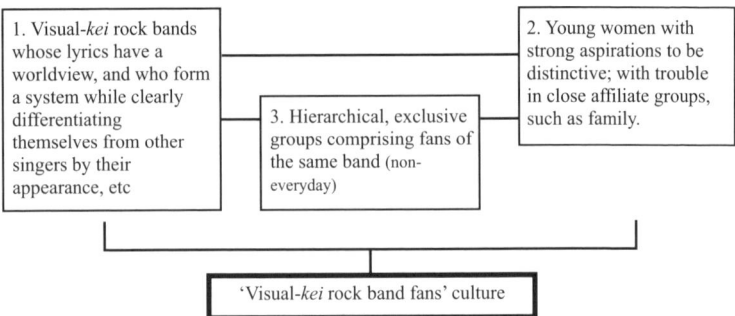

for each viewpoint, and, by comparing the results of the analyses, elucidated the characteristics of each respective 'media-and-group culture.' I further deepened my understanding by comparison of the mutual outcomes. Before introducing the results, when the survey methods are enumerated for each viewpoint, they read as follows.[8]

Analytical methods relating to 'media-and-group culture'

1. Analytical methods relating to media messages
   - Qualitative content analysis (relating to media messages such as television and magazines)
   - Quantitative content analysis*
2. Analytical methods relating to agents
   - Interviews relating to basic attributes (sex, age, place of residence, family composition, academic background, et cetera)
   - Interviews relating to character and personality traits
   - Interviews relating to life history (when did they start to use what kind of media, and in what did they become interested?)
   - These points could also be grasped through a questionnaire survey*
3. Analytical methods relating to ways of grouping
   - By use of participant-observation, snowball sampling,[9] sociometric tests[10] and the like, grasping the characteristics of the ways of grouping
   - Interviews relating to how the parties themselves position such groups[11]

Figure 2.4 is one that diagrammatically illustrates the outcomes, but, when I summarise points to do with '(Analytical example 1) "Johnny's"-type male idol fans,' as the characteristic of idols constituting '(1) Media messages,' first I can cite the idols' having a close-friend-like image, rather than one of an object of yearning, or of manly toughness. Accordingly, in terms of the content of their songs, as well, rather than having an especially profound world-view, they tended to centre upon things from the familiar, everyday world, and they tended to place more emphasis on dancing rather than lyrics (the general objection that idols' songs have no substance probably hits the mark on this point). Moreover, because these idols formed groups with several members, and have an overall consistency as 'Johnny's-type' boy bands, as well, being able to take one's pick from among them was also a characteristic.

Among fans as '(2) Agents,' there could be seen many females who had low self-esteem, and were not very positive about relationships with the opposite sex; and for that reason, even in their '(3) Way of grouping,' they formed network-like groups that spread endlessly, while deftly avoiding competition with other fans of the same idol, known as *dōtan* ('in charge of the same'), rather than in a shape that had a central leader and clearly-defined hierarchical relationships. (Due to space limitations, I leave further details to a separate paper: see Izumi Tsuji 2004, et cetera.) Such characteristics arguably are ones that become clear-cut by overlapping the three perspectives. Moreover, when comparison is made with other 'media-and-group cultures,' an even deeper understanding can be achieved.

By contrast, in the case of '(Analytical example 2) Visual-*kei* rock band fans,' as '(1) Media messages,' their characteristics consisted of the lyrics having a unique world-view and the band members being differentiated from other singers to an almost extreme extent in terms of appearance. Accordingly, their '(2) Agents,' also, often happened to have strong aspirations to be different, such as not wanting to do the same thing as others, or having had some kind of major experience that ended up giving them a unique world-view (family discord, for instance), and for that reason, in their '(3) Way of grouping,' too, they formed somewhat exclusive groups consisting only of fans of the same band, such as could share a world-view.

Furthermore, speaking of the relationship between these two 'media-and-group cultures,' there were also some fans of visual-*kei* rock bands who had originally been fans of Johnny's-type idols, and these had a 'consciousness that their position had improved,' as it were. In other words, many people had had an interest in Johnny's-type idols when around lower-secondary-school age, but after that, when they became upper-secondary students, they not only became fans of something specific, but their interests shifted to a variety of culture (also including becoming positive about relationships with the opposite sex, and so on); and, if they were still fans of idols, they were regarded as being in a slightly inferior position. The issue of 'whether they would become able to appreciate "things that had substance" (whether they had a strong desire to be different),' or 'whether they were positive towards relationships with the opposite

Perspectives on media-and-group culture 33

Figure 2.5: Visual-kei rock band fans gathered at Jingu Bridge (Jingū-bashi) in front of Harajuku Station © Sōichirō Matsutani

sex (whether they were popular with males),' and the like, had become the basis of such consciousness, and it was widely shared by the respective fans, also.

As such, if we were to widen our object of comparison even more to encompass other 'media-and-group cultures' such as those female types that are dubbed *gyaru-kei*, who are positive in their opposite-sex relationships, or, again, females with a strong interest in fashion magazines, and apply the multi-method approach, then it would be possible to extend our understanding even deeper.

Conclusion

Examined in this way, the multi-method approach can be seen to have provided an understanding of 'media-and-group culture' in contemporary Japanese society by deep and broad exploration. As we saw in this chapter, also, rather than simplistically pitting the perspectives of the empirical school and critical school against each other and having them compete for supremacy, one could say there is call for selection of an appropriate way of seeing to suit the time and occasion, while discerning the respective merits and demerits of the two schools' perspectives.

Unlike an 'aloof' way of interpretation such as the conventional ones, which customised their explanations in an easily-understood manner by pinpointing some specific cause, in future it will be necessary to accumulate the kind of perspectives that will continue to delve deeply and broadly, just as if reflecting upon things as 'our own business.' In this aspect, the multi-method approach is still in the trial-and-error stage, and probably needs more polishing; and that is also likely to lead to further development of our grasp of 'media-and-group culture.'

To add one last comment, such a multi-method approach is something that can be utilised not only in qualitative analysis, such as introduced in this chapter, but also in quantitative analysis. In fact, from the late 1980s to the early 1990s, a group led by sociologist Shinji Miyadai implemented a questionnaire survey targeting university students. This was a large-scale project in which they apprehended what in terms of Figure 2.3 above would be their '(2) Agents' pattern' and '(3) Grouping pattern' through questionnaires, and at the same time compared these with their '(1) Media messages pattern.' As a result, they discovered the existence of the two patterns called '*otaku*' and '*shinjinrui* (new Homo sapiens)' in 'media-and-group culture' (Miyadai et al. [1992/1993] 2007).

Even today, this is a study greatly worthy of emulation. Nowadays, however, when segmentation of 'media-and-group culture' has markedly advanced much further than at that time, the task for the moment is to build up a store of numerous qualitative analyses, is it not? Once ample knowledge had been thus obtained, then it would be possible for large-scale quantitative projects to be undertaken once more. For that very reason, it will be necessary from now on to continue tenaciously with approaches to 'media-and-group culture.'

Notes

1 Also see Chapter Six of this volume, as it examines in detail the flow in such empirical school approaches
2 The targets were members of the 'Kazumasa Oda Appreciation Society' of a certain university in Tokyo, and students of a different women's university. Of the sixty members of the Appreciation Society, forty-four were male, while the women's university students numbered 153. Though none of the latter belonged to a fan club, appreciation society, or suchlike, as the majority (84%) replied that they owned at least one Kazumasa Oda CD, or liked him (46.8%), a comparison is made in this analysis between male and female fans from among the male members of the Appreciation Society and the women's university students (Matsui (ed.) 1994). The analytical methodology used here to sort the gratification types into three categories is called factor analysis (for details on this, see Chapter Thirteen).
3 For a detailed explanation of the difference between qualitative and quantitative analysis, see Chapter Four of this volume. Moreover, I would

like to state additionally that early uses and gratifications studies from the 1940s centred upon qualitative research.
4 Hall's own original paper is by no means lengthy, but see Minamida (2005) for a very readable introduction in Japanese.
5 In understanding the 'media-and-group culture' that constitutes Madonna fans, it is vital to comprehend the situation in which young women of the present day are placed. As a detailed analysis of the current situation of young women in Japan is developed in Chapter Ten of this volume, please refer to it at your discretion.
6 In concrete terms, this refers to male idols such as SMAP, KinKi Kids, V6, NEWS, KAT-TUN who are affiliated with an entertainment company called Johnny's Office.
7 This refers to rock bands in which members wear a distinctive kind of makeup, and are especially characterised by their appearance. Specifically, though now disbanded, the group called X-JAPAN is said to have been the first of these.
8 Here, in addition to the one the author actually used, survey methods that could be employed vis-à-vis each respective viewpoint are also introduced, this being in accordance with the aim of this book, that is, to conduct a broad examination of ways of understanding 'media-and-group culture.' As such, those which the author did not use in the actual surveys are marked with an asterisk (*).
9 For example, in the process of repeating the request: 'Please introduce other fans with whom you are friends,' when finally looking back at what sort of people were introduced, the characteristics of the way such fans get together become visible. For details, see Izumi Tsuji (2004).
10 In more easily comprehensible terms, this is akin to a 'who-do-you-like quiz' once often practised at schools, and so on. It is a method which elucidates the characteristics of the internal mechanism of a group by, for example, distributing and collecting questionnaires that ask respondents to write in the names of good friends, up to a set number of people, and then displaying the results diagrammatically.
11 What the author concretely employed was an interview method relating to the proportion of space that similar fans occupied in the contacts list on the mobile phones owned by targets, or how important they were seen to be. For details, see Izumi Tsuji (2004).
12 By all means refer to Chapter Seven of this volume for a detailed analysis of communication among young female readers of fashion magazines.

3 Perspectives on expressive culture: what do cultural works give people, and how do they link people together?

Katsuya Minamida

We live our lives daily as if surrounded by cultural works. Today, too, through media and computer networks, works that have been created by somebody are being viewed. From the fact that the entire IT industry, the so-called winning team in this, is hastening to enhance its content, it can also be seen that cultural works = intellectual property have a powerful unifying force in contemporary society.

What is important, however, is probably not such things. In the midst of our daily lives, when we are troubled, angry, joyful, or when we love somebody, cultural works are there as something to support those feelings, as manna for our hearts. We must think about cultural works as things connected to such workings of the heart.

Could sociology be said to have sufficiently presented any method for analysing such mental mechanisms up till now? In this chapter, I will consider various problems that arise when one has made expressive culture such as artistic culture or popular culture, and especially its very 'works,' into a topic for research.

First of all, I will make a rigorous distinction between the 'person–work' relationship and the 'person–work–person' relationship that constitute the forms in which we come into contact with cultural works, and elucidate their respective structures and mechanisms. Moreover, I will conduct a review of the disciplinary system which has undertaken each of them, meaning that disciplines including literature, aesthetics, sociology, and media studies will probably tender a bid. Finally, based on this, I will show a new sociological conception of cultural works. This chapter has been prepared for people who unconsciously become completely absorbed in the world-view of cultural works.

Communication in expressive culture

Expressive culture as a research topic

In contemporary Japan, many people are familiar with works of expressive culture created for a mass audience, such as music, films, comics, novels and games. Japan's production and shipment volume in the field of music, for example, is second in the world after the United States (Contents Business Kenkyū Kai 2005, pp. 164–5); its animation and games are exported to every country on the globe, and Japan has reached a point where it brags of being a major nation in content terms. Today, especially, when we are a decade into the twenty-first century, enormous numbers of people create works due to the advance of digitalisation, and the media and industries which transmit these have become markedly diversified, almost to the extent that it would be no exaggeration to say that we are living surrounded by crowds of works that somebody has expressed somewhere.

For many people, a liking and taste for cultural works begins to solidify from their upper high-school years. When they become university students, they are likely to spread their wings even further and carve out a new interest, or dig deep into the roots of one particular genre. University life could be called the period when people can be most engrossed in that interest. In that environment, many students seem to want to choose the expressive culture which engages them as their topic when set the task of writing a graduation thesis or report. Actually, it is a significant theme that enables one to gain a greater variety of knowledge the more one becomes absorbed in it.

It is also true, however, that there are many examples of failure, in which things did not run smoothly. By choosing something that one likes as a target of research, one loses one's ability to keep a distance from that target. In other words, one might be preoccupied with admiration for the work in question, for example, or become incapable of dispassionate discussion, which ought to be possible if one alters one's viewpoint. Naturally, this is not a problem that arises solely when making expressive culture one's object. That being said, it also could be argued that it occurs because the motivation for selecting expressive culture in the first place tends to depend on a sense of personal preference. Dissertations that rely upon a 'sense of personal preference' become 'subjective opinions.' It is at times like these that the negative diagnosis is handed down that they are so-called 'analyses of favourite things' (Miyadai et al. 1991, p. 58), characterised by egocentricity and lack of objectivity.

Next time, conversely, how would it be to try being strongly conscious of objectivity? In such a case, this would mean elucidating the approval rating of a cultural work by means of a survey, without touching upon its internal properties, or expounding the workings of the media and content industries which encircle the work. In that case, though, the charm of that work which one really wanted to communicate – the motivation which originally inspired one to begin the research – falls away.

I would like people who harbour the kind of dilemma described above to read this chapter. As many texts that ponder expressive culture from media discourse or industry discourse have already been published, I will not make that my main topic here. Without demolishing a sociological standpoint, I will consider how to construct a narrative that surmounts subjective opinion while closing in the essence of a work, or something similar.

The two points of contact between cultural works and people

First, then, let me show on a theoretical basis what kinds of things can be considered in relation to the communication brought about by cultural works. Expressed in exceptionally simple images, the connection between cultural works and people takes the two forms shown in Figure 3.1.

First, let us begin by thinking about A) The 'person–work' relationship. Each individual comes into contact with a work mediated by media, or a live performance conducted before their eyes, by mobilising their eyes or ears, or sometimes the senses in their skin. Confronting the work results in the individual's having the experience of being impressed, feeling sympathy, being shocked, or suchlike. Further, the person might not stop at that, but will sometimes commit to memory who it was that created the work, and take an interest in the author's persona, or care about what genre to which the work belongs. The individual experience which that person has enjoyed gives rise to the comfortable feeling that it suited their sensitivity; and, in certain cases, the person might empathise with the message imbued in the work, or imitate the actions of the

Perspectives on expressive culture 39

Figure 3.1: A) The 'person–work' relationship

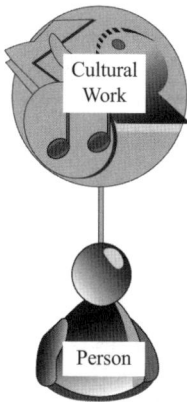

Figure 3.2: B) The 'person–work–person' relationship

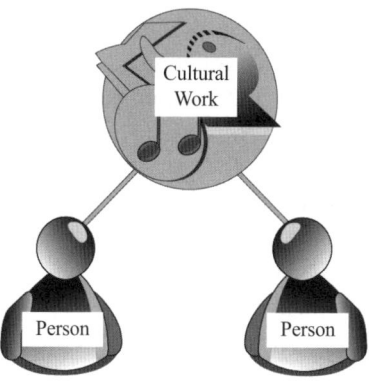

author delivering the work, or overlay the behaviour of the people in the work upon their own life.

As for B) The 'person–work–person' relationship, individuals who have thus experienced a connection with a work communicate with others about the cultural work. In the A) relationship, the work which was the subject of the message becomes a tool for communication, and individuals take up the proper names of the work and its author, employing them as a topic when making conversation. On that occasion, individuals might go no further than to state their impressions of liking or disliking the work, but they sometimes talk about the quality of their own experience in the format of a critique or commentary. Then again, at certain times, they might adopt the style of academism. In such a way, individuals who prefer a particular work or author might collude with others who like similar works or authors; or compete with others who prefer different works or authors; or gauge the social distance between themselves and others who do not share their preference. When this kind of communication arises with sufficient frequency, it comes to be recognised as an explicit genre, or a 'school' dubbed such-and-such a *-kei*.

The categories into which works have been categorised become guidelines for reference when individuals next choose a different work. By following those guidelines, individuals further expand their volume of experience (again, the A) relationship). As they do this, the proper names of works, authors and genres become devices for self-expression akin to their own possessions, and are applied to yet further communication (the B) relationship, once more). In short, the A) and B) relationships come and go.[1]

Furthermore, here, we are applying a simplified model as an ideal type in our consideration, but it would not matter if the subject that linked with a work in the A) relationship were not an anonymous individual. The same goes for people who take on the role of advertising a work extensively: company employees, professional writers, disc jockeys or 'talents,' part-timers who write pop-copy for record shops or bookshops, bloggers, or even the work's very author. Day in and day out, words that tell of the experience of works are produced by those countless subjects, using diverse forms including critiques, reviews, advertising, interviews, diaries, and daily conversation.

Similarly, the B) relationship is not solely assuming the individual on a one-to-one basis, either. Through speech and articles mediated by such media as television and magazines, through the 'liner notes' and commentaries attached to pamphlets and packaging, and through the BBS posts from multiple people on the internet, interaction comes into being day after day.

By sorting out the connection between cultural works and people by means of a theoretical standard, as above, I think that I have succeeded in showing that the connection is a vastly-expanding realm of human activity. From here on, I wish to return to my main topic, and focus concern upon the question of under what kind of academic system that connection has been handled. Pursuits which verbalise the experience of A) The 'person–work' relationship include literary criticism, cultural critique, literature and aesthetics, while attempts to survey B) The 'person–work–person' relationship include culture-industry discourse, media research and sociology. Similarly, to 'talk about culture' sounds simple enough, but everything – from methodology to analytical procedure – changes according to the viewpoint from which the phenomenon is perceived, namely, A) or B). Moreover, through making a rigorous distinction between these two connections, the reason why research into expressive culture has not gone well in sociology will be understood, and the methodology for coping with this is also likely to become visible.

The 'person–work' relationship

People who gaze at works

Let us first think about methodology that focused upon A) The 'person–work' relationship. After people have had an experience such as being impressed, sympathising, or being shocked by a cultural work, they try to give an explanation to that experience with a self-styled interpretation. From the start, a work is simultaneously a site of expression for the one who created it, and a framework of sensitive reception for the person who perceives it (Caune 1997); and the receivers of the work have spun together numerous words about their own sensitivity, which is hard to express in language, with a passion to rival or surpass the author of the work. When this is systematised as an academic pursuit, it is called by such nomenclature as literature, film studies, musicology, or aesthetics.

Incidentally, by what means might cultural works rouse people's sensitivity, bring about the experience of being impressed, and so on? The academe seeks to find an answer to that question. As one major trend, there is a way that focuses upon the 'form' of a work, namely, its style, format, or structure. In poetry, this means rhetoric and literary style; in novels, plays and films, the narrative structure; in plastic works, it means form; in photographic and moving images, composition and placement; and in music, the structure of the musical sounds written in the score. As the history of a genres is amassed, it is the role of these disciplines to scrutinise, discover the hidden order within, and record the various forms which exhibit systematic regularity. They also link with technology (the accumulation of techniques), and also become practical guides when the receivers of works accomplish transformation into creative authors.

If we paid attention only to form, however, we would be unable to account for why cultural works are so attractive to people's minds, so analysis of their 'content' becomes necessary. Language that expressed the spirituality and vicissitudes of the author or characters in the work, originality in depiction of the setting, contemporaneousness which synchronises with the historical aspect, a spirit of innovation which discloses a new world, and the like, are positions which decode the interior portion of the expression engraved in the work. These academic practices are called criticism or critique, and have even spawned independent occupations.

The more such scholarly occupations are refined, however, the more they are shadowed by certain issues. When an assessment of a particular cultural work is to be made, some criterion is always required – namely, whether it is 'something good' or 'something bad.' Whether a work is one with enough constituents to turn history on its head, or one that is only expressing spirituality on a low dimension, no matter what kind of thing it is, a work cannot be assessed without a benchmark for evaluation. Is the experience of being impressed really something that can be measured by such a yardstick, though? Let me express it in another way. In whose eyes is the work, to which a value is about to be enthusiastically applied by the lining up of such assessment criteria, a good thing or a beautiful thing? Ultimately, this is a matter for the subjective sense of the person who is the receiver of the work, and who is going to describe it. The deciding factor as to what constitutes a superior work is the aesthetic criterion which the work's receiver has set up *a priori*.

In the present day, in conventional literature and musicology there is a surfeit of objects that defy evaluation. Light novels that are worthless in literary terms, three-chord punk rock that does not bear mention on the basis of a symphony – it is all too easy to dismiss them because they do not fulfil academic assessment criteria, but if we take heed of their influence in real society, we cannot ignore them when we talk about cultural works. Nonetheless, if we were to discuss these facets of pop culture with conventional scholarly logic, then their subordinate nature would simply be laid bare, and there would be little fruit for our efforts. In the worst case, talking about a work would inevitably become a 'so-called tool for self-inspiration which projected our own desires amid a reality where we would not be free' (Miyadai et al. 1993, p. 133).

Criticism and sociology

Of course, even if discussion by people who scrutinise works were to approach criticism, critiques or 'tools for self-inspiration,' it would not mean that such an occupation were futile. Discourse on works or authorship thus penned might disclose to a different reader or viewer a new potential reading of the work, and that dissertation might be fed back to the author at some time and become a guide to new creation. Comment in which a deep reading is made through keen insight can itself also be called a work. Currently, along with the penetration of the internet, there is a great deal of criticism and critique vis-à-vis pop culture works, including review sites, as well. While there is no lack of situations where their merits and demerits are questioned,[2] the potential for such action to enrich the culture of works overall cannot be denied.

That being said, in cases where one writes one's own thoughts vis-à-vis a work, not as an individual in a blog or coterie magazine, or as a professional critic in an industry magazine, but in the shape of a sociological paper, one is warned against that sort of subjective discussion based on one's own assessment of a work. This is not because the study of expressive culture is not appropriate for sociology. Sociology derives from an academic postulate which it has regulated along with its history.

Frankly speaking, sociology has a mission to observe the state of people's awareness. As Max Weber states, sociology deals with the 'conceptually "ideal type" of subjective meaning attributed to a hypothetical actor in a given type of conduct. In neither sense can it be used in an objectively "valid" or as a metaphysically fathomable "true" meaning' ([1922] 1962, p. 29). The reason for this is that patterns of recognition differ according to social strata, and there is no such thing as 'valid' or 'true' recognition.

> Herein lies the distinction between the behavioural sciences, such as Sociology and history and the orthodox disciplines, such as

Jurisprudence, Logic, Ethics, or Esthetics, whose purpose is to determine the 'true' and 'valid' meaning of the object of their analysis (Weber [1922] 1962, p. 29).

In other words, the identification of an aesthetic essence in cultural works is not the job of the sociologist. The research objective of sociology is to find out how something constituting an aesthetic essence is decided upon among differing social strata, and how it is managed in actual society. Sociologists use imaginative power to ponder the relationality in people's behaviour. Conversely, unless they put a seal on any interest that would cleave its way through into something comprising an aesthetic essence, they will fail to keep their sociologically analytical stance.

Weber also propounds the concept of being 'value-free' as being a preparedness to maintain academic objectivity. He is not suggesting that scholars depart from their own values and be free when they are dealing with a target: he is proposing that they become aware that they themselves are clad with all kinds of values in their daily lives, and with that knowledge, discuss the workings of the hearts of people, including themselves, who simply cannot escape from values.

In that sense, the stance of 'analysing something one likes' arguably does not need to be criticised in itself. Sociology is a discipline which observes events that take place in society, and diagnoses and suggests things vis-à-vis society. When observing events, sociologists should mobilise all resources relating to the target of observation. Then, having decided to make one realm of the expressive culture in which they themselves are immersed into their object of study, when they observe enthusiastic action, the target of observation they can best understand in relation to the mental mechanism of enthusiasm and changes in behaviour is the inner tendencies of none other than themselves. They have secured an informant for observation in a far more practical and effective manner than by observing others. Their own self becomes the target of observation, as it were.

It is not that dealing with pop culture or subcultures is an issue, nor that 'analysing something one likes' is a problem, either. What is important is that one recognises that one is oneself situated within the 'person–work' relationship; and that one searches for a method of discussion while relativising one's subjective opinions, aesthetic instincts and assessment criteria as far as possible.

Cultural research that takes a fresh look at the meaning of works

In the present day, meta-level observation which questions the significance of a work having been criticised, rather than the meaning of the work itself, is not the monopoly of sociology. The humanities, which have a history of literature, aesthetics, and the like, have continued to grope for a style in which they can push forward their descriptions in a form suited to the temporal circumstances, in an interdisciplinary manner, and from a relative positionality.

One theory that emphasises the receiver of a work is Wolfgang Iser's ([1976] 1978) 'theory of aesthetic response.' Iser states that as a work only starts to exist as a work when a viewer comes into contact with it, most attention should be directed at the receiver when analysis is carried out. The work comes to life by being read by a receiver, and that work will attract future receivers, and Iser made the description of how the receiver engages in dialogue with the work and its author the objective of his theory of aesthetic response.

Moreover, literary scholars who took note of 'intertexuality' pushed the relativisation of works a step further. In their research, they did not regard works to be the creative property of a single author, nor as products that could stand alone. Works were 'made possible by prior works that they take up, repeat, challenge, transform' (Culler [1997] 2009, p. 43). It was asserted that any one work would have a connection with many other works, and when thinking about a work, one must pay attention to the interrelationship between texts.

This idea of intertexuality was one which the symbolist Julia Kristeva ([1967] 1986) first propounded, but the image of a text coming and going along a vast textual horizon is one linked to the current in which Roland Barthes proclaimed the 'death of the author' (Barthes 1966), and Jacques Derrida proposed the 'play of difference' (Derrida [1972] 1981, p. 14). Barthes claimed that works which had gone out into the world were interpreted in many ways that departed from the author's original intention, and stated that one should pursue the pleasures of free interpretation. What is more, Derrida argued that, regardless of the presence or absence of the author, the reader takes meaning freely from the text, and there is, therefore, no transcendental meaning that would determine the text's aesthetics or dominance, there being nothing but a 'play' of meaning around the text.

Such theories are called 'post-structuralist,' 'deconstructivist,' and so on, but in recent years they have tended to come under critical scrutiny (Takeda 2001, and others). One reason for this is that there are misgivings that those various theorists might have been too committed to repudiating the uniqueness of authors and works. The way of thinking that situated each person's interpretation of a text through their own reading as being its 'tactics' had significance as critical momentum in an age when it was believed that there was a privileged reading; but, on the other hand, it gave rise to the vulgar understanding that 'readers could do what they liked.' Pulling out the ladder in rejecting authoritative assessment criteria (once a transcendental judgement that was the province of scholarship) has invited a situation in which there was a rash of dubious hermeneutics (the various little local gods).

So, what kinds of things could be considered as research to which sociological methods could be applied, while closing in immanently upon the 'person–work' relationship? Though with some reservations, the viewpoint of 'reflection theory' could be said to be close. Reflection theory is a way of reasoning applied to social comment, and so on, which regards individual works as 'mirrors to reality,' based on the premise that cultural works reflect life and society. This reasoning has been rooted in literary criticism since ages past, so there is nothing novel about it; and there is also a tendency for rejection of naïve reflection theory, which simplistically connects reality and the world of works. However, a method which utilises not the naïve reflection theory of the 'masterpieces that express a sick age!' school, but the narrative development of cultural works as raw material for carrying out a sociological explanation of concepts, has established a regular foothold since Lewis Coser's *Sociology through Literature* (1963). In Japan, scholars like Kei'ichi Sakuta and Shigeki Tominaga have propounded a 'sociology from literature' which aims to 'enable the very discovery of sociological thought' by 'bending an ear to what literature says' (Inoue 2000, pp. 134–5). This is something that uses cultural works as an 'intellectual catalyst' (Miyahara 2001, p. 28), as it were, when pondering social life, and there are more and more examples that consider not only literature, but also comics and animation, as metaphors for the real world (Fujimoto 2001; Tanimoto 2006, and others).[3]

When this method is adopted, however – and this also ties in with the discussion in the next chapter – there is probably a need to examine fully what kind of representativeness that work could hold.

The 'person–work–person' relationship

The loss of shared assumptions

Next, I would like to think about the 'person–work–person' relationship, which would be the main theme for cultural sociology. This relationship, which understands cultural works as media, as a process of production–distribution–consumption, and as a tool of communication for human interaction, is something with which it is easier for sociology, which inquires into the organisation of society from the relationship between one person and another, to become acquainted. The task of apprehending expressive culture by means of this relationship is, however, hampered by certain difficulties.

The network which binds together the 'person–work–person' relationship is recognised as a 'taste group' when the focus is upon 'persons,' and as a 'genre' when it is on 'works,' but the rift between people who have interest in or knowledge about such groups, and those people who do not, is unexpectedly violent. Frankly speaking, for people who do not know the genre which connects works, this becomes something hard to understand.

Let me postulate, by way of example, the site of university education. In tutorials and seminars in media courses and the like, when students make presentations on topics they pick themselves, the weeks when pop culture and subcultures are the theme sometimes are a little lacklustre. Students who have chosen that topic throw themselves enthusiastically into preparing for their presentation, but the more zealous their engagement, the more an atmosphere of 'impenetrableness' is fomented among the surrounding people, and when it is time for questions and answers, silence ensues. (Here, it is lucky if students wake up to a sense of boundaries, namely, that the subcultures in which they are engrossed are little-known, contrary to their expectations.)

In a different week, when the theme of advertising, television and reportage has been set, in discussion time comments will be obtainable from the milieu in their own way, regardless of the relative merits of the presenter's content and presentation technique. The point is that the volume of utterances during discussion is influenced by whether the topic is something constantly touched upon in regular everyday life, or is something whose absence would not be missed.

Alternatively, something similar could be said if we assume a lecture setting. One of the pleasures of sociology is that of submitting a new perspective, one that betrays a commonsense interpretation. This is a learning outcome which only begins to function on the premise that the students who comprise a class have a shared knowledge of the theme of the lecture. When attempting to say something that overturns a conventional interpretation in relation to a subculture, however, as the other students are ignorant of the 'conventional interpretations,' they have first to be taught that particular subculture's commonsense narrative, and so it takes twice the effort.

Formerly, students had to know about the literati of the Meiji era (1868–1912) and the composers of classical music as part of their 'general education.' Cultural research was established upon such a foundation, but that no longer applies. Though this is probably not a difficulty confined to the sociology of culture, in circumstances where common premises have been undermined in recent years in a variety of aspects, it can still be considered a disadvantage in the case of lectures on cultural situations with a specialised character.

Thinking back, in the case of pop culture and subcultures, how can one judge that these constitute knowledge which it is not particularly necessary to share? In order to ponder this question, I would like to start my discussion by explaining once more the structure of the theoretical 'person–work–person' relationship.

What proper names constitute

Sociology places the understanding of relationships between people at its very foundations. At such times it often uses a conceptual relationship model, but because it is comparatively easy to apprehend relationality, as in, for example, parent and child, in the case of 'the family,' boss and subordinate in the case of 'organisations,' and working class/upper class in the case of 'cities,' it is thus also easy to typologise. Of course, I am not suggesting that everything can be explained by concise typology, but Claude Lévi-Strauss' kin-

Perspectives on expressive culture 49

Figure 3.3: Patrilineal/matrilineal kinship structures

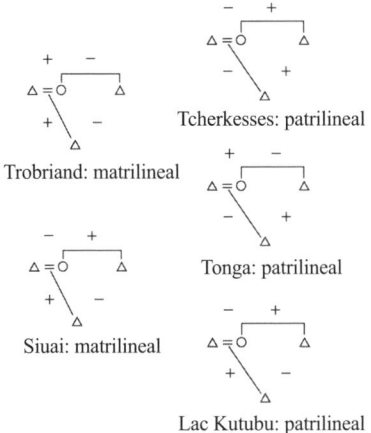

Source: Lévi-Strauss 1958, p. 4.

ship structure shown in Figure 3.3, for one, and Ernest W. Burgess' concentric zone theory (concentric zone model) in Figure 3.4, for another, became the basic model for their respective topics (cultural anthropology and urban sociology), and formed the foundation for discussions acknowledging relationships, as in how such things as exceptions are taken into account.[4]

If one were to endeavour to construct a model of the relationship between expressive culture and people, it would become something expressing the content of the connections among actual taste groups, as in Figure 3.5, for example. In the case of taste cultures, the thing that joins one particular individual to another particular individual is none other than precisely the topic of culture (in the example in the figure, the topic of Japanese rock music). In other words, the positioning of those respective persons' empathy and disaffection will be determined by their taste decisions as to who or what they like and dislike among the proper names in circulation in that cultural sphere (the author's name being taken up in the case of novels or music; or, with films or comics, the name of the work, in many instances). When a taste group or genre is formed, such a way of communicating is at its base. Naturally, if we take into consideration external or attributive factors such as media or industry, social class or gender, then the need for drawing a complex structural chart will arise, but fundamentally it can be argued that

Figure 3.4: Burgess' concentric zone model

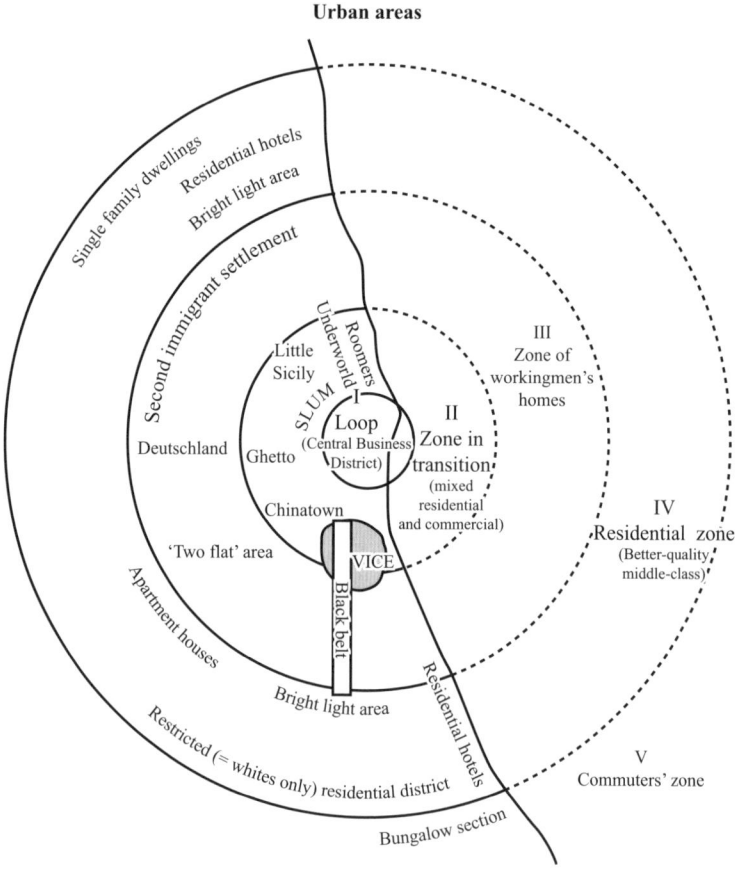

Source: Burgess 1967, p. 55.

the structure of culture consists of a 'relationship that would not be possible without the mediation of proper names such as the names of works or musicians.'

Nonetheless, it would be a fairly difficult job to explain the state of that relationship, and how significant it was to find out about it, to people who hardly knew any of the proper names illustrated in Figure 3.5. By way of experiment, if we try to explain a little about the relationality in Figure 3.5, the person ('he') on the top right side prefers Japanese rock (J-ROCK), he also often reads music magazines like *ROCKIN' ON JAPAN*, and, in his own opinion, he has a broad-ranging understanding of rock. As proof of this, he can

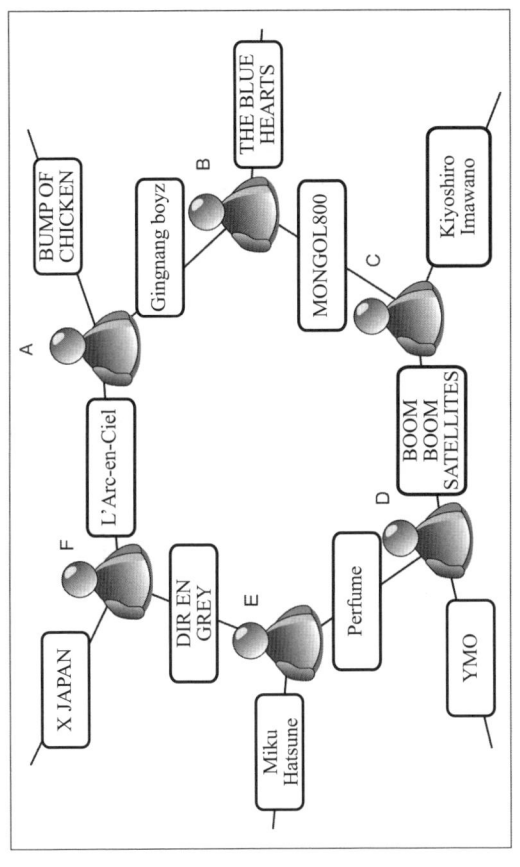

Figure 3.5: Relationship model of cultural taste groups, exemplified by Japanese rock music

talk also to someone on the mid-right who likes punk, and someone on the upper left, who prefers visual-*kei*. Yet though being in the L'Arc-en-Ciel category, he does not have a preference for a heavy metal style, and so will not necessarily get on well with a person on the upper left. On the other hand, a person ('she') on the lower right often attends rock fests featuring Japanese music (festivals in which Japanese artists appear), and she thinks that any sound that can be danced to, even punk or techno, is good music. Her knowledge is limited, though, and she cannot follow the talk of rabid fans of either. A techno fan on the lower left would be more likely to feel he had something in common with someone on the mid-left who was deeply-knowledgeable about the music of the internet generation, and though the techno fan's understanding would not extend as far as the virtual idol, Miku Hatsune, he would feel that these were closer to himself than orthodox rock fans – and so the list goes on. However hard they might try to explain in minute detail the disparities and groupings vis-à-vis the space thus established, it would probably only sound as if they were chattering on about the things they liked.

What is more, one could say that this social space is such a fragile structure that its essence would be modified if even one of its entrants were to change. As the foundations of society lie in communication among people, there are differences in the strength and density of the social foundations which establish that communication.

If we think about the economy or the law, for example, the strength of its communication is extremely robust, and could be called the basic social foundation for humans to run their society. If we were to imagine a being that carried out no economic exchange (communication) at all, could that person be really called a social entity? It is not impossible to live without conducting any monetary exchange. We could, for instance, postulate a baby, or someone stranded on a desert island. Such individuals are not, however, so-called 'social entities.' The castaway could only become a social entity by returning from the desert island and engaging in economic exchange. The same applies in the case of the law. Ordinarily, we live without much consciousness of the law, but once it is revealed that we have broken the law, we will immediately be restrained and punished. Whether people observe or break the law is an important criterion for social communication.

Perspectives on expressive culture 53

By comparison, 'cultural tastes' are an extremely tenuous type of communication. Herbert Gans once called groups that are connected by cultural tastes 'taste publics' (1974, pp. 10–11), but cultural tastes never constitute anything but the feeblest kind of connection. Even if the communication of expressive culture were to be interrupted, people would not have their sociality erased because of that. The reason why culture cannot be called the mainstream in sociology is not simply that its object is pop culture, which seems fickle, but because a fundamental part of it has a weak social 'foundation.'

Nonetheless, this does not mean that it is entirely impotent as a social foundation: the space of connections composed as in Figure 3.5 has spawned all kinds of cultural behaviour. In the case of musical performers, for instance, they have mutually constructed 'sound modes' in a timely manner, while referencing past examples. Alternatively, in the case of record fans, their network might form a critical group. In other works, their organically-composed mutual relations have built a discrete culture. In short, things that are irrelevant to people with no interest in them have become a network of unsurpassed importance to people for whom them are important.

When we research culture, we must not lack imagination towards the things that these proper names comprise. Moreover, we must simultaneously bear the risk that a common understanding will be lost in our attempts to document, to the greatest possible extent, a spatial structure that has proper names as its social foundation.

Noting social factors like politics or social stratification

In their 'person–work–person' relationships, people present the proper name of an author or work to another person as something connected to themselves, and effect communication. At those times, on what basis might people have chosen that proper name? One possibility is that they want to explain the orientation of their own interest to another person. Consequently, that might constitute an action aimed at making someone else understand their character and convictions. It is also likely to be a choice made under the influence of immediately-previous messages from the media which they usually access. Furthermore, on different occasions, there are also cases where there is a commercial aim, namely, to generate profit through advertising that work. In some areas or countries, this might mean that a background such as religion, politics or race is impacting upon the choice.

In order for one to apprehend the mesh-like 'person–work–person' relationship, when a certain work is under discussion, it is necessary to think about each individual's 'backbone' and their collective social character. One can soon imagine that the demographic which reads mobile-phone novels would differ from that which reads pure literature, but one will then tackle the task of pondering such issues as where that disparity arises, what social stratum comprises its central support base, and to what the propensity of an individual to have that preference is related.

Moreover, having such a perspective also means shifting one's concern from one which (appears to) pit an overzealous knowledge of a genre of works against that of others, to one of the background social factors (external or attribute factors). Part of the kind of research which is conscious of the link between taste cultures and sociality, and describes its space, is undertaken by the cluster of research styles called cultural studies in recent years.

Cultural studies, which became popular in Japan from the 1990s onwards, had its birth in Britain, where Birmingham's Centre for Contemporary Cultural Studies (CCCS) was established in the 1960s, and took up the social meaning of mass culture as an academic cause. In his major publication, *The Uses of Literacy: Aspects of Working-Class Life with Special Reference to Publications and Entertainments* (1957), Richard Hoggart, the inaugural director of CCCS, explained about the social character of the British working class, using as his material things ranging from items of daily use to the pulp fiction and popular music its members preferred; and he analysed the meaning of the behaviour of the people who lived in that class. Dick Hebdige, in his book *Subculture: the Meaning of Style* (1979), focused upon the style of such subculture groups as Teddy Boys, Mods, Skinheads, and the like, noting how each group appropriated music or fashion as items, altered them to fit their own style, and went on to combine with other groups. Hebdige states that these actions can be called a mode of resistance against the trumpeting of the mass media and traditional codes (dominant ideologies).

Having pointed out the fact that cultural works, which tend to be overlooked as nothing more than a pastime, sometimes act as symbols indicating the properties of a social class, race or nation, cultural studies spawned many followers, and even today, research is being produced that analyses the ideological nature hidden in films, novels, music, animation and so on.

There are, however, claims that in their over-emphasis of that political nature (with the result, in short, that the background becomes the main topic, rather than what the works communicate), these methods deviate from actual fan mentality. Moreover, this can also lead to a reducing of the abundant meaning held by cultural works to ideologies such as social class or gender, and this is often dubbed fundamentalism.

Pierre Bourdieu is one sociologist who applied statistical and interview survey methods from a different angle from cultural studies, with the aim of constructing a systematic cultural theory. He dealt with people's tastes in cultural works as being an important factor in human behavioural principles, and, far from reducing them to an ideology, he mapped those tastes on a structural model of social space stratified by diverse segmentation principles.

In his chief work, *Distinction* ([1979] 1984), Bourdieu introduces the concept of 'cultural capital.' Taste is not simple individual preference or its manifestation, but is closely linked to the rise and fall of individuals' social status. If we call the concentration of wealth and its utilisation in effective settings activities of economic capital, then, in the case of cultural tastes, also, we can liken the actions of having (= concentrating) good taste and displaying (= utilising) it in a social arena to the logic of capital-management activity. In other words, such things as obtaining a concert ticket, owning a painting, acquiring knowledge of cultural history, or having a discerning eye that sees the aesthetic disposition of a work, can all be positioned as acts of accumulation of cultural capital.

In a questionnaire survey Bourdieu conducted, the result emerged that the propensity to appreciate works with socially-recognised legitimacy increases along with a rise in academic qualifications, reaching a peak in the dominant social class that is endowed with abundant academic capital. Middle-brow tastes, including that for major works in the minor arts, is seen with high frequency in the middle classes, and vulgar popular works with a low artistic evaluation are preferred by the working classes, in inverse proportion to academic capital. By defending such works as its own possessions and mocking the aesthetic judgement of other classes, each social stratum cultivates an ever-firmer sense of class boundaries. Due to the emergence of such a mechanism, the class-specific tastes (habitus) internalised by each class continue to be reproduced over generations (Bourdieu [1992] 1996, pp. 179–80). (This reasoning has led to Bourdieu sometimes being disparaged as a 'fatalist.')

In the case of literature, for instance, rather than expounding each separate literary work in terms of its essence, its aesthetic qualities or its emotional effect, Bourdieu's theory gave rise to the perspective that having an outlook on its essence, aesthetic sense, or emotion – including the very discourse which takes the view that there is a hidden ideology in that work – has become a dividing principle that spawns social disparity.

Even if not the factor called social class, there are some social vestiges engraved in works and in the senses of the agents who judge them. Difficulties would accompany any as-is application of Bourdieu's logical composition to the situation in Japanese society, but consideration of what kind of social disparities are linked with taste fields is an indispensable step in getting to know the 'person–work–person' relationship.

Rivalry between two viewpoints

The conception of a science of works of art

Thus far, I have made a contradistinctive introduction of scholarly research which exposed the A) 'person–work' and B) 'person–work–person' relationships. Though ways have been discovered by my forerunners, if either of these is made the sole focus in discussion, that would create its own difficulties; while if it came to research that incorporated both viewpoints, it would be even harder. When speaking of A), one must omit sociality to a certain extent, while when speaking of B), one cannot help once making a detour through a process of reduction to social factors. Though admittedly the threshold has been lowered with the advance of interdisciplinary exchange, a huge chasm lies between the fundamental attitude of literature, which takes the position that 'cultural works speak to society,' and that of social sciences/sociology, which take the position that 'society creates cultural works.'

In his book, *The Rules of Art*, introduced in the previous section, Bourdieu explains the above polarities by the terms 'internal readings' and 'external readings' ([1992] 1996, p. 193). An internal reading is one in which a logic is concluded solely between a work and the person that refers to it, while an external reading calls upon explanatory or interpretative principles external to the work itself. Sociological research, which excels in treating the language of critiques and criticism not as 'truth,' but as one example among a plethora of 'discourses,' conducts social analysis using the people who surround cultural works as a type of raw material. The majority of these, however, stop 'reading' cultural works as works – in other words, they establish their social analysis credentials by means of 'external readings' which carry out phase-swapping in cultural works. On the other hand, this is also an attitude which abandons any explication of 'things that cannot be expressed except in that work,' or the 'instant of a work's creation.'

Vis-à-vis this limitation, I am of the opinion that it might be possible to make some consideration by focusing on the 'producer' of culture. In the same volume as above, Bourdieu proposes a 'science of works of art' that would conquer the opposition between 'internal readings' and 'external readings.' He assumes a space for the production of works (the field of cultural production) which is above social space, and makes an issue of the mobility of the actor in social behaviour. The actors in social behaviour in what Bourdieu calls the 'field' of cultural production are all producers of a work, including its senders, receivers and introducers, and they, in a space upon which certain structural limitations have been imposed, daily continue to create 'works,' the 'value of works,' and 'cultural meaning.'[5]

Of course, though Bourdieu's conception is not something designed to give some sort of answer to 'things that can only be expressed in that work,' it is a methodology which enabled the incorporation into debate of the question of how 'things that can only be expressed in that work' are socially organised. While referring in a timely manner to the body of works previously created, producers of the 'meaning' of cultural works continuously shape cultural space, while demonstrating internal questions in culture, such as who has approached closest to, or surpassed, the big names; who is radical; or who will seize popularity, in a form related to external issues such as social prestige, or the interests of social class positioning. Taken from a viewpoint that focuses on the producer of meaning, far from being a mere 'tool for self-inspiration,' self-projection in which cultural receivers' own thoughts are invested in a work is precisely what becomes an important factor for shaping culture. The discourse of 'self-projection' is a necessary activity for carrying out an expression of opinion (an internal issue) relating to a cultural work, after having been corroborated by an interest, namely, social position (an external issue).

Such a conception is not one concluded merely by the creation of a theoretical framework. One needs to apprehend the boundaries of the sites where the meaning of works is spawned, and diligent overall scrutiny of people's behaviour within them. To reiterate, if one is connected with some kind of pop culture, subculture or artistic culture, then one ought objectively to recognise the state of one's own disposition, and ponder the parameters of one's own words and actions, or how to respond to sympathetic and antithetic opinions, and so on. After that, one will go on to amass ideas as to what members comprise one's own and other people's fields of interest, and what kind of social disparities these produce.[6]

Cultural experience as socialisation

The objective in this chapter was to consider how to construct a narrative purged of subjectivity, while homing in upon the essence of works, yet without compromising a sociological standpoint. I would also like to think about methods of observing the condition of people's direct contact with culture from a microscopic viewpoint, in addition to the abovementioned macroscopic or mid-range perspective. I suspect that a number of methodologies – ethnographic research into subcultures, self-awareness theory, and so on – will be found, but what Shun Inoue calls 'narratives as cultural elements' also exist as applicable methodologies. Focusing on the 'narratives' disseminated through sagas, novels, or mass media such as film and television, Inoue states as follows:

> From our childhood, we are surrounded by them; we often internalise them as frames of recognition and interpretation, and through those frames, have given order and meaning to the events and incidents in life. Those narratives, moreover, are used as models for our own narratives, or as their raw materials (structural elements). At the same time, though, by indicating the way a 'proper' life-course should be, or the way to create a 'proper' narrative, they also become restraining factors when we make our own narratives (Inoue 2000, p. 162).

In their growth process, people become aware of the entity called the self through a variety of human relationships, and equip themselves with the rules of society. In sociological terminology, this is dubbed 'socialisation,' and it is this standpoint which argues that the power of such socialisation not only is provided by means of the human relationships in the society in question, but also exists in fictitional narratives. This is natural, if one thinks about it. We do not necessarily understand how to deal with feelings of romantic love, for example, even after having tried out various patterns with actual others (of course, there might be some people who have done so). We gain a preparatory idea of, or vicariously experience, the subtleties of emotion that arise in the process of romantic love, as well as most patterns of conversation and courtship, from narratives such as novels, television dramas or comics. In circumstances like the present, where the world is awash with cultural works, it would probably be difficult to find a person with no such experience whatsoever. In short, cultural works have the power to regulate the direction of meaning-creation in our lives.

Nonetheless, taking a viewpoint like this is suitable in analysis of cultural works that have a narrative, such as novels or films, but it is hard to handle in cases where it is difficult to verbalise the message of the work, such as in paintings or music. It is not possible, however, to ignore the aspect of socialisation through contact with those works, as is extensively seen in declarations such as: 'My soul was saved by one picture,' or 'I owe my current self to the influence of music.'

An example would be the sort of experience someone might have at life's crossroads, when their head rang repeatedly with sounds by a musician they had always revered. As if led by a phrase in those sounds, they make a decision as to which road to take in their future. Alternatively, the scenery depicted in an illustration sometimes provokes an intense feeling of *déjà vu*; and there is the impact of a verse in a poem. Words of greeting or farewell, scenes engraved with a slice of everyday life, and phrases expressed in carefully-chosen words, all remain as indelible impressions for a devotee of that poetry, and are felt to be things that are close to the person's own experience. Rather than forms of cultural enjoyment which depict an unwavering ego as their narrative, it is those that empathise (or not) with a fragmented self-image – in short, with the musical phrases at each different moment – that might better suit the present day.

The life-narrative method is probably appropriate for exploring the essence of cultural works that make up the restraining factor upon our creation of our own narratives.[7] By an assiduous exploration into people's subtle disposition as a record of individual narrative, the relationship between people and works is incorporated into sociological debate.

What kind of social space does expressive culture shape in contemporary society, and how does it relate to people's consciousness? This is a still-undeveloped research question, and one worth tackling.

Notes

1 Conversely speaking, without this coming-and-going, works would not secure social recognition. Even if a work were a shocking one that ripped apart an individual's world-view, or one which was amply felt to reach artistic heights, if it were not shared with other people, this would be synonymous with it being socially non-existent.
2 In recent years, the phrase '*ichioku sō hyōronka* (all-Japanese-are-critics)' was coined, and is often mentioned in critical contexts. It goes without saying that this is linked with the spread of the internet.
3 In this volume, Chapter Eleven, which has explored real urban/rural space from the comic-book works of Naoki Yamamoto, corresponds to this method.
4 Lévi-Strauss' model is one of the several structural models that he drew, and it shows the basic types of kinship solely by mean of the four simple symbols: □ (male), ○ (female), + (cordial relations), and – (relations of enmity, confrontation, restraint, and so on). Lévi-Strauss, who explained the behaviour of ethnic groups (which, when viewed short-sightedly, look complex) by consolidating their cross-component connections, is deemed to be the 'father of structuralism.' In addition, Burgess' concentric zone model is one which models the appearance of urban expansion, and also explains that the ratio of upper-class residents rises as the zones spread further from the centre. Gentrification, in which upper-class people gather in the centre of a city, has become a talking-point in urban sociology in recent years, but it is also a discovery made possible by the very existence of the Burgess model.
5 See Minamida (2001) for an example of application and development of Bourdieu's theory of 'field.'
6 In this volume, the people who converge upon rock festivals are surveyed in Chapter Nine. Plunging into the field, to start with, will probably lead to numerous discoveries.
7 In this volume, a practical example would be the examination in Chapter Eight of animation (*anime*) addicts.

4 Perspectives on the culture of generations and life-phases: the quantitative approach and qualitative approach

Daisuke Tsuji

Lately, even in elementary school classes, it is no longer unusual for students to administer questionnaires or conduct interviews for data collection. Such survey methods naturally form the very 'foundation of the foundation' for learning sociology and putting it into practice. However, sociological surveys do not merely mean distributing questionnaires and tabulating the data, or summarising what one has heard said in interviews. What is important is the imagination and ideas to situate and give meaning to surveys and their results in a sociological context; and surveys which lack these things are nothing but meaningless 'rubbish.'

Here, by setting up the practical example of an investigation into 'love rings,' I will conduct a simulation on how to conceive and pursue a survey so that it does not end up as such 'rubbish.' At the same time, I will explicate the merits and demerits of a quantitative approach such as a questionnaire survey, and a qualitative approach such as an interview survey. These two types of approach are often regarded as conflicting, but I wish to reinterpret them rather as mutually complementary sociological methodologies for opening up the potential for understanding the other.

Investigating the culture of a generation: with 'love rings' as subject matter

The departure-point for surveys: little questions

Broadly speaking, there are two ways of describing and expressing things. One is the method which states things in a quantitative way, by converting them numerically, such as in: 'maximum air temperature: thirty-eight degrees; minimum air temperature: twenty-eight degrees,' and the other which couches things in a qualitative manner, without quantifying them, such as in: 'it was sweltering hot from morning to night.' Accordingly, social survey methods also are classified roughly into approaches that utilise quantitative and those that use qualitative data. In this chapter, I will deal with questionnaire surveys as typifying the former, and interview surveys as representative of the latter, and consider their respective merits and demerits.[1]

There will probably be many readers who wish actually to conduct such surveys in order to write reports or graduation theses, so I would like to advance my discussion by setting up a concrete example – that of 'love rings' – to make it easier for readers to grasp a practical image of how to plan a survey and carry it forward.

The items which I have arbitrarily dubbed 'love rings' are rings worn on the left-hand ring finger to symbolise that the wearer has a lover (boyfriend or girlfriend). These are probably nothing out of the ordinary for the young people of today's Japan, but when I (who was born in 1965) first found out about love rings, I was somewhat surprised. This was because, as a member of the middle-aged 'old man' generation, I had imagined almost as a matter of course that the only thing that could be worn on the left ring finger was an 'engagement ring' or 'wedding ring.' 'Love rings,' in that sense, are truly part of the *younger generation's culture.*

Whether originally quantitative or qualitative, surveys begin on the impetus of such little surprises, doubts or feelings of discomfort. These are lying about around us in any amounts, but we tend to overlook them in our hectic everyday lives, thinking them insignificant issues. Of premier importance is a scholarly sensitivity, enabling us to get a firm grip upon them. After all, Newton's law of universal gravitation, too, had its starting point in his questioning of an extremely trivial occurrence, namely, an apple falling from a tree.

Sociologically developing little questions

The second important thing is a sociological sense that repositions those little surprises and doubts in a larger sociological context.

Here, it seems, is the stumbling-block for most people, and especially for university undergraduates. When I tell students: 'Let us treasure our little questions, and think up survey plans from there,' the sort of design that they tend to conceive is: 'to survey, by means of a questionnaire, what proportion of university students wear a love ring; whether there is a gendered disparity; and what type of ring is popular.' Let us assume we carried out this questionnaire survey, obtaining results showing that fifteen percent of all students wore a love ring – ten percent of male students, and twenty percent of female students – with the most popular type being a simple silver one, and second-most-popular being such-and-such, and so on. The problem is: what on earth did we learn from that?

What we can obtain from surveys is never anything but fragments of truth, nothing more than 'data.' 'Data' might satisfy our simple curiosity as to what proportion of students wear a love ring, for example, but in that case, it would end with: 'Hmm, so it's around fifteen percent,' and that little question would vanish without growing any larger.

The important thing in order to expand our little doubts into interesting problems with some depth to them is to ask the *reason* why people wear love rings, more than to ask about *facts* such as what proportion wears them. In response, we could conceive of such personal reasons as: 'Because I want to make [our] love into a visible form,' or 'I want to prevent my own gorgeous boyfriend/girlfriend from being approached by anyone else.' However, even though these might be reasons explaining individual conduct (wearing a love ring), they would not necessarily be reasons that explained the behaviour of the social group called the current younger generation. Even in the younger generation when I was once a university student, there was a psychological need, that is, a desire to make romantic relationships take a visible form, and so there were some young couples who wore matching outfits – the so-called 'pair look' in Japanised English. They did not wear a ring on their left ring-finger, however. The difference between the younger generation of former times and that of today is something that cannot be explained in individual or psychological terms. In other words, the point is whether the question of 'why?' can be asked by positioning it not in the psychological context of an individual, but in the social context in which the individual is placed.

Pondering the sociological context of love rings

What becomes necessary at these times is sociological literacy and general knowledge. In my own case (though I do not really mean to boast that I am overflowing with sociological knowledge), my problem-concern as to love rings was one connected to the following context.

According to research in family sociology, the relationship between romantic love and marriage is said to have changed greatly in post-war Japanese society. Formerly, marriage meant not so much a tie of affection between one individual and another, but a connection between one household and another. In the pre-war, and for a while in the post-war, also, arranged marriages (*o-miai kekkon*) were the mainstream, while love-marriages (*ren'ai kekkon*) were in the minority. Thus, romantic love and marriage were two different things. After that, however, the proportion of love-marriages followed an upward trajectory, and now, arranged marriages have become the minority, instead. In short, marriage has become an extension of romantic love – not something separate from the latter, but continuous with it.

Moreover, in the aspect of sexual awareness, too, huge changes can be seen. According to NHK's survey on 'Japanese people's consciousness,'[2] responses saying that couples 'should not have sex until marriage' fell from fifty-eight percent in 1973 to twenty-four percent in 2003. On the other hand, responses saying that sex was permissible 'if the couple loved each other' rose from nineteen percent to forty-four percent. This kind of awareness was especially strong the younger the informant, reaching seventy percent among males aged between twenty and twenty-four, and eighty-two percent among females in the same age bracket. In short, love and marriage had ceased to be separate things.

If the homogenisation of marriage and romantic love progresses in this manner, then what a 'wedding ring' on the left-hand ring finger symbolises will become identical with romantic love – meaning that one has a partner bound to one by affection. Is it true to say that this is where the reason for the emergence of love rings lies? In other words, through the homogenisation of love and marriage, a ring on the left ring-finger has become applicable to both marriage and romantic love, has it not?

I have roughly contextualised the problem in this way. By those means, what is at first a little piece of 'personal curiosity' develops into a 'sociological issue' likely to attract the notice even of people with no interest in love rings themselves. At the same time, it becomes clear that the love ring – which seemed a silly thing – is an object that truly deserves to be called 'culture.' In lexical terms, culture is 'a form of activity that transverses both the material and spiritual, reflecting the values shared by the constituent members of human groups,'[3] and so the form of activity constituting (the wearing of) a love ring is none other than something that reflects the values shared by the current younger generation as to romantic love and marriage.

Substantiating a hypothesis

It goes without saying, however, that this by itself is still an impractical desktop theory, remaining at the 'hypothesis' stage to the bitter end. It is necessary to collect *evidence* to prove whether the hypothesis which one has thought up corresponds to reality – in other words, one must 'demonstrate' it. One of the procedures or methods of such demonstration is the social survey. For a start, let me use an example of a questionnaire survey to show briefly how to substantiate a hypothesis (I will deal with questionnaires in detail in the third section).

If one follows the way of thinking or hypothesis such as that mentioned above, it will be envisioned that a higher proportion of people who think that 'marriage is an extension of romantic love' will have the idea that they 'want their lover to wear a ring on their left-hand ring finger' than those who regard these as 'two different things.' As such, in the autumn of 2005, I handed out questionnaires incorporating questions relating to these issues during a lecture, and had students answer them. The results are as in Table 4.1.

When we examine this, we see that in the case of female students, a higher percentage of respondents with the view that 'marriage is an extension of romantic love' wanted their lover to wear a love ring than did those who thought love and marriage were 'two different things' (fifty-three percent as opposed to thirty-three percent). In the case of male students, however, the ratio was almost the same (fifty-four percent versus fifty-seven percent). Seen overall, alas, it

Table 4.1: Awareness vis-à-vis views on romantic love/marriage and love rings

	I want my lover to wear a ring on his/her left-hand ring finger		
	Yes	No	
Male students			
I think that marriage is an extension of romantic love	54%	46%	100% ($n = 46$)
I think they are two different things	57%	43%	100% ($n = 14$)
Female students			
I think that marriage is an extension of romantic love	53%	47%	100% ($n = 58$)
I think they are two different things	33%	67%	100% ($n = 24$)

would be hard to argue that these are results which cleanly support[4] the hypothesis. Without giving up at this point, let us resolve to proceed a little further.

Conducting an interview survey on 'love rings': a qualitative approach

Exploring a hypothesis by a survey

Of course, it is rather rare to be able to explain a certain social phenomenon by means of one rationale (hypothesis). It would probably be more natural to think that the wearing of a love ring also was due to a layering of multiple reasons. Moreover, even if the homogenisation of love and marriage were to become the reason why people thought that it *does not matter* if they wear a ring on their left-hand ring finger even without being married – a negative reason that forms a prerequisite for a love ring – this would probably not become the positive reason of *wanting to* wear a love ring, or *wanting the other party* to wear one. Accordingly, it is necessary to find a further, different hypothesis as to the reason why the present younger generation wears love rings.

The interview survey is the type that suits such a hypothesis-exploratory (heuristic) survey. By contrast, the kind which is conducted after having decided upon a hypothesis in advance is a hypothesis-confirmatory survey, exemplified by the way the questionnaire survey in the previous section was conducted. It is not that a questionnaire survey cannot be used in a hypothesis-heuristic manner (similarly, it is not that an interview survey cannot be used in a hypothesis-confirmatory manner, either), but as it means discovering a hypothesis from the response data from certain fixed question items, limitations naturally arise. In comparison with interview surveys, the range and level of freedom with which one can explore for a hypothesis cannot help being reduced.

Below, I would like to employ as raw material an interview survey by Shiori Kawakami, who wrote her graduation thesis on the theme of love rings in my seminar class.[5] However, to facilitate understanding of the flow of the narrative and its points, I have in my own way restructured and adapted the way the survey was carried forward and the argument put together. As this is not something which reproduces or cites Ms Kawakami's work and discussion, please bear in mind that any criticisms it deserves should be directed at me.

How does one conduct an interview survey?

The people cooperating in the interview survey (called the 'informants') are thirty university students, aged between eighteen and twenty-four, who are wearing love rings. As the current objective is to try to find a clue to a hypothesis from what they say, it is desirable that they speak as freely as possible. This kind of free-talking interview format is called an 'unstructured interview,'[6] but there is a problem in that it is hugely swayed by the interviewing skill of the interviewer. That is to say, the content that can be elicited changes according to the liveliness of the conversation. For that reason, essentially, interviewers are required to have had prior training in demonstration classes and the like.

In cases where there is not sufficient leeway to do so, and the interviewer is not accustomed to interview surveys, it would probably be a good idea not to conduct the interview in a completely free-talking format, but to prepare a number of questions to ask all of the informants. First, have an informant answer the initial question, and if it seems the conversation will continue on from there, have them speak freely. If the interviewer poses the next question when the conversation lapses, the burden will be lighter on the interviewer than if the latter had tried to sustain the flow by ad libbing. This method is called a 'semi-structured interview.' On this occasion, that is what it was decided to use, and basic question items which were thought advisable to grasp, such as when the informant began to wear a love ring, their motivation, or what the informant felt wearing it, were made ready.

If the informant's consent can be obtained, the interviewer will record the content of the interview on an IC recorder or tape. However, as informants often feel reluctant or nervous if an audio recorder is placed in front of them from the beginning, after having made general conversation for a short while and making the mood of the venue more relaxed, the interviewer will then ask for permission to make an audio recording, with the combined implication of a signal that the main topic will now be pursued. A recording is only an auxiliary means of confirming content, however, and it is vital to take full notes on the spot. It is actually quite difficult to be taking notes while simultaneously listening to someone speaking. If interviewers take too much time to write things down, they might miss things that were said, or the flow of conversation might break off. What is good training for that purpose is note-taking in regular lectures. Students should not merely copy what is on the board, but summarise and jot down in their own way the content of what the teacher is saying. When the class finishes, they should review their notes while the memory of what was said remains, and add supplementary information or organise the contents. These tasks are absolutely no different from the things one should do on the occasion of an interview survey. There are numerous other points and tricks to remember when interviewing, and for details, refer to such practical introductory volumes as Nagae (2002) and Kasai (2005).

Documenting interview results

Let us now look at the results of the interviews. Having been asked about what inspired them to start wearing a love ring, a certain male student responded as follows:

> I bought pair rings with my girlfriend, but around then, it happened that she was getting a bit anxious as to, like, whether I really loved her. And so, with the sense that she didn't need to be so anxious, that it was okay (because I loved her) (I presented her with one). And when I did that, she, like, was a bit relieved, too.

This 'girlfriend' also agreed to be interviewed, and replied: 'By the two of us wearing rings, even when we're not with each other, when I look at the ring I'm wearing, it's proof of his feelings, like.' Though lack of space here necessitates their omission, there were numerous other informants (eight out of ten males, fifteen out of twenty females) who described the love ring as being the thing which turned their affection into a visible form, for instance: 'I wear it as proof of my love,' or 'Because it is proof of our mutual feelings, it would be doing wrong by my partner if I didn't wear it.'

These answers might very well be ones with limited scope for discovery, as was foreseen, but what was a little unexpected for me was that there was a kind of 'old-fashioned' sense tenaciously remaining, such as in the following example from a female student:

> In my case, I said I wanted a ring. Actually, pair rings would be better, but (he) doesn't like wearing accessory-type things, so I'm the only one wearing one. But every time I see the ring, I feel like 'I am his!' and I'm thrilled.

This is the sort of response that would antagonise feminists, with a woman being a man's possession ('being his'), but utterances with a similar gist were heard from seven female informants. For the record, there were no male informants who mentioned 'being hers' in their answers. Even from the topic of love rings, which could be regarded as trivial, it will be seen that a persistently-remaining androcentric dynamic is still at work in present-day Japanese society, too.

Let me offer an explanatory note here about the notation method for interview results. The question of how to make a written record of an interview is fraught with quite difficult issues. In the above example, for instance, let us assume that the informant actually paused after saying: 'I feel like "I am his!"' then, after being cued by 'Mmm' noises from the interviewer, continued with: 'I *am* thrilled[, you know?]' Such pausing and faltering might indicate that the interviewee is hesitating, wondering to herself (even while being thrilled) whether it is enough for her just to feel she is 'his.' Alternatively, having received affirmative feedback noises from the interviewer, she might have flatly stated that she was 'thrilled.'[7]

In this manner, such hesitation or silence sometimes can indicate the same amount of important information as the content of the utterances. One could go on forever if one tried to reproduce all of these faithfully, but I beg the reader to bear in mind that merely writing down a summary of the content of the utterances is not as simple as it sounds. What to draw out from an interview as being something that deserves note depends on the degree of the interviewer's problem-concern and sensitivity.

Drawing a hypothesis from interview results

Let us return to the main topic. What distinguishes love rings from mere rings presented to lovers is that they are perceived largely to attract the attention of third persons. One female student, for example, speaks as follows:

> If he isn't wearing it (the ring), I get angry. If he's wearing the ring he can signal to the girls around him that he has a girlfriend, and so I think it becomes a 'chick-repellent.' When I meet somebody (male) other than my boyfriend, if I am wearing the ring I don't get asked to do any funny business, and so it's handy, too.

All of the male informants and seventeen out of twenty female informants mentioned such an anti-cheating function. They also said that in some university clubs, there are cases where it 'has almost become an unwritten rule that couples who are seeing each other will wear rings.' In other words, not cheating (not being able to cheat) on a lover also becomes 'proof' of serious affection, as introduced above, and it even seems that an atmosphere (= social norm) has arisen in some groups that if one does not wear a love ring in spite of being romantically involved, then the seriousness of one's relationship will come under suspicion.

In addition, the following kind of point was also made in terms of a love ring's ability to grab the attention of others:

> If even unpretentious people wear a ring (on their left-hand ring finger), I imagine that they surely have a really great personality, or they have some kind of attractiveness. That's why I feel that by wearing a ring, I, too, am viewed in a favourable light by everyone around me.

Similarly, a different informant commented:

> When I see even somebody I don't know at all wearing a ring, more

Perspectives on the culture of generations and life-phases 71

often than not they make a better impression on me. Recently, that's come to my notice. Previously, apart from the times when I was meeting my boyfriend, I used to take mine off, but I've started to wear it at other times, too.

While such a feeling was something that I could never have expected, at the same time, it also did happen to ring a bell.

It refers to the fact that people appear to have become more oriented towards close interpersonal relationships such as friendships in more recent years. It is a commonly-held view that human relations have been weakened in general, but various kinds of social statistics show that friendships are tending to be more and more intense. Compared to times past, people's number of friends has grown, and their level of satisfaction with friendships has also risen. On the other hand, it seems as if people also have heightened anxiety about friendships breaking up. When carrying out interviews with students, one often hears such voices as: 'When I am eating alone in the university cafeteria, I cannot bear to look as if I haven't got any friends, and so I absolutely always use my mobile phone to find somebody to eat with me.' On top of that, one even hears it said: 'If I had to dine alone, I would rather hide in a toilet cubicle and do it.'

Can people sustain close relationships – not only with friends, but with lovers, too? It has come to carry considerable weight within values-consciousness, after all. Love-rings, I suggest, are also a culture in which the values and anxieties of such an emphasis on relationships are reflected. For that reason, are love rings perhaps seen as 'proof' that an intimate relationship is being maintained – at times, also becoming a 'cultural norm,' and even turning into a tool for actively advertising to others that one is fulfilling a relationship value?

This is the new hypothesis relating to love rings which was unearthed from the interview survey.

Conducting a questionnaire survey on 'love rings': a quantitative approach

Comparison and contrast of quantitative and qualitative approaches

One reason why interview surveys are useful in exploring for a hypothesis is the high degree of detail in the information that can be drawn from them. In comparison with the sort of quantitative data we saw in Table 4.1, in the first section, the results of the interview survey seen in the previous section are likely to impart a sense of vividness and reality. By contrast, even if we could mentally absorb the logic of such data as in Table 4.1, we would feel it to be bland and lacking in a sense of reality. This is because it handles the diverse and abundant realities relating to love rings in a way that merely cuts away and reduces them to the limited aspects of whether informants think marriage is an extension of romantic love, and whether they want their lover to wear a ring. However many questions one puts in a questionnaire survey, the level of detail in the information that is obtained cannot help being basically lower than in an interview survey.

On the other hand, though, the range of information it can gather is wider than with an interview survey. For example, approximately how many female students who felt that they 'belonged' to their boyfriend due to their love ring were there in the entire university that constituted the survey field? How would it be in all of the universities in Japan? It takes too much effort to go around conducting interviews to obtain such information, and in practice, it is often impossible. On those points – the degree of detail in the information, and the range of collectability – quantitative questionnaire surveys and qualitative interview surveys could be said to enjoy a mutually-complementary relationship.

Furthermore, sometimes questionnaire surveys also clarify connections which are hard to see from the results of interview surveys. As discussed in the first section, for example, a consciousness which perceives romantic love and marriage in a homogenous manner could be regarded as potentially linked to wearing a love ring, but no matter how many interviews were conducted, one cannot imagine that there would be any informants who, when asked why they wore a love ring, would reply that it was because they thought marriage was 'an extension of romantic love.' This is because it is not the type of factor of which the parties in question could be aware (or articulate). In an interview survey, a fearsomely high level of expertise is required to unearth such factors and connections which are so difficult to recognise.

Verifying a hypothesis by a survey

Let me now introduce the process for verifying the hypothesis discovered in the previous section by means of a questionnaire survey.[8]

Perspectives on the culture of generations and life-phases 73

In the current case, the first thing to note when compiling a questionnaire (survey sheet) is to avoid questions in the following format:

> Question X: For what reason(s) do you wear a love ring? Circle as many of the following as are applicable.
> 1. Because I think that marriage is an extension of romantic love.
> 2. Because I think that close relationships with lovers and friends are worth more than anything.
> 3. Any other reason

There is probably no need for me to explain in detail about the stupidity of such a question. On being exposed to the word 'love ring,' the informant is unlikely to know what it means, and even if the word is understood, the informant would be unclear as to why the given options constituted reasons for wearing a ring. However, when one has first-time interviewers think up questions, designs that are almost as bad sometimes do actually emerge, even if not quite so awful as the above example. This is because novices tend to be unconsciously convinced that things which the interviewer understands will be understood by the interviewees, as well. I recommend that when one compiles a questionnaire, one first has a third party (ideally, someone such as a specialist teacher well-versed in questionnaire surveys) check for the presence of any questions whose meaning is not comprehensible, or which cannot be answered.

Again, in the above example, even if the informant does understand the meaning of the question, a huge drawback still remains, namely that as the question format only targets people who wear a love ring, information about the people who do not wear one will not be obtainable. Even if ninety percent of those who wore a love ring were to reply that 'marriage is an extension of romantic love,' if ninety percent of people who did not wear one also thought the same, it could not be argued that there was any connection between wearing a love ring and a consciousness of homogeneity between marriage and romantic love. In order to confirm a hypothesis, it is crucially important to set questions in a format that enables comparison and contrast to be conducted. This, too, is considered obvious, but is a trap to which novices in compiling questionnaires are surprisingly susceptible.

In the present case, an appropriate question format would be the following, for instance:

Question X: If you had a lover, would you (a) want your lover to wear a ring on their left-hand ring finger? Would you (b) want to wear a ring on your own left-hand ring finger? Circle the applicable number in each case. You would:
a. want your lover to wear a ring on their left-hand ring finger.
   1. Yes 2. No
b. want to wear a ring on your left-hand ring finger. 1. Yes 2. No

Question Y: Do you think that marriage is an extension of romantic love? Or, something unconnected to it? (Circle only one answer)
1. I think it is an extension. 2. I think it is unconnected.

Question Z: Do you think that if you did not have a familiar someone with whom you could have an intimate association, then your lifestyle and life would be worthless? (Circle only one answer)
1. I think they would be worthless.
2. I do not think they would be worthless.

If people who had answered 'Yes' to Question X (a) and (b) had a higher propensity to answer Question Y with 'I think it is an extension' than people who had said 'No,' or if they had a greater propensity to answer Question Z with 'I think they would be worthless,' then that would be evidence to support the respective hypotheses.

Additionally, if one were to use a method called multivariate analysis, then it would be possible to analyse the extent to which wearing a love ring (Question X), views on marriage/romantic love (Question Y) and relationship values (Question Z) were each related. The ability to analyse the associative structure of such multiple factors in a collective manner could also be called one of the advantages of quantitative questionnaire surveys. For more detail, I urge you to read of an introductory book on statistics, but for readers with a humanities background, Shin Takahashi's *Statistics Understood through Comics* series should be easy to tackle. In spite of the *manga* format, the basics of statistics are painstakingly explained in an easy-to-understand manner, without any dumbing-down. The sole English version was published in 2008, but for readers of Japanese, it would be a good idea as far as the order in which the volumes were read to start with Chapters One and Two of the third volume (Takahashi 2006), *Factor Analysis*

Edition (in which the basics of the basics of social survey methods are explained), then to return to the first and second books in the series (Takahashi 2004; Takahashi 2005). Also, if I were to cite one book that should be read as an introductory guide elucidating the whole range of survey-sheet design, sampling, administration and analysis, I would recommend Morioka (2007).

Now, when one has distributed the survey sheets that one has created in this way to the targets, and input and processed the answers thus gained into a computer,[9] a result such as in Table 4.1 – called a cross-tabulation table – can be obtained. Thanks to having decided upon a question format such as the above, comparison and contrast by means of a cross-tabulation table becomes possible, and one will be able to get concrete proof (results confirming the hypothesis) as to whether it is appropriate to position love rings (Question X) in a social context characterised by homogenisation of marriage/romantic love (Question Y).

Discerning the reliability of survey results

The results shown in such cross-tabulation tables and the like are still not, by themselves, the goal of a questionnaire survey, however. The next thing deemed necessary is to discern the validity and reliability of those results, that is, how far they can be trusted. Let me explain, taking as my example the results pertaining to the female students in Table 4.1.

Of the female students whose view was that marriage was 'an extension of romantic love,' fifty-three percent said they wanted their lover to wear a love ring, while this was thirty-three percent in the case of students who had said that love and marriage were 'two different things' – certainly, there is a difference of twenty percent. Yet there were only twenty-four students overall in the 'two different things' faction, and thirty-three percent of that number means only eight persons. The addition of just four more people would bring the proportion up to fifty percent, which would be little different from the fifty-three percent in the 'extension' faction. With such a margin that just four people would bring about, could it really be said in the end that there was any difference between the 'extension' and 'two different things' factions in regard to love rings?

It is possible to answer this question by using an analytical method in statistics called a 'test.' A test is a method of calculating the probability of differences and associations accidentally emerging in an actually surveyed target (sample), even though there are no differences or associations in the group as a whole (parent population) that could be the survey target. In social statistics, generally, when there is greater than five percent probability that it will fall within such a margin of sampling error, then it is seen as 'no significant difference.' Incidentally, if we test the results of Table 4.1, as they fail to pass this criterion, this means that there is 'no significant difference.'

In order to assess the reliability of survey results by means of a test, it is a precondition that the sample has been initially chosen from the parent population by random sampling. If the parent population that one wishes to scrutinise were present-day Japanese university students, then it would be necessary to choose an unbiased sample from a list of all students by means of a method akin to drawing lots. Unless this condition were fulfilled, even supposing that results which cleared the criterion by testing were obtained, at most these would be no more than tentative criteria with an added restriction, to the tune of 'supposing they were *taken as being* results of a survey conducted by random sampling.'

The questionnaires which I conducted with the attendees at my lectures could never be a randomly-chosen sample even of the entire student body of that university, let alone of all the university students in Japan. For that reason, no matter how much one applied sophisticated statistical analysis, the reliability and validity of those results would never be anything but fairly limited. In fact, there are even some experts in quantitative surveys who go so far as to say that the results of surveys not conducted by random sampling are nothing but 'rubbish.' If this be so, then as long as one cannot do random sampling, would it perhaps be better to concentrate on qualitative surveys such as interviews?

Beyond the quantitative/qualitative conflict

The issue of social surveys and generalisability

Such a criticism of being 'rubbish' is one with the capacity to be directed also at interview surveys. This is because they harbour the same difficulties as to how far interview results obtained from some informants will apply to the group as a whole – that is, be generalisable. I wish to parry this kind of 'random-sampling-supremacism' with two swords.

The first is the possibility of generalisation that does not depend on random sampling. Let us assume that I conducted the questionnaire in the previous section at the university where I work, and that you, too, who read this and took an interest also implemented it at your own university. Consequently, in regard to the new hypothesis which was discovered in the second section, supposing that a tendency to want to wear, or have a lover wear, a love ring (Question X) was seen at both universities to rise in direct proportion to strongly holding values (Question Z) that emphasised close relationships, then it should be reasonable to think there would be greater possibility for generalisation.

As I had not introduced the verification outcome for this hypothesis (the association between Question X and Question Z) until now, there may be some readers who are bothered by this. If so, I urge them to try doing a survey themselves. It does not need to be a questionnaire – an interview survey would do just as well. A survey based not on the hypothesis that I indicated, but one that you put together would be fine, also. As well, I would like you to publish your survey results on the internet. Survey research is not something that is concluded with just one survey, in the first place, but something in which those involved accumulate expertise as a type of collaborative activity, and there is gratification in the process itself. I do not venture to verify my hypothesis here because it is intended to be an invitation to take part in that process.

My second sword is an issue that is more deeply connected with the essence of quantitative/qualitative surveys. In other words, it is the question of whether social surveys are ultimately meaningless unless their (quantitative) generalisation is possible.

Certainly, sociology is a discipline which has made society (groups) that transcend individual persons its object of study from the beginning. For that reason, even if, for instance, there were an informant among those interviewed who said: 'If I don't wear a love ring, I will be possessed by the devil and die,' assuming that person were the only one like that in Japanese society, it could be thought impossible to say that this was a sociologically important survey result (if not in psychiatric terms).

Conversely, however, one could also inquire as follows. Let us suppose that, having conducted an exhaustive survey of all the young people in Japan, we had apprehended the overall image and general image of the young people's cohort – that such-and-such a percentage was wearing a love ring; and the largest associative factor was values that emphasised relationships; and the next associative factor was…et cetera. That, however, was a social image that nobody had known about until the survey was done. While remaining in ignorance, every young person could be expected to have been living their separate social reality to do with love rings. A social image that no-one knew about, and was never alive in anybody – is not such a thing just a type of hypothetical construct fashioned by a survey? Does it fail, from the very start, to grasp the actual image and way in which human beings live their social reality?

Developing the capability to understand the 'other'

On this point, in my opinion, the goal for which sociology essentially ought to aim is the social reality lived by each individual human being; and qualitative surveys need to take priority over quantitative surveys in order to approach that reality. What is important on such occasions is firstly to comprehend (by means of highly-defined information gained from qualitative surveys) what kind of reality each respective person – the 'other' – is living: in more detailed and precise terms, this means opening up one's style of understanding. At this stage, the question of how far this style of understanding actually can be generalised is not much of a problem. Even if there were only one 'other,' it would be vital to develop the capability to understand that person, because that very thing is what underlies the business of our social life, and is also the fundamental issue in sociology.

What then becomes a problem is the very question of how we can expand our ability to apprehend the realities that others live. People each live their respective individual realities. However, if these were totally individual realities, each belonging uniquely to one person, then they would be no different from delusions. It would be a good idea to think, for example, of the informant above who said: 'If I don't wear a love ring, I will be possessed by the devil.' In such a case, we probably have no alternative but to give up hope of understanding, thinking that the informant was someone who for some unknown reason was convinced of that.

Suppose, however, that it had become clear from our questionnaire survey that people with values which emphasised relationships had a greater tendency to want to wear love rings, and this informant was a person who was hypersensitive to interpersonal relationships, and suffered great anxiety – how would it be then? Under the *general* pattern of understanding in which sensitivity to relationships leads to love rings, would there not be some glimpse of the ability to understand even to the slightest extent (even if empathy were out of the question) the delusional reality this informant was inhabiting?

Only when we have been able to recognise, within individual reality, a social aspect that transcends individuality, it becomes a comprehensible social reality for the first time. Quantitative surveys can give us a clue for fathoming the condition of the mechanisms and forces that provide that kind of aspect. To reiterate, the mechanisms and forces that can be fathomed from those surveys are certainly a sort of hypothetical construct. If, however, a new ability to understand the reality which each individual other is living could be developed through that hypothetical construct, then by rights it could be called a hypothetical construct with soci(ologic)al significance.

In the present day, in which the younger generation and its culture are often depicted as 'incomprehensible' others for the older generation, it is probably an extremely important task to develop that ability to comprehend. Whether quantitative or qualitative, a social survey is not simply a means for exploring and verifying a hypothesis or theory, but nothing more or less than a practice that strives to open up our potential to understand the other.[10] Even if its object is only something that could be regarded as trivial as love rings, that practice is something with ample scope for success.

Notes

1 As analyses based on the results of questionnaire surveys are also expanded in Chapters Five, Ten and Thirteen in this volume, and those based on interview surveys in Chapters Eight and Nine, I urge the reader to compare these from this kind of perspective, also.
2 See NHK Hōsō Bunka Kenkyūjo (ed.) 2004, pp. 45–9.
3 From Kindaichi (chief ed.) 1997.
4 In statistical terminology, a result which 'supports' a hypothesis means a

result that matches the expectations drawn from the hypothesis.
5 Kawakami (2006–07).
6 By contrast, an interview in a form whereby informants are required to reply (choose answers) to set questions is called a 'structured interview.'
7 Arguably, not only was the survey result: 'When I feel "I am his!" I am pleased' elicited from the informants themselves in the case of this example, but was also generated amid reciprocal action from the interviewer providing affirmative back-channel feedback. The theory and methodology of the 'active interview' has also been developed from a viewpoint that re-interprets the interviewer as someone who participates in this manner in reciprocal action equally with the informant, and produces the interview (result) in collaboration with the latter. For details, see Holstein and Gubrium (1995); and for a critical examination of it, see Tsuruta and Komiya (2007).
8 This does not imply that verification by means of a quantitative survey of a hypothesis thus explored in a qualitative survey is a typical method. Conversely, there are times when a method of qualitatively verifying what has been quantitatively explored is adopted; and there are quantitative–quantitative and qualitative–qualitative ways of handling it, also. In addition, in surveys that take a qualitative approach, there is also a deeply interesting approach called 'grounded theory,' in which a process of exploration and verification of a hypothesis is consciously repeated, and theory is constructed (made to converge with theory) from within that process. For details, see Glaser and Strauss (1967), for a start.
9 For analysis of input data, it is convenient to use statistical software such as SPSS or SAS, but if one is not in an environment such as a university where either could be used, then fairly high-level statistical analysis has become possible recently even with regular spread-sheet software such as Excel. Moreover, statistical freeware called 'R' has also been published on the internet. On statistical analysis using the various software programmes, please refer to any of the numerous published introductory manuals or internet-based explanatory sites.
10 For readers who would like to ponder further as to what kind of undertaking and practice social surveys constitute, I suggest Ishikawa, Satō and Yamada (1998); and Imada (2000).

Part II: Addictive Media Culture

5 Why do people become addicted to mobile phones?: the sociology of email communication

Kensuke Suzuki

Now that we have entered an age of a hundred million mobile telephones, the 'mobile' has become a data-telecommunication device that is almost the basis of our very lifestyles. On the other hand, it has also come to be pointed out that, in concert with this rapid dissemination, a phenomenon called 'mobile dependence' has been spreading among young people whereby they become unable to part with their mobile phones. This chapter explores what kind of phenomenon mobile dependence might be, and especially considers the reasons for youth coming to the point where they cannot extricate themselves from mobile email interaction.

In spite of the fact that the devices have become 'smart' – high-functioning, in other words – the reason for our inability to relinquish the means of written communication that constitutes email is that it is something which enables each of us to present the entity that is 'I/me' in a fashion that reflects ourselves. On the other hand, however, it is also a breeding-ground for the anxiety that we might be actually estranged from the personal relationships that have grown that way. A factor in mobile dependence is this kind of anxiety that each of us 'might be isolated.'

Mobiles turning into email devices

What do you do with your mobile?

In daily life, we often use the word 'mobile' – *keitai*, in Japanese, meaning 'portable.' Moreover, we have no doubts whatsoever that it means 'mobile telephone,' to the extent that the terms '*keitai*' and 'mobile' have even made it into dictionaries now.

However, though we call fixed- or land-line telephones '*ie-den* (house-phones)' in Japanese, we are unlikely to call one a 'fixed (*kotei*),' nor to abbreviate 'public phone' to 'public.' Only 'mobile telephone' loses the 'telephone' portion, which ought to be the more important word, and is abbreviated to 'mobile' (and this expression has already been exported overseas as '*kei-tai*').

This is probably a manifestation of the fact that, for us, a mobile has become a tool that goes further than being a mere 'telephone.' Inside that small device there are jammed enough functions to fill a user's manual several hundred pages long, and we walk around 'porting' all of them. In particular, in the data in the 'White paper on mobile telephones 2006' (Mobile Contents Forum 2006), as for 'functions often used on a mobile phone,' 66.8 percent of people surveyed replied 'talk,' while an astounding 100 percent replied 'mail.' We no longer mainly use mobiles as telephones, but as terminals for email.

Moreover, since the appearance of the so-called *i*-mode (mobile internet service) in 1999, internet connection via mobiles also has come to have important significance. It was because mobile phones developed the capability to connect to the internet that it also became possible for the abovementioned 'mail' to be sent and received as email, crossing between carriers; and recently, there are increasing numbers of users who employ such communication services as electronic bulletin boards, blogs and social networking services (SNS). Content-delivery, including image, video, music and text, is also becoming established as a familiar thing.

In an age where mobile phones already number 100 million, it is starting to be taken for granted that every person will own one. As far as the internet is concerned, mobiles' singularity is obvious when compared to personal computers. According to a survey on trends in communications usage conducted by the Ministry of Internal Affairs and Communications, in the 2005–06 Japanese fiscal year, while there were 66.01 million users of the internet from personal computers, there were 69.23 million people using it from mobile phones, PHS and mobile data terminals, and it became a talking-point that connections from mobiles had overtaken those from personal computers for the first time. In 2006–07, 80.55 million people connected to the internet from personal computers, and 70.86 million from mobile phones, meaning that connections via personal computers again topped those via mobiles, but the 60.99 million people who utilised both accounted for almost seventy percent of the total. As it is unclear from this whether the device they were using on a daily basis was their personal computer or their mobile phone, however, it is also necessary to note the impossibility of comparing the two simply by these figures.

Are 'mobiles' a universal phenomenon?

As mobile phones have spread to such an extent, it might be perceived as a matter of course that everyone all over the world is using them all the time. Yet using a mobile to connect to the internet, or to send and receive email, is by no means a natural usage method. Certainly, *i*-mode services have been expanded outside Japan, too, and the mobile-to-internet connection service called WAP (Wireless Application Protocol) can also be used in many countries. In addition, more and more mobile phone models in use in Japan can be taken overseas and used without modification.

As for email, however, the mainstream method used outside Japan is called SMS (Short Messaging Service), in which a maximum of 140 characters can be sent or received; and there are also many countries and areas where talk rather than text (email) is seen to be the mainstream when their ratios are compared.

Why do such dissimilarities arise? A cultural discourse-type of explanation, namely that 'mobiles suit Japanese people's lifestyles' has been proffered, but rather more important are the differences in the historical, market-structure and economic conditions under which mobile phones have spread.

It was in 1987 that products dubbed 'mobile phones (*keitai denwa*)' made their debut in Japan. Later, in 1994, the system of outright purchase of the handsets began, and following an increase in carriers, a reduction in call charges, and the like, the number of units on contracts broke through the sixty-million barrier in 2001, overtaking the number of line contracts for fixed-line telephones.

What was important in this process was the fact that ultra-low-priced handsets called by such names as 'zero yen cellular' or 'one-yen cellular' arrived on the market. Though the development cost of a mobile phone is usually several hundreds of millions of yen per unit, and the price of a handset from fifty to eighty thousand yen, such drastic price cuts were possible because mobile phone carriers that wished to increase the number of users of their own companies' lines were paying 'rebates' to dealers in anticipation of subsequently recovering their capital through call charges.

As a result, in Japan, conditions emerged in which anyone could obtain a high-functioning, latest model for a bargain price. It was because the hurdles were low at the stage when handsets were spreading that many people came to use such cutting-edge functions as *i*-mode, ringtones and games. Overseas, by contrast, in many cases sales incentives were prohibited, handsets were being sold at the list price from the start, and so on, making a considerable financial outlay necessary in order to use the latest functions. For that reason, in many areas the situation continued where mobile phones were 'symbols of wealth,' or things that enabled users 'only to do talk and SMS.'

Recently, high-functioning units such as the 'Blackberry' and 'Sidekick' have been popular, mainly in the United States. As these cost a whopping $300 to $500, however, switching to them is no simple matter, unlike in Japan. It is also necessary to note that these handsets were ones called 'smartphones' that had functions akin to those of a personal computer. Japanese mobile phones had become high-functioning in a form that absorbed such devices as a music player, camera and games which young people regularly carry around, but in many cases, the music and games could only be used on a mobile. In other words, mobile-specific functions and environments which had no compatibility with personal computers had evolved.

For this reason, though compartmentalisation emerged overseas, based on economic disparities – namely, a choice between 'highly-priced, high-functioning devices that were almost personal computers, and devices that focused on low-priced talk' – in the Japanese case, a difference arose between 'people who mainly used a personal computer, and those who dealt with everything on their mobile phone.' The survey by the Ministry of Internal Affairs and Communications cited at the outset could also be said to be one that reflects the unique Japanese environment. People critical of the Japanese mobile phone market, which has been left behind by the global standard, sometimes refer to the situation as the 'Galapagosisation of Japan,' or suchlike.

'Mobile dependence' and adolescent youth

As a prerequisite when discussing Japan's 'mobile' culture, one must first understand that its uniqueness is something born from market differences. So, what sort of thing is the culture it has spawned? Here, let us take a look at the culture of 'mail,' which boasts a 100-percent usage ratio.

What is often mentioned in relation to mobile-phone email is the issue of so-called 'mobile dependence,' which problematises young people's incessant exchange of emails. Certainly, if we are going to use the term 'mobile dependence' for a state in which, for example, people can never abandon their mobile, or continue emailing back and forth without being able to stop, then it is likely that such behavior will be seen particularly among the younger generation.

According to a survey by the Metropolitan Police Agency, 84.7 percent of female lower-secondary students arrested by police during the survey period reported that they did not feel at ease without their mobile (Keishichō 2004). As suggested by this data, a mobile-dependent mentality has a tendency to be attributed to a problem of so-called 'delinquent' or 'lower-class' individual users.

Yet such a semblance must be called arbitrary. It will not be clear from this whether 'mobile dependence' is the fault of mobile phones, or else is due to some other factor; and even if mobiles were partly to blame, for example, it would still remain hazy as to what young people are gaining from 'mobile dependence.' Unless one takes the extreme position that 'electro-magnetic waves from mobile phones have damaged their brains,' there is likely to be some sort of rational reason for mobile dependence, as well.

One of the clues to unlocking the puzzle is the view that the combination of 'mobile phones' and 'youth' may have provoked dependence. Richard Ling and Birgitte Yttri have demonstrated that teenaged youth in Norway deem the task of mutually checking on each other's peer relationships through SMS on their mobiles to be necessary (Ling and Yttri 2002).

A girl they interviewed speaks as follows:

> If I get a text message I am curious. I want to be included, so, like if I am in the shower and I get a message, I, you know, have to read it.

If I write a message and don't get a response immediately then it is like, you know, ehhh... (Ling and Yttri 2002, p. 149).

In a different study, the following email exchange between Finnish youth is introduced:

I'M REALLY STRESSED OUT AFTER SENDING TONI THE MESSAGE. I REALLY SHOULDN'T HAVE! HE HASN'T SENT ANYTHING BACK. MAYBE IT'S OVER NOW. ARE YOU ANXIOUS ABOUT TOMORROW?

PatiencePatienceMyFriend! Maybe he's getting back from the fun fair and hasn't had time to answer yet. But should I be stressed if you are?:) I'm not (Kasesniemi and Rautianinen 2002, p. 186).

Adolescence in contemporary society is a period in which young people learn how to relate to society through mutual communication with their peers. For that reason, the question of whether they can get along well with their age cohort becomes the most important thing for them. The sentiments and email exchanges such as the above-mentioned are an everyday spectacle in Japan, as well, but this means that 'mobile dependence' is a universal phenomenon seen all over the globe, including in Japan, regardless of the uniqueness of the Japanese market structure. Perhaps the maintenance of a state of 'connectibility' with friends through email has become a big factor in 'mobile dependence'?

The meaning inherent in textual communication

Before verifying the above, it is necessary to consider why the means of maintaining that 'connectibility' has taken the form of the textual communication called email. If we mean to keep up a condition of connectibility, we ought to be able to see our friends and classmates who live nearby anytime, yet in a majority of cases, *keitai* mail exchange on mobiles is conducted with 'intimate others' such as family or friends (Mobile Contents Forum 2006). Why, I wonder, must we deliberately maintain a state of 'connectibility' with intimate others even as far as by email?

What we must note here are the characteristics of the medium called 'textual communication.' The ability to send and receive messages whenever one pleases, irrespective of the situation of the person on the other end, is often cited as the advantage of emailing. In the examples seen above, however, it is deemed mandatory to reply to emails as soon as they are received, so this property of 'not having to be concerned about the condition of one's opposite number' is not exercised. Moreover, if one wants to be constantly connected with the other person, there ought also to be the alternative of telephoning them, but for whatever reason, emails are used in preference.

One large factor is that it costs less to email than to make a phone call. Is that the only explanation, though, for email having spread to the current extent? I suggest that there is 'something' which cannot be achieved without the medium of 'text,' and that this is the factor behind the preferential use of email.

Actually, as long as the focus is on means that comprise textual communication, we will see that this began to spread even earlier than mobile telephony. The so-called 'pocket bells (pagers)' which were fashionable in the 1990s could be called its forerunners. Pagers were a service that the then Denden kōsha (Nippon Telegraph and Telephone Corporation, later to become NTT) initiated in 1968. Initially, they were simply devices which rang in order to tell company employees who were on outside jobs to contact their office. In the process of addition of numerical and textual display functions, young people began to use them as communication tools among their friends. In fact, until about the year 2000, using both a mobile phone (or Personal Handyphone System = PHS) *and* a pager was a regular practice among youth (Okada 2002). In other words, the present-day mobile phone is also fulfilling the role of a 'mailer' that has absorbed this textual communication function of the pagers.

For this reason, several fascinating phenomena can be seen in pagers' textual communication when analysing current mobile email. The one which I wish to introduce here is the importance of the meaning held by 'symbols' in textual communication.

A programme entitled 'Beru tomo juu-ni moji no seishun (Pager friends: youth in twelve characters),' telecast on the NHK General Television network in November 1996, was a documentary which followed some upper-secondary-school boys who publicised their own pager numbers in a magazine carrying information on individuals (like a magazine version of a dating site). Its ending scene showed the figure of a boy who, having had his first date with a high-school girl he had befriended through pager interaction, was overjoyed to find a ♥ symbol attached to the 'Good night' message that had always arrived from the girl.

Why is the presence or absence of a heart mark so vital? Of course, it is because one can read from it that the girl had gained a favourable impression of the boy as a result of the date. Yet the heart mark itself is nothing more than a simple symbol. Why did the boy read so much meaning into the symbolic heart mark, and become so joyful?

If that becomes clear, then the essence of the question as to whether we endeavour to maintain a relationship of 'connectibility' with intimate others through 'textual communication' is also likely to come into view. From here on, I will thus look at what kind of influence 'communication by means of text' exerts upon personal relationships, through past studies.

Community in the early days of the internet

The internet in the age of text

Research relating to mobile dependence could be said to have only just begun even in Japan, but there has been a varied accumulation of research on a similar phenomenon, '(inter)net dependence' prior to this, also. Of course, as internet technology and fashions change frequently, and users are continuing to increase, one cannot know if past studies on internet dependence will have currency even now, in their present form. There are, however, some parts of research on internet dependence that are informative in analysing the state of dependence that focuses upon mobile email. This is because mobile email centring on text messages is situated in an environment that is similar to the internet in its early days, when it could display nothing much more than text and simple images.

In her 1999 book, psychologist Patricia Wallace has pointed out that internet dependence became a problem in the late 1990s, along with the spread of the internet. In her view, surveys and researchers differ in their assessment of the incidence of a state of dependence in which online communication can become 'a serious time sink and… lead to compulsive overuse' (1999, p. 99), but there are psychological factors at play there.

The key is 'synchronicity.' The thing to which people in a state of internet dependence are especially 'addicted' is real-time communication, such as synchronous online chat. In this, Wallace sees the signs of what psychology calls 'operant conditioning' – in other words, when users post some text, they may get a response immediately, or may not. The 'not knowing' is the factor that keeps participants glued to the internet (1999, pp. 182–3).

Certainly, in a condition of email dependence, also, what is often said is that each party continues to reply to their counterpart's email, and the exchange can never end. Here, too, the 'synchronicity' of communication – the fact that a person and their opposite are exchanging messages in real time – achieves importance.

Another thing which drew attention on the internet in the age of text was the MUD (Multi-User Dungeon). MUDs are online games played only with text, and, as in commonly-found role-playing games, the players become fighters or sorcerers and have adventures in fictional worlds. Moreover, while the same feature is seen also in present-day online games, participants not only were able to play the games, but also to enjoy communication with other participants that was unconnected to the games themselves. For that reason, MUDs were regarded not so much as simple games, but rather as online virtual communities.

Much of the research relating to MUDs has insights useful in the analysis of internet society in the current age, as well. However, what we must focus upon here is the communication that was carried out in that context, and especially the intriguing behaviour to do with how people present their 'selves' online.

Online self-presentation

What MUD scholars particularly observed was players' online sexual behaviour. Clinical psychologist Sherry Turkle introduces the story of a student by the name of Stewart who held a 'wedding ceremony' with a female player called 'Winterlight' whom he had befriended in a MUD called 'Gargoyle.' Online, Stewart went by the name of 'Achilles.'

> On their first virtual date, Achilles took Winterlight to an Italian restaurant close to Stewart's dorm. He had often fantasized being there with a woman. Stewart used a combination of MUD commands

to simulate a romantic evening at the restaurant. Through these commands, he could pick Winterlight up at the airport in a limousine, drive her to a hotel room so that she could shower, and then take her to the restaurant...In real life, Stewart felt constrained by his health problems, his shyness and social isolation, and his narrow economic straits. In the Gargoyle MUD, he was able to bypass these obstacles, at least temporarily (Turkle 1995, pp. 194–5).

Precisely because netspace is anonymous, people's ability to engage in different kinds of behaviour that transcend the limitations of reality is a frequently-seen phenomenon even now. What I wish to emphasise here, however, is the fact that a 'wedding' can be held there. Naturally, this marriage is something that only exists online, and has no meaning except among the MUD participants. This kind of event is not at all extraordinary, however. Far from it – though admittedly only taking place in text, every conceivable kind of 'virtual' sexual behaviour, including sex, orgies, partner-swapping and rape, was being carried out in MUDs.

When we ponder the meaning of sexual behaviour held by online communication, the role played by gender there becomes something of enormous importance. Let us examine this with the example of a male psychiatrist called Sanford Levin, introduced by media scholar Allucquére Rosanne Stone (1995). Levin inadvertently awoke to the appeal of acting as a woman in a MUD. If he behaved as a woman, then online female players would readily reveal the kind of 'girls' secrets' that they would never divulge to men.

Having begun to participate in a MUD in the guise of 'Julie,' a psychologist with a disability, Levin eventually came up against a huge problem. As he, a non-disabled person in the real world, continued to pose as a woman with a disability, others began to realise that 'Julie's' behaviour was not natural for someone who was disabled. Yet Levin, with many online friends already, found it impossible to discard his 'Julie' persona. Conversely, when he had participated in a MUD as a player called 'Sanford,' who reflected his real self, he had been unable to make any online friends.

These examples tell us all sorts of things as to what significance an online 'self' has for the individual who plays it. One of these is that it is possible for a person's online self to become a larger presence than their real self. The reason for this lies in the fact that our 'identity' is secured through 'approval' from others. In other words, when their self-image presented online gains stronger approval than their one in the real world, it becomes impossible for that individual to know which one they can call their real 'self.' It will be easily appreciated that such a thing is a commonly-occurring phenomenon if we think of the case in which a person cannot tell the truth about themself, even if they think their real self is a gloomy one, because they have been recognised as an 'amusing fellow' among their friends.

Another deeply-interesting point is that when a self-image which has been presented is online, it can become something that drastically departs from a person's real self. In Japan, people who falsify their gender portrayal on the internet are called '*nekama*,' that is, those who play (portray themselves as) the opposite sex online (formed from *netto* (internet) and *okama* (effeminate transvestite),' but from the early days of the internet, such people existed in large numbers in other countries, as well. This does not mean, though, that tragedies such as Levin's always arose. By playing a gender role online that differed from theirs in the real world, people's outlook also broadened through the kind of bodily experience that they could never know simply by living an ordinary life.

The internet, which liberates humans from reality

The reason why attention was drawn to online sexual behaviour is that falsifying deviant behaviour and gender is easier there than in the real world. This is because the distance between reality and the online realm can become markedly great, especially in relation to sexual behaviour.

Of course, there was also criticism vis-à-vis such behaviour from both inside and outside of the internet. If it is revealed that users have falsified their gender, they are open to severe criticism from those around them, and there have also been people who have reacted to incidents of rape which occurred online with about the same degree of shock as with a real case. However, the kind of psychologists and media researchers I have cited here and the online inhabitants who appear in their research, even while recognising the negative aspects of the internet, still appear to be addicted to the 'pleasure' it brings.

What was the object of their 'addiction'? It is the medium's capability, namely, by connecting to the net, people might eventually lose their boundaries as human beings. In the real world, we are limited by various boundaries such as our own sex, appearance and physical ability. Online, however, we can depart from such restrictions, and become a completely different person.

Why was having such a capability considered so wonderful? Historically, it could be said to originate in the 'hippy'-like tendency of the people involved in the birth of the internet. For the hippies in the 1960s who aimed for liberation from a controlled society, and to drop out from modern society, the computer technology which emerged in the latter half of the twentieth century seemed to be something that would provide them with a Utopia. In an essay that spelled out his own online experiences, journalist Howard Rheingold notes that internet communication gives rise to 'virtual communities' akin to the communes formed by hippies (Rheingold 1994).

What has flowed into twentieth-century media discourse is the hippy-like ideal which says that new technology may banish the various conditions which limit real individuals, and give rise to a connection between human beings as an entity in itself. That has also been incorporated as a part of the ideology in discourses that debate the internet. For that reason, the phenomenon of internet addiction may also be viewed not only with the perspective that it is a dangerous thing which will neglect real life, but also with the expectant eye that it will give birth to a new society.

The meaning of the heart symbol

In pondering the diverse phenomena occurring on the internet, it is absolutely vital to understand that prior studies had the common themes of the 'potential for a new society' and the 'wavering of human identity.' In our lives, in which a lifestyle with the internet has become an everyday thing, such themes perhaps will look overblown, but especially when researching our society and culture, there is call for a viewpoint which goes beyond merely looking at the extent of dissemination, or individual fads.

We have seen that it was possible for users to manifest themselves as different entities from real individuals because the internet in the age of text was an anonymous space in which even gender could be falsified, and it has provided participants with a kind of pleasure, but how does this relate to becoming addicted to text messaging, with a focus on email?

What is important when users become completely different entities from their real selves is the quality of the data sent and received over the internet. If the information flowing there consists of a three-dimensional image of themselves and their own voice, then people cannot falsify their own appearance. It is precisely because data is something which is divorced to a certain extent from reality, such as 'text,' we can also become 'a completely different person' on the Net.

If we think in this way, then it becomes plausible that the pleasure provided by text-centric communication conducted over the internet could also be adapted to the world of mobile-phone email, which similarly involves the mutual sending of messages by text. In other words, by utilising text – a data-poor means of communication – we can deftly manage our communication by lying to our counterparts about our own data, or sending out information in a limited manner.

Sentiments about 'videophones' uttered by one upper-secondary student I interviewed express this concisely. In her words: 'Videophones are permissible because [the people using them] are entertainers who appear in commercials. I couldn't possibly show the unmadeup face I wear at home to my boyfriend!'

It is not that the girl is presenting a false version of her own attributes to her boyfriend, as Levin did. By her use of textual email rather than a mode of communication such as a videophone which would show her 'real self' as is, what perhaps is being undertaken here is the act of presenting her own condition in a conveniently stage-managed way. Even in cases of communication with an intimate opposite, it is therefore possible for a condition to arise in which 'text-only messaging is more convenient.'

This might solve the question posed at the end of the first section about the 'heart symbol.' In short, here, the heart symbol placed after the 'Good night' is precisely the self which the girl choreographed in her own way by means of text. The 'alternative me' in emails, expressed through text and symbols, manifests itself in exchange of email with another person as an entity that is 'more like "me" than I am myself.'

If we follow that line of thought, it means that the symbols, emoticons and embellishments such as 'deco-mail' which are frequently employed in emails are being used as a means for expressing a self that is separate from the real me, but yet is the most 'me-like me' of all. Even if our mobile phones become high-functioning and we obtain a means of communication as sophisticated as a personal computer, the reason for our inability to relinquish the form of text-messaging called 'email' is that there are things which only email can do.

Mobile dependence and friendships

From the results of a survey on students

Reasons for a need for 'interaction via email,' which is a factor in mobile dependence, can be considered from such preceding studies. Why, then, might people in a state of mobile dependence have to maintain connections with friends through their mobiles in the first place? In order to elucidate this point, it is necessary to think specifically about the personal relationships of the people who are connected by using mobiles.

There can be diverse ways of examining that issue, but here I shall base my discussion on the student survey which I jointly conducted with Daisuke Tsuji and Akihiro Kitada. The data I cite below is the result of analysis targeting students who owned a mobile phone, taken from a questionnaire survey of 424 students carried out between December 2006 and January 2007 at multiple universities in metropolitan Tokyo and the Kansai area (around Osaka-Kyoto-Kobe).

First, let us look at the data concerning mobile email. In terms of the number of email messages sent and received per day, forty-six percent of respondents fall in the 'ten or more' bracket. There are also some whose daily email exchange is huge, comprising as many as 100 or 200 messages, but more than half of the students limit their exchange to ten or fewer emails per day. However, in response to the question of whether they try to reply as promptly as possible to email from 'friends,' fifty-eight percent of students indicate agreement, which implies that mobile email is being recognised as synchronised communication.

In addition, the survey also included such items as: 'When I am out of signal range, I feel somewhat unsettled,' and 'I check my mobile numerous times to see if there have been any incoming mail.' Thirty-three percent and forty-three percent respectively responded with agreement to these items.

Figure 5.1: Number of mail messages sent and received per day

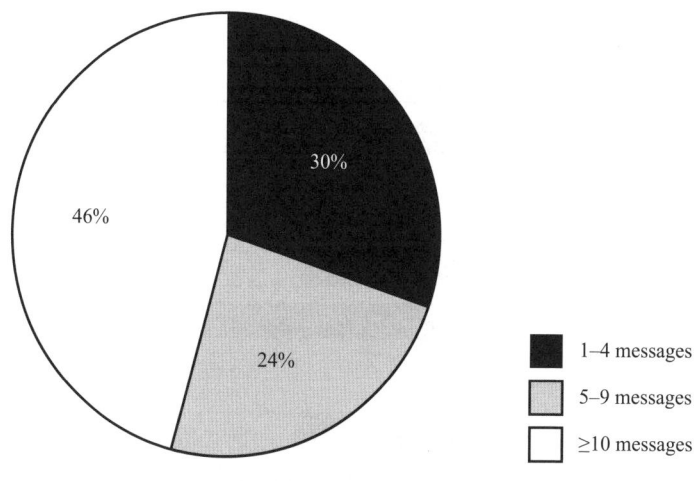

Figure 5.2: I reply promptly to mail from friends

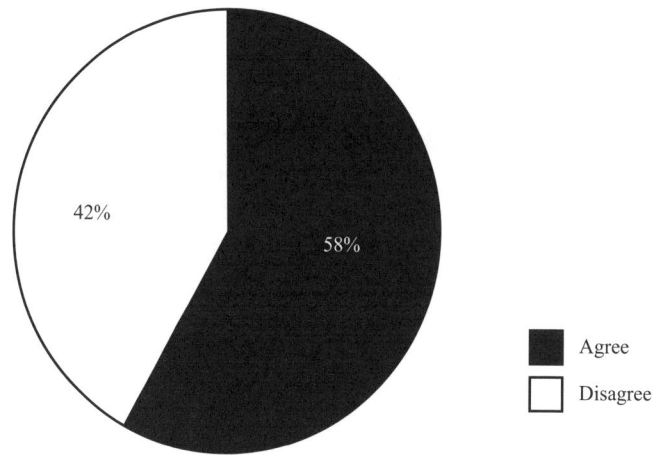

If we were to show a state of mobile dependence by these indicators, namely, 'replies immediately to emails,' 'anxiety due to the condition of the signal,' and 'frequent checks for incoming mail,' then students who replied that they agreed to all three of the above indicators will account for fourteen percent of the total.

Figure 5.5: Mobile dependence and mail usage frequency

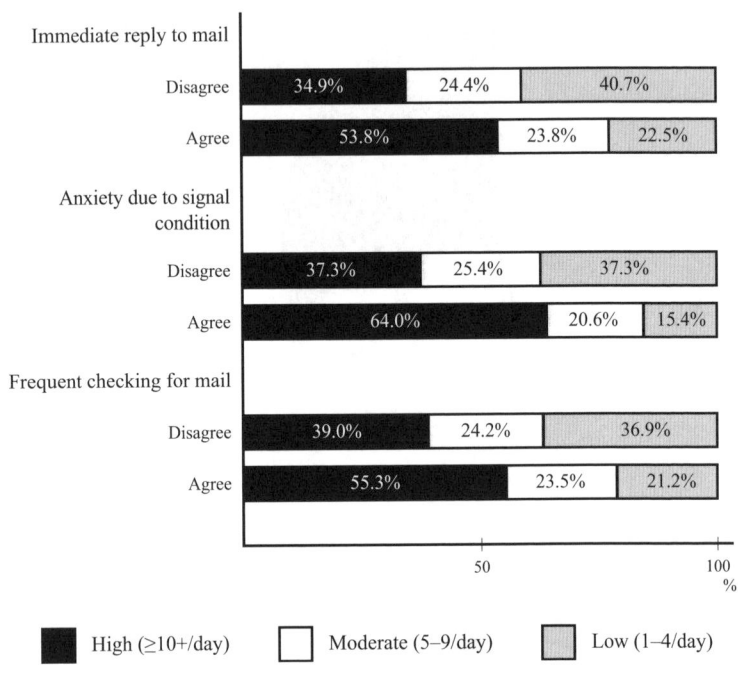

Though students' mobile dependence cannot be said to be a majority condition, it can be seen to have a certain volume.

So, how do these indicators and the frequency of exchanging emails relate to one another? Cross-tabulation of the abovementioned 'number of emails sent and received per day' with these indicators yielded the result that with any of the indicators, students giving an 'Agree' response had a significantly larger number of email messages sent and received (a 0.1 percent standard in a chi-square test).

Among students who check their mobile phone numerous times per day for incoming mail, while 55.3 percent send and receive ten or more emails, thirty-nine percent do not report that many. Alternatively, while sixty-four percent of students who replied that they 'feel unsettled when out of signal range' sent and received ten or more emails per day, those who did not accounted for only 37.3 percent. From this, it can be appreciated that mobile dependence has a correlation with the number of email messages sent and received.

Figure 5.6: Frequent checking for incoming mail and fear of loneliness

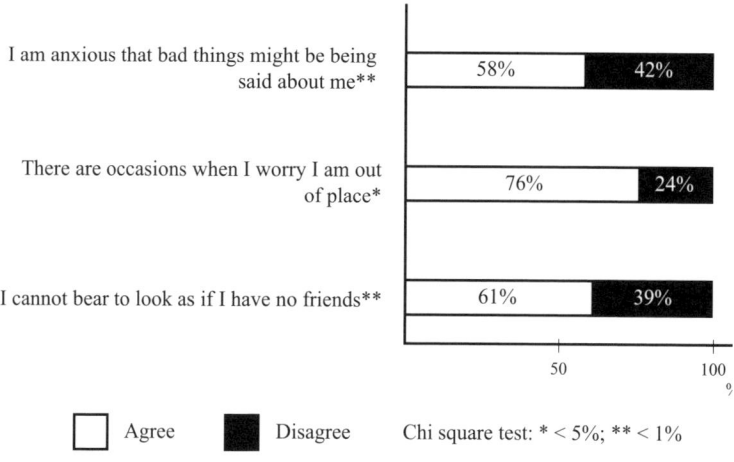

A correlation between feelings of loneliness and the number of email messages sent and received has been made clear in research by Isao Nakamura (2003). According to Nakamura, it can be seen that active users of mobile email tend to have active face-to-face and interpersonal relationships, while conversely, the less active in face-to-face relationships a person is, the less active their email interaction tends to be.

When we look at the number of email messages sent and received not as the issue of a condition of 'now being lonely or not,' but in relation to a feeling of loneliness that constitutes a 'fear of becoming lonely,' it is important that a correlation be recognised between these two, as well. In other words, as mobile email is something that assuages a fear of loneliness, frequent use of mobile email is promoted, and feelings of loneliness also fade as a result.

How, then, are this 'fear of loneliness' and mobile dependence connected? In the survey, we had items such as: 'I cannot bear to be seen by those around me as having no friends,' 'There are times when I am concerned that my own behaviour might be inappropriate,' and 'I am worried that friends or acquaintances might be saying bad things about me.' When we conduct analysis using these indicators, it will be seen that the more that students agree with indicators of mobile dependence, the stronger their anxiety about

Figure 5.7: Anxiety over signal condition and fear of loneliness

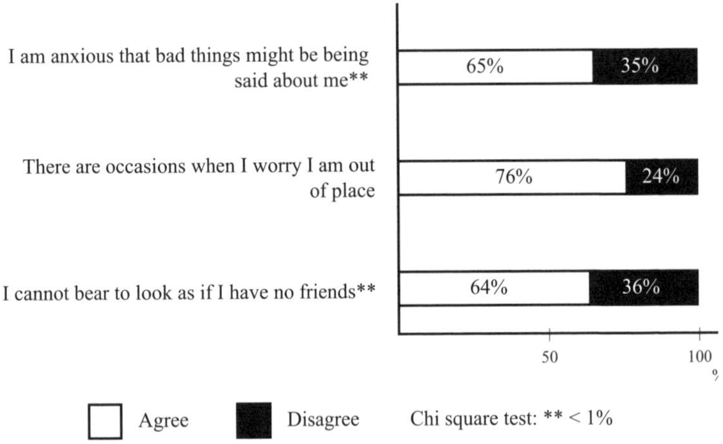

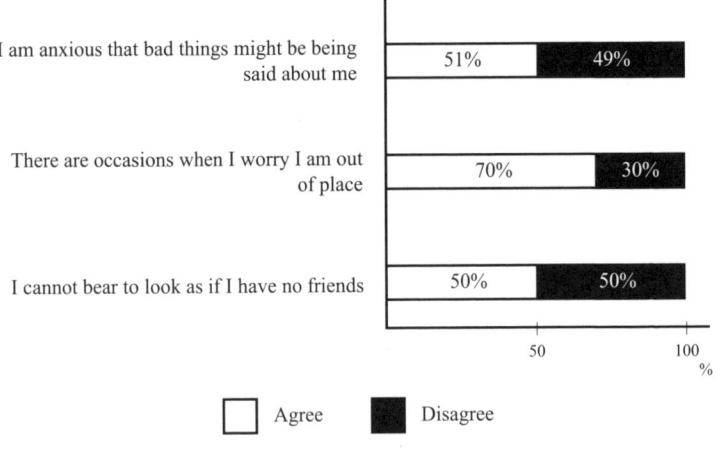

Figure 5.8: Immediate reply to mail and fear of loneliness

loneliness will be. Responses to the question on concern that their own behaviour might be inappropriate reached seventy-six percent among those who 'frequently check for incoming mail.'

What must be noted, however, is the fact that not all of the indicators cited here have a significant connection with mobile dependence. Responses are divided half-and-half between the 'I cannot bear to look as if I have no friends' and 'I am anxious that people might be saying bad things about me' items vis-à-vis the 'I reply immediately to emails' indicator. It could be argued that there is still room for further refinement of indicators considered to be factors in mobile dependence.

Character conversion/switching aspirations and anxiety over loneliness and isolation

In any case, what becomes clear from the above analysis is that the phenomenon of mobile dependence is a phenomenon related to a fear of loneliness. Particularly in terms of its relationship with the survey items in question, we could say that the fear is not one of being lonely *per se*, but of 'realising one's own loneliness.' The feeling arises of wanting always to be connected with someone and to maintain a condition of connectibility, in order to avoid noticing one's loneliness, and the mobile phone becomes a tool for satisfying that emotion. I argue that the factor which provokes the birth of mobile dependence lies therein.

Why, then, are people afraid of noticing that they are lonely? A popular explanation might be that 'young people's personal relationships have become tenuous.' Research on youth friendships shows, however, that there is no justification for this 'rarification-of-personal-relationships discourse.' Rather, a hypothesis has been presented heretofore by multiple scholars, arguing that young people's personal relationships have perhaps become 'selective relationships' in which they switch connections and their own personality (character) to suit the circumstances (Tsuji 1999).

Accordingly, when I conducted a survey about how such aspirations to switch friendships and personalities relate to loneliness anxiety, something deeply interesting came to light. The following correlations between indicators were seen: vis-à-vis 'I cannot bear to look as if I have no friends,' 'I want to associate with friends intimately, including in private matters' ($\rho = -0.234$); 'I want to widen my circle of new friends further' ($\rho = 0.173$); and 'Fitting the mood is more important than the content of the conversation' ($\rho = 0.135$); and vis-à-vis 'I worry that I might be out of place' and 'I am anxious that people might be saying bad things about me,' 'My character changes according to which friends I am talking with' ($\rho = 0.101/0.186$, respectively).

What this shows is that it is not merely the question of a state of 'being lonely' that breeds anxiety about loneliness. People want to associate intimately with friends, and also to broaden their personal relationships. If they try to expand their personal relationships, however, they must strive to change character and align themselves with the opposite party. This implies that anxiety over whether that 'alignment' is going well develops as a result, and this is linked with the fear that 'actually, I might not be considered one of the "in-group."'

Here, what can be seen is the dilemma that 'conforming to other people in order to avoid loneliness has the reverse effect of breeding anxiety over isolation.' Mobile phones certainly are a tool for compensating for feelings of loneliness, but it is probably difficult to use them as tools for compensating for the isolation anxiety that develops in consequence. The more widely people's personal relationships extend due to mobile phones, the more they have to continue to maintain a condition of permanent connectibility, and sustain the behaviour of replying immediately to emails. Is that not the mechanism which gives rise to mobile dependence, perhaps?

Conclusion: for research into mobile-phone culture

Thus far, I have elucidated the connection between youth and mobile phones and the factors in mobile dependence from theoretical and empirical aspects. Theoretically speaking, as mobile dependence – and especially addiction to textual communication – is constricted by the means called 'text,' it emerges that this makes it all the easier for people to present themselves in a manner that reflects the persona that best suits themselves. When the 'self' thus presented is flung into a broad circle of friends, however, 'anxiety about isolation' arises due to that very connectivity. What becomes clear from an empirical aspect is a cycle in which people constantly check their connection with others in order to compensate for such isolation anxiety.

Previously, when it was beginning to be revealed that the internet spawned dependence among people, researchers and net users still gave a positive appraisal to the internet's opening of new relationships between people and their potential to become a different self from their current self. That, however, was an expectation that a 'future which had hitherto never existed' would arrive, and an assessment born of a rift between the new society and the previous one.

For young people of the future, who will have to build personal relationships in a situation where the internet and mobile telephones have 'been there from the beginning,' such expectations are ones that could probably never be harboured.

It is implausible to hold such expectations. Perhaps it can be argued, for that reason, that there is call for theoretical frameworks and empirical approaches that are appropriate to the present age, where the meaning of those expectations has changed, while still taking past theoretical studies into account?

Finally, I wish to comment on the points to note when researching the new media with which I have dealt in this chapter, and the society and culture which have emerged as a result. In many cases, media such as the internet and mobile phones have spawned a new culture of usage centring upon youth, which is undergoing change in short cycles. For that reason, conditions change greatly before any firm demonstration can be accomplished in terms of academic research, meaning that the step from hypothesis to verification will be unable to keep pace.

In addition, even if such a culture of usage were a 'self-evident phenomenon' for the people who are within it, in occasional cases it would appear to be something completely incomprehensible for those who are not. Accordingly, the problem also arises of a standard for determining whether a certain hypothesis was valid in the first place. Though people outside a culture of usage may sometimes make misguided analyses, those within that culture who well understand the circumstances are not necessarily able to present an objective and valid hypothesis, either.

In order to deal with this problem, while always keeping one foot inside a culture of usage, researchers must maintain a sense of distance which enables them also to appraise it with an external eye. Moreover, they must examine the validity of the results of their analysis based on that sense of distance by comparing them once more with the actual feeling they obtained inside the culture of usage.

Such a stance consisting of 'shuttling between the positions of party concerned and researcher' is one that has been taken for granted in research in cultural anthropology and the like. In this chapter, too, I trust I have honed the phenomenon of email exchange by subjecting it also to objective verification through quantitative surveys, while describing it in a form close to the actual feeling of the parties concerned.

In the current age of advancing globalisation, so-called 'primitive societies' might have been lost from the world, yet we can still find incomprehensible cultural spheres here and there even within the societies that we ourselves inhabit. Is not the kind of research that delves into such cultures perhaps what we are seeking?

6 How has the style of television viewing changed?: the active receiver and the transformation of the subversive riposte

Keiichi Nabe

Though television's presence has arguably faded in the sense of its newsworthiness, due to the spread of the internet and mobile telephones, it is still the most familiar medium in our everyday lives. How do all of you readers usually watch television, I wonder? You could concentrate on a single programme and watch it from beginning to end, or you could occasionally glance at the screen while doing something else. Alternatively, you could watch while talking with family or friends, and it would not matter if you watched while restlessly using the remote control to channel-surf, either. In this manner, various ways of viewing are possible according to the individuals and situations involved, and the very fact that such viewing methods are permissible might be said to be a special feature of television viewing seldom found in other media experiences.

In this chapter, using '*tsukkomi* (subversive riposte)' as a keyword, I will examine how television, which allows such a diversity of ways of watching, has changed its principal viewing style along with the times. When, and in what form, did the viewing audience which provides the subversive ripostes appear? Moreover, how has the subversive riposte transformed since then, and how has the content of television programmes changed in tune with the subversive riposte's transfiguration? Here, I wish to ponder these questions.

The critical viewing audience's immersion in television

The 'Hakkutsu! Aru aru daijiten (Discovery! Encyclopaedia of living)' data-fabrication issue

In January 2007, a huge incident occurred which shocked the

television industry. In a telecast on 7 January, a lifestyle information variety show entitled 'Hakkutsu! Aru aru daijiten (Discovery! Living encyclopaedia)' (Fuji Television Network) claimed that *nattō* (fermented soy beans) were effective in dieting, and, along with experimental data, introduced such actual examples as people having lost weight in two weeks if they ate one pack of *nattō* each morning and evening. It was revealed that, in fact, the blood tests, serum triglyceride measurements and so on which formed the basis of this data had not been carried out, and the data itself was a 'fabrication.' As soon as this was announced, the sole sponsor, Kao, instantly decided to withdraw its sponsorship, and the programme itself ended up being cancelled.

Though this incident provoked the re-posing of the longstanding question of 'broadcast ethics,' it is not in an attempt to think about this issue that I have mentioned the incident here. What I wish to focus upon here is the phenomenon which arose all over Japan after the 7 January telecast. One newspaper reports it as follows:

> Starting from the day after the telecast, supplies of packaged *nattō* grew short at the point of sale in supermarkets in every area. In early evening, there were even some shops that put up a 'Sold out' notice. Looking astounded, one person in charge of a middle-ranking supermarket said: 'The next day, twice the usual quantity sold, and on the eleventh, products stopped arriving from the major manufacturers. We heard that a fixed quantity would come in from the twelfth, but I have never had such an experience' (Asahi shinbun 2007, 12 January).

How did you feel to read this article, I wonder? How enormous the influence of television must be, to be able to change people's behaviour so readily! The mass media are a brainwashing device that exerts a powerful effect upon human thinking. It frightens us to think thus. There might be people who have felt this way, or perhaps others who have turned their eye towards the viewing audience and gained the following kind of impressions: whatever the circumstances, those people who rushed out to buy *nattō* are too naïve; we must not take what we hear on television seriously; or, we have to read messages from the mass media more 'critically.' All of these opinions are valid, but I would like you to stop and think at this point. Does television operate unilaterally vis-à-vis its viewing audience, and does it have sufficient influence to change even its audience's way of thinking? In addition, do contemporary viewers so meekly accept the messages that television emits?

The mature viewing audience

If we examine surveys on television viewing in recent years, an image that differs from such a 'naïve viewing audience' will emerge. According to a survey that national broadcaster NHK conducted in 1997, for instance, when given such question items as 'Part way through, I see the trick in a programme,' or 'I feel that even with the same issue, different newscasters and programmes have different ways of telling it,' the proportion of people who replied 'Yes (Often + Sometimes)' was as high as sixty-eight percent; and in the 2002 'Survey on fifty years of television,' more than thirty percent of people, regardless of age bracket, had the view that 'even if [they] see that it is a pretense, if the programme is entertaining, then it is permissible' (NHK Hōsō Bunka Kenkyūjo 2003, p. 216). Moreover, in a 2005 survey on 'The Japanese and television,' 28.4 percent of people indicated agreement with the statement: 'I think that what the mass media conveys is mostly factual,' this being a fall of 8.8 percent from 37.2 percent in 1985; while conversely the proportion of people disagreeing rose to 49.5 percent, showing a 6.2 percent increase in comparison with 43.3 percent in 1985 (Shiraishi, Hara and Terui 2005, p. 32).

If we examine these figures, we can see that most of the present-day viewing audience is not accepting what is being said on television without criticism or reflection. Viewers know that a certain degree of staging is being carried out in the production of television programmes, and they are also aware that things which cannot be called 'facts' are contained in the messages which the mass media release. In that sense, the modern viewing audience could be said to be one that has 'matured.' Accordingly, we cannot simplistically conclude that the collective phenomenon of *nattō* selling out arose due to many people having unquestioningly swallowed information disseminated from television and the mass media.

If that is the case, then it means that a curious situation developed, namely that a viewing audience with a critical, cool eye towards the mass media responded immediately and obediently to conveyed messages. A phenomenon has arisen in which, while making the gesture of maintaining distance from the reality fabricated by television, the viewing audience becomes totally immersed in such a reality. How should we understand this paradox? In this chapter, by pursuing the changes in television viewing in Japanese society, with its fifty-odd years of history, I wish both to shed light on how this 'mature viewing audience' was spawned, and to ponder the question of why the viewing audience, which holds this critical perspective, becomes absorbed in the reality constructed by television.

Models of mass communication

Characteristics of mass communication

First, with reference to the media theory of J. B. Thompson (1995), let us look at the features of so-called 'mass communication,' including not only television viewing, but the reading of magazines and newspapers, or listening to the radio or compact discs (CDs). Firstly, in mass communication, the sender and receiver of a message do not share the same context. The 'context' mentioned here indicates the temporal/spatial circumstances in which messages are sent and received. In mass communication, messages are conveyed towards people who are not present in the 'here and now,' and so it can be said to be communication whose temporal and spatial range is greatly expanded in comparison with face-to-face communication.

The second characteristic which can be listed is that the receivers are in unspecified large numbers. Not only face-to-face communication but also actions such as writing a letter or making a telephone call are usually directed at a specific other. By contrast, an action such as publishing a magazine or broadcasting a television drama do not make their target an other who can be specifically stipulated by name. Of course, at the planning stage of new magazines and dramas, a certain amount of focus upon readers or the viewing audience is carried out, but this does not mean that the receivers are totally limited by such speculation on the part of the sender. Nothing prevents elderly men from watching dramas produced with young women as the target audience. As long as the conditions of having a television set or being literate are met, then any kind of other can potentially become a receiver in mass communication, and for that reason, senders cannot completely control the type of receiver.

As the third characteristic of mass communication, I can state that the flow of information is unilateral. In face-to-face communication such as conversation, it is usually impossible for one party to continue speaking arbitrarily. Communication progresses by allowing the roles of sender and receiver of messages to alternate in sequence, as in when one party finishes talking for a moment, the other party starts to speak in response. This is the type of conversation that is regularly carried on, and so we can recognise 'mutuality' in it. On the other hand, the receiver in mass communication merely passively accepts the messages sent by the mass media, and cannot turn into a sender and send messages back to the mass media on an equal footing, as is possible in conversation. What the receiver could do is nothing much more than to send an email or letter to the broadcasting station or publishing house, or to telephone them, and in this sense, the relationship between sender and receiver in mass communication cannot help being asymmetrical – this meaning that its character will have a more strongly monological rather than a dialogical hue (Thompson 1995, pp. 23–31, 84–5).

Now, we have seen the features of mass communications in terms of three points. In sum, mass communication is communication that unilaterally conveys a large volume of information towards an unspecified large number of receivers with whom the mass media (the sender) does not share a context. Due to the convergence of these characteristics, a secondary effect not seen in other types of communication is brought into being in mass communication, namely, a situation in which there is no mutual monitoring between sender and receiver.

In the case of communication where a party mutually exchanges messages with a specific other who shares a context such as a conversation, its participants endeavour to understand how their own utterances have been received by the other party by observing each other's reactions. If they feel that the other party is not seriously listening to their own utterances, then they are likely to call the other's attention so that the other will listen; and if they think they are being misunderstood, they will probably try to convey their true intention by such means as expressing themselves in another way. The ability to attempt course-correction in communication in this manner through mutual observation is a major feature of face-to-face interaction.

By contrast, in the case of mass communication, such mutual monitoring is actually impossible. This is because the receivers are in a different context from the sender, and so the receivers' reaction does not enter the sender's field of vision; and it is also almost impossible for the receivers to send a message back instantly. This does not necessarily become a stumbling-block to the progress of mass communication, however. Rather, from the standpoint of the sender, there is the advantage of being able to keep on sending messages without the need to be much concerned about the receivers' response. From the receivers' perspective, on the other hand, it is not possible to intervene in the process of transmitting messages, or their content, meaning that large amounts of information are transmitted irrespective of receivers' hopes and desires (Thompson 1995, pp. 97–8).

The powerful effects model and minimal effects model

If we think about the characteristics of mass communication in this way, it is probably natural in a certain sense for it to lead to the view that the sender in this communication will be in a stronger position than the receivers. In actuality, when we look back at the history of mass communication research, we see that in its early stages, it was argued that the influence exerted by the mass media upon people was extremely large.

In October 1938, an incident which brings home the seriousness of the effect of the mass media occurred in the United States. CBS Radio produced a radio drama based on H. G. Wells' novel, *The War of the Worlds*, but in order to draw the interest of listeners, it adopted the directorial method of conveying witness accounts of an invasion of Earth by Martians through news flashes. The effect of this staging was all too dramatic. All over America, people fell into a great panic, with listeners who accepted the news flashes within the drama as being 'real news' fleeing from their homes, broadcasting to the neighbours about the Martian invasion, calling ambulances or police cars, and so on. This incident was later surveyed in a study by researchers including Hadley Cantril, and summarised in a book of his called *The Invasion from Mars* (Cantril [1940] 1971), which we can regard as one example of the powerful effects model that understands the influence the mass media exerts on the general populace as being something extremely large.

A while after the heyday of this powerful effects model, the theory that the influence of the mass media is not so great made its appearance. P. F. Lazarsfeld and others analysed voting behaviour in the 1940 U.S. Presidential election, resulting in the revelation that fifty-three percent of the electorate had already decided upon a candidate in the early stages, and that no more than eight percent had changed their preferred candidate. Moreover, those who changed had relatively low frequency of contact with the mass media, and such people reported that influence from other people was greater than that from the media. From this stemmed the proposal of the 'two-step flow of communication' theory, which says that the effect of the mass media first reaches 'opinion leaders' who are in frequent touch with the media, and, as a continuation of this, is transmitted to the majority through the 'personal influence' of such leaders (Lazarsfeld, Berelson and Gaudet [1944] 1948). In this model, the effects of mass communication are deemed to be insufficiently powerful to cause a dramatic change in many people's opinions, remaining at the level of 'reinforcing' each person's way of thinking, and it is therefore called the minimal effects model.

The discovery of the active receiver

In this way, the powerful effects model and minimal effects model indicate contrasting views of the effects which the mass media exert. Nonetheless, though both theories are extremely important in apprehending mass communication, there is one point to which they have not paid enough attention. This is the question of how receivers understand the messages emitted by the mass media. I have pointed out that there is not much mutual monitoring between senders and receivers in mass communication. This implies that senders transmit messages without caring about receivers' reactions, giving rise to an image of receivers as a presence that merely accepts those messages. In such an image, it is the mass media side – always the sender – that is the active one, while receivers are consistently depicted as a passive presence.

Seen from a different angle, however, the situation in which there is no mutual monitoring can also be considered to be to receivers' advantage. This is because not having their responses observed by the sender means that receivers can decide with a certain degree of 'freedom' how they will engage with the messages that are sent and received, by exercising their own judgement. The viewing audience may concentrate on watching television, or may equally indulge in 'multi-task viewing' in which they cast occasional quick glances at the screen while doing other things. For that reason, senders always end up being placed in the unstable state of not knowing how their receivers are accepting and understanding their messages. With this idea, we will see that it cannot always be claimed that senders are in a stronger position than receivers in mass communication.

If we assume that receivers are not merely passively accepting the messages which the mass media sends out, then how should we apprehend mass communication? The theory proposed by way of an answer to such a question was Stuart Hall's 'encoding/decoding' model (1980). Encoding describes the process in which the mass media, which is the sender, gives meaning to incidents and events and 'encodes' it into messages, while decoding indicates the process in which receivers 'decode' the messages that have had meanings added in that manner. The important thing here is that decoding by receivers is relatively autonomous from senders' encoding, and for that reason, there is always the possibility that messages will be decoded in a form that diverges from senders' 'intentions.' Not only that – as receivers have differing ideas, hobbies and interests according to their social position, namely such things as age, sex, social class and occupation, the meanings decoded by those receivers cannot be one-dimensional by any means, and could be said to be opened into multiple interpretations.

If we follow a model such as Hall's, even if receivers in mass communication are in a passive position in terms of the transmission of messages, if we look at the angle of meaning-decoding in the messages, we can regard receivers as an active presence. Moreover, such a transformation in the image of the receiver leads to a change in the way we understand mass communication itself. In other words, this means that mass communication will be reinterpreted not as a monological process in which senders unilaterally transmit messages, but as a space for dialogical 'negotiation' carried on between encoding and decoding. Accordingly, in mass communication where the relationship between sender and receiver is fixed, though it arguably lacks the kind of mutuality seen in everyday conversation, we can find some manner of mutuality in that receivers are carrying out active interpretation as decoders of meaning.

Transformation of the viewing audience

A viewing audience that spectates and appreciates

In light of the theoretical considerations in the previous section,

Figure 6.1: Street television in the early 1950s © Sankei Shinbun-sha

here I wish to take a look at changes in television viewing styles in Japanese society, in chronological order. Japanese television broadcasts uttered their natal cry in 1953 upon the opening of the NHK Tokyo station. The characteristic of television viewing in those early days, as demonstrated in such sights as the watching of live telecasts of professional wrestling on street televisions along with throngs of spectators, lay in the 'spectating' of performances and events hitherto unable to be seen without going to their actual venues (see Figure 6.1).

If we look at questionnaires that inquired as to how people were watching television in those times, we can see that watching television was a 'formal event' for people of the time, and that they were viewing every enthusiastically for that reason, as evidenced by such responses as: 'Every day, I would be a spectator of the street television in the station plaza, going without dinner,' and 'I watched at a neighbour's house, kneeling in the formal manner. It would never do to have lain down to watch, or anything like that' (NHK Hōsō Bunka Kenkyūjo 2003, p. 207). In 1959, the 'Crown Prince's Wedding Parade' was telecast, followed by the Tokyo Olympics in 1964, and on each occasion, television's diffusion rate displayed dramatic growth, and television shifted its main location from the streets to ordinary homes, but there still was not a great change in the viewing style, which involved the enthusiastic spectating of events through the medium of television.

From the late 1960s onwards, television completely blended into the everyday, and the viewing style whereby people watched in their living rooms with their families became established. As if in reflection of this, in the 1970s so-called 'home dramas' such as 'Kimottama kāchan (Feisty mum),' 'Arigatō (Thanks),' and 'Terauchi Kantarō ikka (The Terauchi family),' all from the TBS network, recorded high audience ratings, while the TBS variety programme 'Hachiji da yo! Zen'in shūgō (It's eight o'clock! Everybody get together)' and the historical drama 'Mito Kōmon' (again from TBS) garnered overwhelming support from primary-school students and middle-aged to elderly age groups, respectively; and they were dubbed '*o-bake bangumi* (monster programmes)' (NHK Hōsō Yoron Kenkyūjo 1983, p. 57). These programmes were all made based on solid scripts and direction, and the fans regarded those various programmes as 'works' and 'appreciated' them with concentration. Even speaking from the functional aspect, the remote control had not made its debut at that time, and it was difficult to indulge in channel-surfing (changing channels at will), which is done nowadays as a matter of course. For that reason, it was usual for the viewing audience to watch one programme from beginning to end, and were forced into appreciative television viewing, one could say.

A viewing audience that inserts subversive ripostes

Appreciative viewing such as this is thought to have been the general viewing style of the Japanese populace until about the mid-1970s. In the 1980s, however, a hitherto unseen, new style of television viewing emerged. This was not a style in which receivers accepted the messages transmitted from the television without modification, but one where the viewing audience decoded them using its own interpretive frame, and created 'new meanings' that the sending end had not intended.

The programme which became the perfect target for such a new mode of television viewing was TBS network's 'Suchūwādesu monogatari (A flight attendant's story),' broadcast from 1983 to 1984. This drama series was a 'tale of sheer determination' in which a trainee flight attendant, Chiaki Matsumoto – played by an idol of those days, Chiemi Hori – continued her efforts throughout severe training with the aim of becoming a fully-fledged flight attendant, while having romantic feelings for her instructor, Hiroshi Murasawa, played by Morio Kazama. This drama series won enormous success, with a high audience share of twenty percent on average, and 26.8 percent (Tokyo and environs) for its final episode. This 'success' was not necessarily one that eventuated because the majority of the viewing audience was attracted and moved by this tale of will-power, however. Rather, the main reason for its having earned such popularity was its exaggerated and clumsy directing, unique to dramas from the Daiei studios, and the fact that Chiemi Hori's acting, which could by no means be called skilful, was 'laughter-provoking.' In other words, the viewing audience 'saw ["A flight attendant's story"] not as a tale of perseverance, but skewed its message, and watched it as a type of parody' (Inamasu 1991, p. 15).

Such a way of watching television could be said to personify the 'active receiver' mentioned in the previous section. The point of the 'active receiver' discourse is that the receiver does not constantly accept the meaning loaded by the sender as it stands, and for that reason there is potential for slippage to occur between encoding and decoding. The sending side telecast 'A flight attendant's story' as a 'moving tale' of overcoming numerous trials and growing to become a fine flight attendant, but the viewing audience was consuming it as an '*o-warai* (comedy)' show. The gaze in this kind of television viewing is no longer that of a 'spectator' who grasps the programme as an artistic work and appreciates it as such. Conversely, here the viewer cunningly finds stereotyped dialogue and exaggerated staging or acting and inserts a subversive riposte: in other words, the perspective of a malicious 'observer' is being foregrounded. Erving Goffman divided people who watch plays and theatrical performances into 'onlookers' and 'theatregoers,' and made a distinction between the sympathetic 'laughter by the onlooker' which is triggered by the humorous characters on stage, and 'laughter of the theatregoer' generated by staging bungles and actors' mistakes (Goffman [1974] 1986, pp. 130–1). It is probably arguable that this sort of observer's gaze, which inserts its own subversive ripostes, could be one where the perspective of the theatregoer has been applied to the television-viewing setting.

In about the mid-1980s, in response to that unexpected reaction from the receivers, the senders' end began to make the viewing audience's insertion of ripostes a prerequisite, and programmes made in a form that actively harnessed the audience's gaze as observers started to appear. Nihon Television network's 'Tensai Takeshi no genki ga deru terebi (Genius Takeshi's Energising Television!!)' which was broadcast from 1985, was a programme that symbolised this. The distinctiveness of this programme lay in its construction of a non-everyday sort of 'festive space' by taking up in mockumentary style the sort of topics that were hardly worth attention, such as reviving a run-down shopping arcade, or making a little-known university famous, or searching for '*o-jōsama* (young ladies),' and by the viewing audience also venturing to join in such projects. Here, a hitherto unseen sender–receiver relationship is created in which the producer, who uses the directorial style of a documentary for inappropriate material, colludes and conspires with the viewing audience, which has spotted that it is a parody of documentary programmes (Kobayashi 2003, pp. 163–4).

A similar thing could be said in regard to the Fuji Television network's 'Yūyake nyan nyan (Sunset miaow miaow)' programme broadcast between 1985 and 1987. This programme is renowned for having spawned 'O-nyanko Club,' an idol vocal group that was a collection of girls still at upper-secondary school, but when recruiting its members, the producers ventured not to choose girls who were good at singing and dancing. Instead, they made the approachability of the 'girl-next-door type' their main hiring criterion. In response, while aware that the girls were neither particularly good singers, nor were equipped with enough charm to be called stars, the fans, too, feverishly cheered them on for those very reasons. Here, too, one can see a conspiratorial relationship between the senders, who intentionally attempt to promote idols that do not have 'real talent,' and the receivers, who, having detected such machinations, are complicit in this 'game of deception' (Inamasu 2003, pp. 162–3).

The responsive viewing audience

A little way into the 1990s, however, a subtle yet decisive change occurred in this kind of conspiratorial relationship between sender and the viewing audience which inserts subversive ripostes. The production that clearly illustrated the sign of this change was Nippon Television network's 'Susume! (later Susu*nu*!) Denpa shōnen (Advance! Radio-wave boy),' broadcast from 1992. This programme won popularity with its 'no appointment' design whereby it doorstepped celebrities and topical people, making all manner of requests and having them carry these out without prior arrangement, but it became an overnight sensation because of a 'hitchhike across the Eurasian continent' conducted by a then completely unknown comedy duo calling themselves Saruganseki. This was a project in which the pair was supposed to hitchhike from Hong Kong to London with only the hundred thousand yen in funds that were given to them. The sight of Saruganseki overcoming the numerous difficulties they faced during the journey and intently heading for their goal struck the hearts of many viewers, and when they finally reached their goal in December 1996, Saruganseki had become so popular that they deserved to be called a 'social phenomenon.'

Some time later, however, it was revealed that Saruganseki had travelled by air during their trip, and this was reported in a critical tone by part of the mass media. In spite of this, the reaction of the viewing audience to such reports was lukewarm. Why was this, I wonder? A prerequisite for the statement that a particular documentary-type programme is 'actually a set-up' to function as a 'criticism,' there must be the idea that there is an 'objective reality' outside television, and that television should faithfully reproduce such a reality without distortion. In the 1980s, though, from the standpoint of viewers who had recognised that the reality created by television is 'fiction,' and had learned the fun of daring to sport with 'fiction,' this kind of thinking which enabled the criticism that it was 'staged' looked all too naïve. Though admittedly there are differences in degree, what is broadcast on television always undergoes some choreography, and in that sense, there can be no such thing as a programme without any 'contrived elements.' As we watch television with a full awareness of this, even if it were disparaged as being 'staged,' we would feel no mental anguish whatsoever. This means that a 'weird viewing style consisting of immersion for the very reason that it is ironical' (Kitada 2005, p. 183) develops here. In other words, a kind of television viewing that could even be called 'defiant' comes into being, with the attitude that 'in the end, television is all a set-up, so isn't it enough if one can be emotionally moved at that moment?'

Seen from the perspective of 'subversive ripostes (*tsukkomi*),' however, the radical recognition of a television reality which supports this sort of viewing must be said to have markedly decreased in power. As we have already seen, in the early 1980s when *tsukkomi-*

type television viewing made its appearance, slippage between encoding and decoding was generated due to the viewing audience inserting their subversive ripostes as observers. The consumption as 'comedy' of 'A flight attendant's story,' which had been made as a 'tale of will-power,' is a typical example of this. In the case of the 'Saruganseki hitchhike,' though, even if there had been no intention on the producer's part to make an emotionally-moving programme, the moving element was brewed with each new episode, ultimately leading to the creation of an 'emotional space' through collusion between Saruganseki, choking with tears of gratitude, and their viewers whose hearts were warmed at the sight. Here, it was not that their gaze as riposte-inserting 'observers' had vanished, but it did weaken and withdraw into the background. To borrow the words of Shōichi Ōta: 'An omitted riposte does fulfil its role as a riposte when the need arises, but basically it functions silently to guarantee the substantial broadening of the riposte's circuit of "emotion," while pretending not to see, so to speak' (Ōta 2002, p. 136). In this case, no longer can any slippage be seen between encoding and decoding. Now, the viewing audience accepts the reality created within a television programme as 'reality,' and has become an entity that sometimes laughs at it, sometimes is surprised at it, and sometimes is moved by it. If this is so, then we must acknowledge a huge paradox here. The reason for it is that the active receiver who inserts subversive ripostes has turned into an entity which, in its true pursuit of that activeness, dutifully responds to televised reality.

Where has the subversive riposte gone?

The three types of television viewing

Heretofore, we have looked at how viewing styles have changed. Finally, in summary, I wish to categorise television viewing in each of its ages and organise its characteristics. The principal viewing mode from the 1950s to 1970s was one in which the viewing audience would 'spectate (*kenbutsu*)' performances and events that took place outside of television, or 'appreciate (*kanshō*)' programmes such as dramas and variety shows which senders produced. For that reason, I want to name such viewing 'spectatorly–appreciative' television viewing. The gaze of the viewing audience here is basically a 'spectator's' gaze, and so there is a strong tendency for the

Figure 6.2: The three types of television viewing

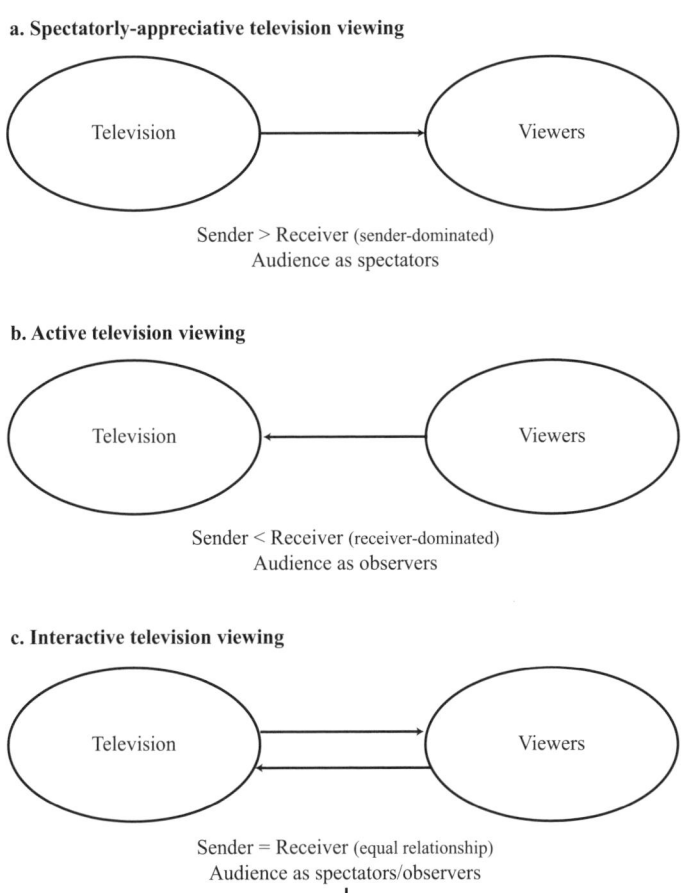

audience to concentrate while trying to receive the information and messages from the sender. Alternatively, if we focus on the power relation between sender and receiver, this can be called sender-dominated communication, in the sense that the receiver remains a presence that enjoys the messages transmitted arbitrarily from the sender (see Figure 6.2a).

Once the 1980s began, the viewing audience stopped being the sort of 'meek' presence it had been before. Receivers accepted messages sent and received from senders in forms such as the senders had not intended, and carried out 'alteration' of their meanings. In other words, the viewing audience watched television more as 'observers' rather than as 'spectators,' inserting subversive ripostes into the minute details of the programmes. Here, the receiver is actively involved in the composition of 'new meaning,' and for that reason, such a way of watching television could be called 'active television viewing' (see Figure 6.2b).

In response to the emergence of a viewing audience which had become a presence that bypassed senders' intentions, senders did not tame the viewing audience, but started to make programmes premised upon the latter's activeness. Here, a complicit relationship is constituted between the senders, who contrive numerous projects in a way that is neither fully serious nor fully joking, and the receivers, who, while recognising such trickery for what it is, venture to go along for the ride. Let us call this kind of television viewing, which is carried out with the sender and the receiver utilising their mutual activeness, 'interactive television viewing.' In this type of viewing, both parties can be said to be in an equal and intimate relationship, in which it is almost nonsensical to ask which one out of the sender and receiver is dominant.

However, this 'interactive television viewing' underwent a transformation in quality in the mid-1990s. In the late 1980s, because interaction was being carried on between the viewing audience, which had the dual gaze of spectators/observers, and the senders that utilised that gaze, the reality constituted there was always vacillating between reality and fiction. In the 1990s, though, as the audience's gaze as an observer retreated at the same time as a widening of the recognition that 'there is no such thing as outside of television,' receivers started to immerse themselves in the reality which television configured. Along with that, the subversive riposte began to operate not as a gesture for maintaining distance from television-like reality, but as a candid response to it (see Figure 6.2c).

The self-contained television space

The subversive riposte is not now a force that modifies meaning, but has changed into an instantly-reactive force to the reality that is spawned in television. Not only that, recently this 'riposte as reaction' has come to be openly shown on the television screen. What symbolises this is the 'Picture-in Picture (PiP)' which has been much used in variety programmes in recent years. A PiP is a small screen displayed in one corner of the main picture screen, and it often shows the reaction of television personalities who are watching a video segment. The response of the performers exhibited in such a PiP is thought to have the function of representing what the sender assumes will be the reaction of the viewing audience. As I stated in the second section, because mass communication lacks mutual monitoring, it is not easy for the sender to apprehend and control receivers' responses. For that reason, in comedy programmes and the like, senders endeavour to elicit the ideal reaction from receivers by inserting a laughter track as a sound effect. A PiP could be said to be a new method of incorporating the viewing audience's response into the television screen.

This means handing the receiver's activeness, in terms of the autonomy to decode, over to the sender. This is because performers now show reactions such as 'laughter,' 'tears,' or 'surprise' in the viewing audience's stead. At the same time, the sender's role also changes. Television performers of today not only have to amuse or move the viewing audience, but on top of that, have to be a presence that laughs, weeps, or is surprised in place of the viewing audience. The reason why personalities in recent years make almost excessively exaggerated reactions in variety programmes is that they have taken on the role of representing the response of the ideal receiver. In this way, both sender and receiver become 'interpassive subjects' (Žižek 2002) deprived of their activeness.

As such, when the viewing audience's gaze and response are incorporated into the television screen, and television space starts to become self-contained, what reactions will the receiver who is on the outside display? Will he or she resonate with performers who laugh, cry or are astonished in their stead, and show a similar reaction, or else stare dumbfounded at the 'private jokes (*uchiwa uke*)' (Ōta 2002, p. 76) bandied about in over-the-top reaction games where the real viewing audience is abandoned? In either case, little remains of the leeway brought to it by meaning-modification through subversive ripostes which active television viewing once made possible.

7 Where is differentiated communication heading?: through analysis of the readers' column in the fashion magazine, *CUTiE*

Sōichirō Matsutani

'That kid's cool, yeah?' Anyone might make a casual remark like this on an everyday basis, undoubtedly delighting some people to be its object, yet leaving others hurt by it. For better or worse, it is because people are not all the same that such words are used and come into existence. People use all kinds of elements – age, sex, external appearance, ways of thinking, personality, behaviour, and so on – to distinguish between you and me, him and her, and Sally and Harry.

Out of these elements, the clothing – that is, the fashion – which everyone wears as a matter of course has become an easily-understandable indicator showing people's sex and generation, their individual orientation and suchlike, from their external appearance.

In this chapter, along with briefly reviewing the history of fashion, I will utilise the readers' column of the women's street fashion magazine, *CUTiE*, to analyse the way fashion has become a tool for differentiated communication. Take the question of what *CUTiE* girls perceive about the girls of the *ko-gyaru* genre, and what attitude they have taken to display their difference, for instance: I will use this to illustrate the kinds of differentiation strategies that present-day young people, using fashion as a tool, have adopted.

Ebi-chan and supermodels

Around 2005–08, a fashion model nicknamed 'Ebi-chan,' Yuri Ebihara, enjoyed explosive popularity. As an in-house model of

CanCam, Shōgakukan's fashion magazine aimed at women in their twenties, she drove the magazine's popularity, along with Moe Oshikiri and Yū Yamada. While the circulation of rival publications *JJ* (Kōbunsha) and *ViVi* (Kōdansha) was falling, *CanCam*'s net paid circulation for the second half of 2006 grew to nearly 700,000 copies, thanks to Ebihara's popularity.

The Tokyo Girls' Collection, which has been held twice annually since 2005, is a fashion show bringing together popular models such as Moe Oshikiri and Anna Tsuchiya, in addition to Ebihara. Though not the sort of show that is directed at mass communications and buyers, as is the Paris Collection or its ilk, it is an event held at a huge hall such as the Yokohama Arena or Saitama Super Arena, drawing ordinary women in their thousands. It is run by a mail-order clothing website for mobile telephones, and the customers' purchasing of a succession of garments via their mobile phones in the midst of the show became a hot topic.

This form of fashion show is extremely rare even in the rest of the world. The products displayed by brands such as ALBA ROSA and CECIL McBEE are not particularly expensive, making it a fashion show of mass-oriented brands, so to speak, which could not be summarised as 'high fashion.'

Naturally, every age has had a specific model leading the times as its trend-setter. In recent memory, fashion models known as 'supermodels,' including Cindy Crawford and Naomi Campbell, have been popular. They appeared in high-profile brand fashion shows such as the Paris and New York Collections, playing an active role towards highlighting the non-everyday, cutting-edge styles that each brand's designers unveiled. Their popularity lay in their very presence, which was far beyond the reach of the regular populace.

The nature of Ebihara and Oshikiri's popularity, by contrast, was dissimilar to that of these supermodels. They were not as tall as the supermodels, and they appeared in apparel of an affordable price. The substance of their popularity was made up not of the charisma of a supermodel, but of a yearning to emulate, namely: 'maybe I, too, can be like Ebi-chan.' In other words, these Japanese models became a point of reference for ordinary women in accomplishing their own social roles, as a familiar ideal that made each ordinary women feel that 'I, too, might be able to be like that.'

The history of fashion and analytical methodology

The limitations of the trickle-down theory

It is indeed unique that this kind of mass-fashion (fashion oriented to the general populace) should have expanded to such an extreme extent in Japan. This stems from the economic structure peculiar to Japanese society, and the fact that Western and Japanese fashions have grown in their respectively differing contexts. If one traces the history of Western fashion, one will end up back in nineteenth-century Paris. Charles Frederick Worth, who crossed from Britain to Paris in 1845, opened his own shop there in 1857. He presented new creations every season, adopting a method of showing them off, moreover, by dressing real people (mannequins) in the garments, and re-sizing them to fit the figures of favoured customers. This system, called *haute couture*, was something previously unthinkable, because high-class apparel hitherto had been something made by designers who ascertained the wishes of the upper class who were their clientele, the initiative always remaining with the customers. Worth, however, strengthened the position of the fashion designer by, for example, only ever accepting orders from clients with whom he himself was satisfied (Kitayama 1991).

Along with the maturation of the mass-production system due to industrialisation, the twentieth century ushered in the age of high-class, ready-made clothing called *prêt-à-porter*. Brands such as Pierre Cardin, familiar even now, came to enhance their value as brands by entry to the *prêt-à-porter* system (Inoue 2006).

Such *haute couture* and *prêt-à-porter* can be collectively called high fashion, having in common their proposal of new styles every season to their wealthy clients, and the upper class's use of these as items with which to forge differentiation from the general populace. A scholar who critically analysed such circumstances was Thorstein B. Veblen, writer of *The Theory of the Leisure Class*. Veblen critically analysed the extravagant purchasing activity of the wealthy in late nineteenth-century America, calling it 'conspicuous consumption = ostentatious consumption.' He determined that they were attempting to highlight their difference from the general populace by means of flamboyant consumption in order to flaunt the fact that they were upper-class (Veblen [1889] 1973).

Similarly, Georg Simmel also came to the analytical conclusion that the fashion phenomenon arises in this way due to competitive differentiation between social strata. According to Simmel's explanation, people are swayed by fashion trends because psychologically, a desire for synchronisation and an opposing desire for differentiation exist simultaneously. In concrete terms, this proceeds in the following way.

Firstly, members of the upper class seek a unique style in order to parade their own social position (differentiation), while this functions at the same time as mutual recognition among their own group (synchronisation). Then, the lower classes imitate that upper-class style as an object of yearning (synchronisation), but when that fashion permeates on a wide scale, now the upper class will discard the existing style and turn towards a new fashion in order again to demonstrate their difference from the lower classes (differentiation). This means that trends change by such a mechanism. Just as water trickles down from above to below, this pattern in which fashions permeate from the upper to the lower echelons is called the trickle-down theory (Simmel [1911] 1976).

This model which Simmel presented in the first part of the twentieth century has limited application to contemporary societies, including Japan, however. The societies that Veblen and Simmel analysed were from the late nineteenth and early twentieth centuries when the high and low in terms of social strata could be clearly demarcated and their social structure was comparatively stable. For that reason, when there is an increase in social mobility, some phenomena that do not fit this theory will also arise.

In the 1960s, the jeans which hitherto had been the style of labourers, and the T-shirts which they had worn as underwear, came also to be incorporated into high fashion. In addition, the mini-skirt that was trendy in London in the same period also had been a style popular among young people who liked rock and modern jazz. Taking a hint from this street fashion, Mary Quant started marketing the mini-skirt in 1960, and it became an explosive hit on a worldwide scale.

What can be seen here is a pattern consisting of the incorporation into high fashion of a subculture (street fashion) popular in a stratum that was not upper-class. In the 1970s, Vivienne Westwood, who had opened a shop along with Malcolm McLaren, spawned the rock band called the Sex Pistols, and punk fashion. This means that fashion came to be generated without being influenced by social strata, or as if by turning those very strata to its own advantage.

From 'vertical differentiation' to 'horizontal differentiation'

If we trace back the history of fashion in Japan, we end up at the time when the Western-style clothing that had flowed into Japan in the Meiji era (1868–1912) became a fixture among the general populace, as well, after the beginning of the Taishō era (1912–26). Nevertheless, the penetration of high fashion was not particularly conspicuous in Japan, where the rich lost their power due to the Second World War. In the process of accomplishment of dramatic economic growth after a poverty-stricken post-war, the general populace sought to 'be average,' aiming for a lifestyle that approached the same level as others = synchronisation, rather than trying to be different from others (society at large). For this reason, differences between strata ceased to be felt in the 1980s, to the extent that it was proclaimed that 'all Japanese were middle-class,' and people tended to be less conscious of the difference between high fashion and mass fashion than in the West.

However, one phenomenon that symbolically indicates the subsequent change is the DC brand boom which arose in the early 1980s. This refers to Designers and Characters (DC) brands, a group of brands including Comme des Garçons, BIGI, NICOLE, and PINK HOUSE, which thrust designers' individuality to the fore, and deployed not mass-, but high-mix low-volume production.

This DC boom was arguably a phenomenon established in Japan precisely at a time when people paid little heed to social stratification. This is because young people sometimes formed long queues and made purchases as if squabbling over expensive but small-volume items, trying to promote the difference between themselves and others. Such young people were sometimes also lumped together in marketing terminology not as the conventional 'undifferentiated, large-scale masses (*taishū*)' that preferred mass-produced goods, but by such expressions as the 'small-unit masses (*shōshū*)' and 'segmented masses (*bunshū*),' whose members each sought 'something that was theirs alone.' Hiroshi Kashiwagi explains such an age in the following way:

> Through the emergence of DC [brands], the desire for so-called orthodox fashion represented by the Paris Collection became diluted, principally among the young. That being said, this differed again from the fashion which the counterculture from the end of the 1960s into the 1970s had produced. The fashion which the counterculture had spontaneously brought into being (though admittedly it was ultimately reclaimed by the logic of the market) rejected the very consumer society that was grounded in market logic, along with the traditional fashion system. DC brands, on the other hand, were fashions established on the presumption of a system of difference in consumer society. It could also be argued that they were something that radicalised the logic of the consumer society system, against a background of that society.
>
> Furthermore, a phenomenon wherein the relationship of centre to fringe in fashion seemed ultimately to have been rearranged into one of mutual difference was triggered by DC brands. In other words, the rivalry of *haute couture* versus mass-produced goods or the class relationship in fashion centring on the Paris Collection vanished, and a situation where everything seemed to be in a relationship of equal difference was created (Kashiwagi 1998, p. 176).

Punk fashion, the beatnik style, and so on, which had originally been popular among the working class, were styles that were incorporated into high fashion. Hip-hop in America, too, was a subculture that grew from foundations of Black, Hispanic and other ethnicities.

By contrast, in Japan from the 1980s onwards, where it was difficult to have consciousness of disparities between strata or ethnicities, there developed a strong awareness of the relationship between self and others through differences in cultural tastes. In a society where people were on an equal footing in terms of class, what came to the foreground was 'horizontal differentiation' indexed by differences in preferred culture, not 'vertical differentiation' such as disparity between strata.

At the same time, this also meant that the stable relationship between self and others was progressively lost. Social space such as agrarian communities where communication used to be carried out on the basis that members mutually shared a presumed understanding (origin and experiential memory) vanished from Japan, where the university entrance rate topped forty percent, the proportion of workers engaged in tertiary industry ballooned, and there was advancing urbanisation and informatisation. Communication without shared assumptions was deemed necessary by people with diverse origins and values, and a consciousness of an opaque sense that 'you and I are different people' came to be strongly perceived (Miyadai [1996] 1997).

In such a social space, fashion functioned as an indicator (a sign that 'you and I are the same type') which displayed one's own attributes (intentionality) to others in an easily-understandable manner. It did not have authority or privilege because it had no foundation in class, and it was also something very fickle. The DC brand boom also became pervasive from around 1983, and developed into the kind of huge boom where there would be long queues at bargain sales, but it died down in the autumn of 1987 (*Ryūkō kansoku* (Trend watching) 1997). Amid a cycle consisting of the creation of a new trend in such a society, a lot of people latching onto it, and its popularity surging then receding, young people acted as mediators in cementing and severing relationships with others.

The street-fashion magazine, *CUTiE*

The characteristics of *CUTiE*

A variety of '*zoku* (tribes)' also arose amid this 'horizontal differentiation.' A '*zoku*' refers to a group of young people who pivot around a subculture, and who are collectively known as '-*zoku*.'

Until the 1980s, these – like motorcycle gangs, and the *fūten-zoku* (vagabond tribe) which had its roots in hippiedom – had been understood as being firmly rooted in a particular social stratum, and as indulging in behaviour that deviated from established society. From the 1980s on, however, a series of *zoku* that had no footing in a social stratum were born. These included the '*shinjinrui* (new [human] types),' *otaku*, '*chīmā* (teamers),' *ko-gyaru* and '*Urahara-kei*'[1] (Mabuchi 1989; Nanba 2007).

Of these, the one this chapter makes its target of analysis is '*Urahara-kei*' ('*Urahara*' being an abbreviation of 'Ura-Harajuku,' the back streets of Tokyo's Harajuku district, a youth fashion mecca) which established its identity with fashion as its resource. Strictly speaking, the chapter analyses the readers of the fashion

Where is differentiated communication heading? 129

magazine, *CUTiE* (hereafter referred to as *CUTiE* girls), categorised as *Urahara-kei*.

CUTiE is a fashion magazine launched in 1989, aimed at a female readership. It is a monthly (twice per month in one period) issued by Takarajimasha (formerly the JICC shuppan kyoku), and is still in publication. More than half of its readership consists of girls in their late teens, with sixteen-to-seventeen-year-olds accounting for twenty-five percent, and eighteen-to-nineteen-year-olds twenty-eight percent (Takarajimasha 2008). Its net paid circulation is an estimated 140,000 copies, and in the past few years, its circulation has been following a downward trend (Zenkoku Shuppan Kyōkai Shuppan Kagaku Kenkyūjo (ed.) 2007).

Though its characteristics have varied according to the times, what has been consistent since its launch has been a tendency to value readers' unique sensibility as 'individualists' by heavy use of clothing in primary colours and layering, for example, rather than a style which, as in *CanCam*, positively promotes their female gender attributes.

The clothes they wear do include some popular brands such as HYSTERIC GLAMOUR or MILK, but since the late 1990s, 'second-hand clothing' has come top in questionnaires as to 'favourite brands,' and stores like BEAMS, a speciality boutique, have been popular from the start, with no excessive brand-orientation being seen. Rather, emphasis tends to be laid on ways of dressing such as 'mixing and matching' and 'layering.' The fashions of ordinary females walking the city streets are also inserted into the page layout as 'street snaps,' and readers use these for reference as to ways of dressing.

Another characteristic of the magazine is its strong affinity with subcultures such as *manga* and music. *Manga* such as Kyōko Okazaki's *Ribāzu ejji* (River's edge) and Moyoko Anno's *Rabu masutā X* (Love-Master X) were serialised in the early and late nineties, respectively. Favoured music includes JUDY AND MARY and SHAKALABBITS. In lieu of in-house models, it has installed entertainers, musicians and popular models such as Tomoe Shinohara, Miwako Ichikawa, YUKI (originally JUDY AND MARY), Anna Tsuchiya, and UKI (SHAKALABBITS) as fashion leaders.

As such, *CUTiE* can be said to be a street-*kei* fashion magazine. *Urahara-kei*, which became trendy from the late 1990s, refers to the cohort that prefers the original brand cluster of shops that set

Figure 7.1: CUTiE, March 2008 © Takarajimasha

up along Cat Street at the end of the avenue called Takeshita-dōri in Harajuku, and which was led at first by its popularity among young men. In concrete terms, brands such as A BATHING APE and UNDERCOVER, which produced goods in extremely small volumes, were the centre of attention, and the fact that they had some manner of connection with pop music – APE's designer, NIGO, having deep associations with musicians, for example – was also a major characteristic. Eriko Minamitani explains that the aim of *Urahara-kei* is '"more than street [fashion], less than high fashion," not being everyday wear or casual wear that is cut off from fashion, either, yet different again from the fashion and designer brands of Paris or New York, which are strongly conscious of novelty and trendiness' (Minamitani and Ii, 2004).

Having not shown much locality until the early 1990s, *CUTiE* began to deal much with *Urahara-kei* style in the late 1990s, X-girl having opened in LaForet Harajuku in 1995, and it increasingly accentuated its 'streety feel' (locality as a symbol).

Targets of analysis and analytical methods

There was one major reason why I made this *CUTiE* a target for analysis. It was because when I was attempting to grasp the intentionality of fashion enthusiasts, the readers' letters' column in *CUTiE* had continued in almost the same form. By rights, it is desirable to compare readers with all kinds of fashion attributes and analyse them, but substantially this was impossible because fashion magazines such as *CanCam* and *ViVi* do not have readers' columns. Though its title may have changed over time, *CUTiE*'s readers' column has taken up two to three pages in each issue for over a decade. Interchange among fellow readers is very lively there, with readers actively stating their own views, and others, in turn, expressing agreement with or opposition to those views, and so on.

The analytical method which this chapter adopts is rhetorical analysis, using this readers' column. It will look at the kind of rhetoric that individual people employ, by which cultural 'horizontal differentiation' never rooted in any social stratum is established.

According to the social constructionist Joel Best, 'rhetoric' is form of language (way of speaking) in which words are used to persuade others in some presumed circumstances (Best 1987). Here, I will analyse the manner of speaking that *CUTiE* readers use to situate themselves as '*CUTiE* girls,' as well as that by which they judge that others are not '*CUTiE* girls.'

As such, my specific focus will be upon *CUTiE* girls' reactions seen in the readers' column for the past decade towards the female cohort of their same generation called '*ko-gyaru*' or '*gyaru*.' This is because when I scrutinised the readers' column over time, '*ko-gyaru/gyaru*' (hereafter referred to as '*ko-gyaru*') frequently appeared as an object from whom *CUTiE* girls strove for 'horizontal differentiation.'

Ko-gyaru and *CUTiE* girls

The *ko-gyaru* (the '*ko-*' deriving from the term for a high-school student, '*kōkōsei*', and 'kid' or 'small') is one of the youth tribes

Figure 7.2: Popteen, October 2007 issue © Kadokawa Haruki Jimusho

that has garnered the greatest attention in about the past fifteen years. It was in 1993 that this expression was used in the mass media for the first time, but it was only from 1995 that it began to permeate widely to the general populace. Those dubbed as such at the beginning were high-school girls with dyed brown hair and skin tanned a golden brown, who wore their school uniform skirt short, and donned loose-fitting long socks. They were seen as socially problematic due to the major role they played as frequenters of so-called '*burusera* (bloo-sailor)' shops which bought and sold teenaged girls' used **bloo**mers (underwear) and **sailor**-suit school uniforms, or else as participants in the prostitution practice called '*enjo kōsai*,' or '*enkō*' (compensated dating), which earned them the nickname of '*burusera* high-school girls' or '*enkō* high-school girls.' They were also sometimes called '*Amurā* (Amurers)' because they emulated the fashions of singer Namie Amuro.

The place where they had always gathered from the beginning, and do so even now, is Tokyo's Shibuya – specifically, the apparel building called SHIBUYA 109 which, since its renovation in 1996, has been tenanted by numerous shops catering to *gyaru*, in addition to the nearby Centre-*gai* street. The various media that focused on these girls collected their data in Shibuya, and fashion magazines took street snaps, as the *ko-gyaru* style was a different kind of street fashion again from *Urahara-kei*.

From the end of the 1990s, these girls came to be called '*gyaru*,' and the *gyaru* style became established not only among high-school students. Though there have been some changes along with the times, it is basically a style whose appeal is a feminine body-line with a lot of exposure; and the headline '*hada-mise* (skin-revealing)' was frequently employed in the fashion magazines concerned. It was in this period, also, that some of its adherents began to subdivide into the streams called '*ganguro* (blackface)' or '*yamamba* (mountain hag),' flashy styles in which foundation designed for Black people was applied to the face, with white eyeliner around the eyes (Narumi 2007).

In appearance, this kind of *ko-gyaru* style was very different from that of *CUTiE*. As previously mentioned, the *ko-gyaru* style preferred that skin showed, and was a style which, if it were summer, consisted of a sleeveless top such as a tank top, with a miniskirt and high-heeled pumps as the bottom. In *CUTiE*, by contrast, even in summer a layered style was preferred, with tank tops being layered, and for the bottom, coordinating pants or a long skirt with thin-soled pumps or sneakers was favoured. One could say they are poles apart.

The positioning of *CUTiE* and *gyaru-kei* fashion magazines among women's fashion magazines as a whole can be classified as in Figure 7.3, with age and genre as the axes. The five genres into which I classify them are 'loose casual,' 'career,' 'conservative → housewife,' '*gyaru*,' and 'goth/goth-loli type.'

'Loose casual' is a type of *Urahara-kei* style, including *CUTiE*, which has generally penetrated. 'Career' refers to fashion magazines aimed at female career-track company employees who grew in number after the introduction of the Equal Employment Opportunity Law (EEOL) in 1986. 'Conservative → housewife' means magazines oriented at women who choose a life-course in which they marry, then quit their job for a time and devote themselves to child-rearing. '*Gyaru*' has already been explained. Here, 'goth/goth-loli type' indicates fashion magazines mostly aimed at female fans of visual-*kei* bands, otherwise known as *bangya*, from 'band girls.'[2]

Zipper is one of *CUTiE*'s rival publications, followed by *SEDA*, *mini*, *spring*, *sweet*, *InRed* in the generation above them. In different genres in the same generation, there are such magazines as the conservative (*konsaba-kei*) *SEVENTEEN*, and the *gyaru-kei* publications of *Popteen*, *egg*, and the like.

For a typical *CUTiE* girl, *ko-gyaru* of the same generation and their fashion style have become the differentiation criteria which characterise her own place in a variety of aspects. In short, with the *ko-gyaru* as her other, she is striving to acquire a self-image as a *CUTiE* girl (or *Urahara-kei*).

Differentiation from the *ko-gyaru* style

Firstly, in terms of differentiation in fashion style, the following kinds of comments can be seen, by way of example:

> Actually, I was an extreme *gyaru* until a year ago. But then I realised it was sort of boring to always be the same as everybody else, and I became a bit more individualistic. At first, the guys around me were really surprised, too, but now they are completely comfortable with it (Tokyo/age not recorded/25 October 1999 issue).

> However you look at it, *yamamba* fashion is not cute!!
> I'm still in third year of junior high, but I absolutely don't want to become like those people. If I see them, I think, 'Yuck, horrible!! Are they women or what?' I think that dying their hair will damage it like mad, and their skin will develop abnormalities when they become adults, too. They wouldn't look cute in anybody's eyes, they're kind of stupid, and so there's nothing good about them! What's more, they haven't got any individuality, either! However you look at it, they're all the same.
> But our *CUTiE* look is different! After all, we do all sorts of layers, make things, and so we can expect an individuality that is somehow different from other people's to appear – [we each have] our particular way of enjoying it, thinking about clothing combinations, and stuff. I think that even from adults' point of view they would understand us. You mustn't compare that sort of fashion with us! (Tokyo/aged 15/17 and 31 January 2000 issues).

Both of the above regard the *ko-gyaru* fashion style as if it were all the same, and conversely promote the uniqueness of their own style. In short, this is rhetoric saying that the *ko-gyaru* style is not

Where is differentiated communication heading? 135

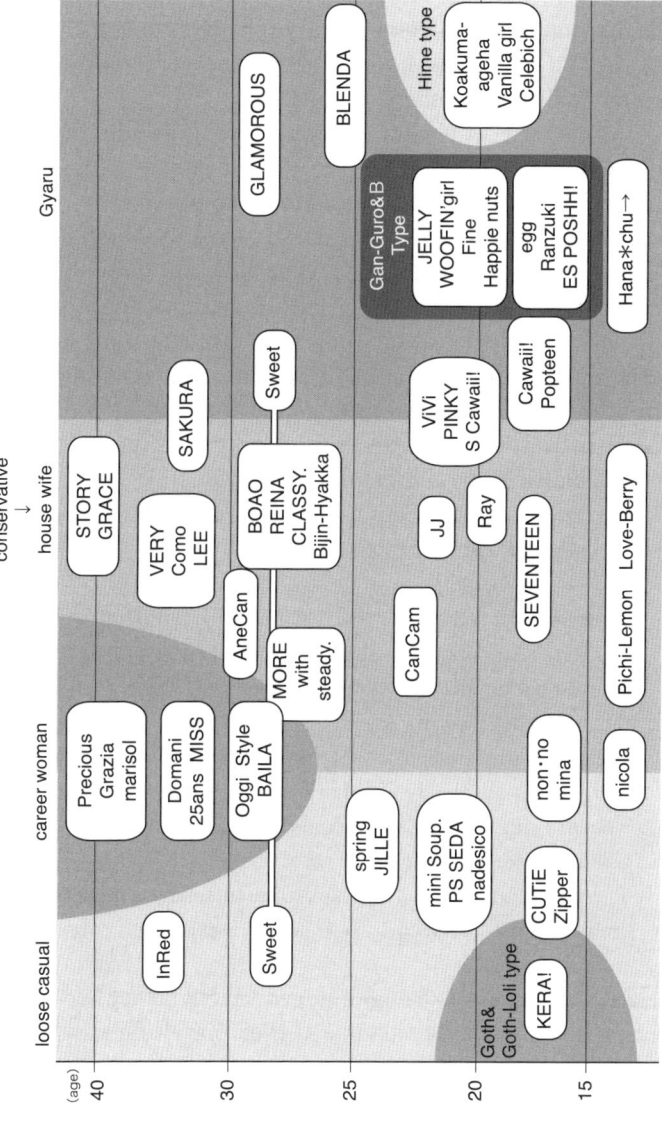

Figure 7.3: Matrix of fashion magazines as of Spring 2008

individualistic because it is uniform, while the *CUTiE* style, by contrast, is fashionable and individualistic.

That being said, whether it is a case of *ko-gyaru*, *CUTiE* style, or *Urahara-kei*, any categorisation as a distinct style derives from having some kind of commonality. The tying-together of elements as the '*CUTiE* look' holds true for the very reason that some commonality with others can be found.

In this case, it is characteristic that 'individuality' has been located as its common feature. As the above readers also state, individuality generally indicates 'the personality/disposition which that individual alone possesses, and which differs from that of others.' Nonetheless, when they are lumped together as 'individualists (*kosei-ha*),' it means being fraught with a huge paradox. This is because it implies they share some features with others, though they ought to be 'different from other people.' In other words, it turns into a situation that should perhaps be described as the 'ordinariness (non-individuality) that means being "individualist,"' or 'commonplace individuality.'

Comments which seem to suggest that readers have awoken to such a state of affairs can also be seen:

> What on earth is the *yamamba* fashion that is proliferating in Shibuya and Harajuku? With white hair as well as their *gonguro* [faces tanned an even darker shade than the so-called 'blackface' *ganguro*], all of them wearing the same sort of egoist clothing, their lips white pearl. Whichever way you look at it, I think that having their lips whiter than their skin is absolutely weird...But maybe that's their style. I kind of wonder if my own *CUTiE* look also appears the same in adults' eyes when they see me – maybe it's six of one and half a dozen of the other? The pot calling the kettle black? I'm suffering a huge loss of self-confidence (Tokyo/aged 20/11 October 1999 issue).

Here, her anxiety is being divulged as to whether her own style is being seen as looking the same as everyone else's, as with *ko-gyaru*. What should be noted in this comment is the question of who triggers her feeling of 'loss of self-confidence' by thinking so. Here, it is described as being 'adults.'

Here, 'adults' can be thought to refer not to specific others such as friends, lovers, or family, but to the gaze of society in general, people who are not she, nor people with the '*CUTiE* look.'

Where is differentiated communication heading? 137

This assumption can be understood as meaning the 'generalized others' explained by George Herbert Mead (1934, p. 154). The term indicates the social expectations (or social norms) internalised by individuals. In other words, it refers to an awareness that 'one must do things in a particular way (because it would be expected in that situation).' Though specific others are not present, 'organised society,' the 'social whole' or the 'community' which internally governs/suppresses the individual can be thought to exist (Mead 1934, pp. 155–6).

Whether the *CUTiE* girl affirms or rejects her own fashion, she nevertheless compares it with that of *ko-gyaru*, for instance, or is concerned over the gaze of society in general. Though the object of attempted differentiation may be concrete or abstract, she still is conscious of the existence of some kind of other, all the same.

The gaze coming from lovers and the opposite sex

So, the concrete others of whom the *CUTiE* girl is strongly conscious are not limited to *ko-gyaru*, but include the presence of lovers and the opposite sex. For females of this generation, which corresponds to adolescence, it is not strange to be very powerfully aware of the gaze of members of the opposite sex. There are cases, for instance, of girls actively choosing the *CUTiE* style in order to be liked by their boyfriends.

> Until just three months ago, I was reading *JJ* and *CanCam*, and dressing like a *gyaru*. But the boy I fell for was reading *Smart*, and I found out that girls like the ones in *CUTIE* (sic) were his type, so I made the MOMENTOUS DECISION to dress totally differently, 180 degrees, stopping wearing suits or making my onslaught with brands, or saying things like 'I want a Prada bag!' and tried my hardest to become the type he prefers! (Gifu Prefecture/age not recorded/6 July 1998 issue).

As far as we can tell from reading this particular contribution, what fashion such as the *CUTiE* style means to her is first and last a tool for satisfying her boyfriend, yet what is seen even more often than such comments is the converse anxiety that a lover or the opposite sex prefers the *ko-gyaru* style over the *CUTiE* style.

> The other day, I broke up with my boyfriend. It was because I'm a Lolita. He likes *gyaru-kei* girls, and though I actually want to wear

Milk, etc., I was trying hard to dress like a *gyaru*. When I was walking through town wearing a suit, arm in arm with him, if I saw punk couples amicably looking at used clothing and suchlike out of the corner of my eye, I was hugely envious...After lots of soul-searching, I told him. His answer was: 'I want to keep on going out with you, but I can't walk along with a woman looking like that – it's too embarrassing.' I was sad, but my mind was made up at that single comment, because for me, Lolita was a policy I still wanted to keep. Ultimately, *I* was more precious to me than *he* was (Osaka Prefecture/age not recorded/20 July and 3 August issues).

Now I don't know what to do! My boyfriend started staying he preferred *gyaru*-like girls, you know? I am a *CUTiE* girl, so I want to keep on with *CUTiE*-style fashion for ever, but what should I do? Because I do adore my boyfriend (Tokyo/aged 14/February 2007 issue).

To summarise briefly, their worry is articulated as: 'I want to be loved by my boyfriend, but I do not want to dismantle my *CUTiE* style.' If these girls who are agonising that their own fashion style is not liked by their boyfriend were to pick one of the two options, they could possibly lose one of them. In actuality, one of the girls *has* made the choice to part from her boyfriend, having been torn between two opposing values.

Not being restricted to fashion, the situation is often seen where women are pressed to select between the two alternatives of self-actualisation (the achievement of their own way of living) on the one hand, and love/marriage on the other. This often appears in the setting of women's social advancement. The way that women vacillate between the path of working as a career woman on the one hand, and that of cherishing their family as a wife and homemaker on the other, has been frequently evoked since the 1986 Equal Employment Opportunity Law.

This was also rendered in Ai Yazawa's popular *manga* work, *Paradise Kiss* (Yazawa 2000–03). Though it was the fashion magazine *Zipper* (Shōdensha), a rival publication of *CUTiE*'s, that carried this work, its content depicted the romance between Jōji, a male student with charismatic talent at a senior high school with a fashion-studies programme, and Yukari, a high-school girl treading the path of a professional fashion model on the impetus of having modelled Jōji's creations.

In the final stage of the work, Yukari is told that Jōji has decided to go to Paris after high-school graduation. Jōji asks: 'Will you come with me?' but Yukari replies: 'I'm not coming, 'cos I've only just begun modelling work, and I'll go to uni and keep studying for ages longer, as well' (vol. 5, p. 143). Out of the two options of her boyfriend and her work, she has chosen her work. That selection outcome would also echo that of the *CUTiE* girl who split up with her boyfriend due to her own choice of fashion style.

CUTiE style as a withdrawal from sexuality

Another thing which these comments have in common is the fact that the males who are/were the girls' lovers prefer the *gyaru* look. The girls are very concerned that *gyaru* fashion stands in a superior position to the *CUTiE* style in men's estimation of females.

> I had my hair cut, from long to a bob. Though I REELY (sic) loved it, and thought it was 'absolutely sweet,' the reaction of my friends and people around me seemed like [huh?], with them making faces as if to say 'weird or what?' I was sad. Even though it was a change of mood I made on purpose. As well, what was more of a shock was that boys' attitude changed. Boys like '*gyaru*,' as you might expect. Somebody like me doesn't merit their time of day. Being judged by your external appearance is painful, isn't it? It made me sooo depressed... (Kanagawa Prefecture/age not recorded/22 June 1998 issue).

As such, the male gaze makes *CUTiE* girls strongly aware of *ko-gyaru*. In other words, what governs the *CUTiE* girl is not only *ko-gyaru*, their own lovers and the opposite sex, but also 'consciousness towards *ko-gyaru* by lovers and members of the opposite sex.'

There is also a theory that in this triangular relationship, differentiation in the shape of a retreat from a *ko-gyaru*-like existence excessively bathed in a sexual gaze from males gave rise to the *CUTiE* girl. In Shinji Miyadai's analysis, girls who felt: 'I want to be a cool kid, but I don't want to take on sexual symbolism!' were 'strange girls (*fushigi shōjo*)' like the 'talent' Tomoe Shinohara who played a large role in *CUTiE* in the late 1990s (Miyadai [1999] 2002).

I did not find any remarks to verify this hypothesis in the *CUTiE* readers' columns, but in a 1997 article in *Bart* magazine, the then chief editor of *CUTiE*, Hiroshi Arai, made a comment that seemed to acknowledge this kind of element. Arai said that because *ko-gyaru* were sexual objects for males, *CUTiE* girls '[came to] dislike giving the strong impression of being [adult] women, or of currying favour with males,' and 'rather than wanting to be seen in a favourable light by somebody else, they [began to] express themselves by means of clothing that they themselves considered cute' (Sakaguchi 1997).

In response to this article, Kensuke Suzuki also argues that the 'individual' style of the *CUTiE* girl (strange girl) is a strategy caused by withdrawal from a *ko-gyaru*-like sexuality.

> In a situation where girls are seen as sexual objects by older men merely because they have donned the sign that constitutes loose-fitting socks, such an action becomes a high hurdle [to surmount] for girls who do not desire to be seen in that way, or who have no self-confidence sexually. However, simply withdrawing from that situation would mean defining themselves as a presence that was one step behind the *ko-gyaru* who swagger around town with seeming self-confidence. As such, they restored their own self-confidence not by means of the kind of sexual relationship that consisted of 'sole acknowledgement by a boyfriend,' but by adopting a strategy of classifying (screening) their interpersonal relationships through fashion, or words and deeds.
>
> The keyword for reclamation of that self-confidence is 'individuality.' In other words, they recover self-confidence by making the self-interpretation that their 'strange self' which cannot get stuck into *ko-gyaru*-like communication – the mainstream – is fine because they are someone who has 'individuality.'...This re-reading strategy, namely that 'being individualistic is a good thing,' may be said to be an element supporting the foundation of the strange girl, as a counter to the *ko-gyaru* (Suzuki 2003).

To reiterate, no opinions that fitted these hypotheses were to be seen from the *CUTiE* girls who comprised the interested parties, yet it would not be strange even if there had been some girls among them – who could be considered almost excessively aware of *ko-gyaru* – that chose the *CUTiE* style via a process such as this. In addition, as Suzuki argues, the '*CUTiE* style as non-*ko-gyaru*,' which initially was the outcome of a negative choice, perhaps can be re-read as a positive choice, namely: '*CUTiE* style as individuality.'

This cannot be verified, and so no conclusion can be drawn, but I wish to bear it in mind as a promising hypothesis.

'Self-enclosed individuality due to self-conformity'

As explained above, *CUTiE* girls, being conscious of such objects as *ko-gyaru* and members of the opposite sex, choose their own style accordingly, yet here and there one also sees opinions that seem to deny such an awareness of others. The following contribution is one example.

> I've never seen *yamamba* fashion, but I think it's fine. And I feel it's not a case of 'the pot calling the kettle black,' but 'a ruby mocking a sapphire (rubies and sapphires originally being the same type of stone).' Both *yamamba* fashion people and *CUTiE* kids have the same desire to be stylish. Maybe their type of sparkle is different? ... Because Ms A.'s (reader's pseudonym) *CUTiE* look is what Ms A. is wearing with the idea that it is 'cool!!,' she needn't worry about comparison with *yamamba* fashion people. Fashion isn't a uniform. Because it's something that people can freely decide about (Osaka Prefecture/aged 17/17 January and 31 January 2000 issues)

> Personally, I don't like *yamamba*, but I don't think I should criticise them, because fashion is a matter of 'preference,' after all. It's a bit inexcusable to say bad things about people whose taste in coordinating is not one you yourself like. It's best to dress the way you like. The only way to make friends with people whose taste in clothing clashes with yours is to do so with other topics of conversation. I think that 'style' means taking responsibility for 'how you are seen,' and to be bold no matter what people say (Tokyo/aged 16/17 January and 31 January issues, 2000)

These are pieces of advice directed at readers who worry about *ko-gyaru* and the like. Fashion is thus described as something that should not be compared to others, 'something that people can freely decide about,' and people should 'dress the way [they] want.' Here, rather than making others the criterion, it is deemed better to make oneself the criterion. Nevertheless, is 'dress[ing] the way [one] likes' the sort of thing that arises spontaneously in the heart without comparison to others, I wonder?

Leaving aside the question of whether it is subjective or non-subjective, or positive or negative, people as a rule construct their own aims while playing up their connection with others. Establishing one's own style in comparison with others close at hand, such as *ko-gyaru*, lovers or the opposite sex, is not something mysterious, as we have seen up till this point. Conversely, the rhetoric which says: 'do not be concerned about other people's style or gaze' harbours a paradox which could also invalidate the reason why the individual in question chose the *CUTiE* style from among multiple options in the first place.

Even so, the reason why such opinions are seen here and there is that the previously-mentioned concept of 'individuality' is strongly supported. The following view, for instance, is extremely impressive:

> I get told things like, 'Gross! What's with that outfit?' or 'You can't have an Alice band with a fringe.'
> At first, I considered moving on from *Urahara*[-*kei*], but then I thought: 'Whatever you are told by others, you are yourself, aren't you!? On the contrary, you should just think nothing of being called gross or weird or something!! I don't think you need worry so deeply [about it]. Because it's your own individuality, after all' (Saitama Prefecture/aged 16/February 2005 issue).

Here, it is stated that 'individuality' is more precious than 'minding others' gaze.' Nonetheless, as previously stated, if a style deemed to represent 'individuality' permeates to a lot of people, then it will readily turn into 'commonplace individuality,' and its originality (its being different from other people) will be lost. If that happens, then apart from by discovering yet another 'new individuality,' one will be unable to transcend that 'commonplace individuality.'

By and large, it will be possible to derive a 'new individuality' by comparing it with the 'conventional individuality' that has become predictable. In other words, it can be derived by measuring distance from others – that is, precisely by differentiation. However, the 'individuality' that this *CUTiE* girl brings forth can be read as being qualitatively different from the 'individuality' thus cultivated within relationships with others. This is because 'individuality' here is being used without foundation as a powerful magic word, more than anything.

Takayoshi Doi argues that in counter to 'social individuality,' which is socially constructed amid comparison with others, the young people of today have an 'aspiration towards self-enclosed individuality,' which is not so constructed. This 'aspiration towards self-enclosed individuality' is 'discovered in one's inner depths just as if it has substance, and perceived as something akin to a rough diamond that deserves to be carefully polished,' and refers to the 'spontaneous impulse' which deems that raw stone to be 'one's real self' (Doi 2003). One gets the impression that the 'individuality' which this *CUTiE* girl mentions is near to this 'self-enclosed individuality.'

It could also be considered a consequence elicited by an individualisation strategy which always aims for differentiation from others. Even if one were to exhibit some 'individuality' (differentiation), if that style were supported and many people were to imitate it (synchronisation), then the initial style would become obsolete. As I have previously stated, because this differentiation process is not culture that is rooted in a social stratum, it is not stable. There is no firm frame of reference for judging which out of the *ko-gyaru* and *CUTiE* styles is superior. When it came to that, one can assume the parties would abandon themselves to an easily-supplied 'spontaneous impulse = self-enclosed individuality' as a result of seeking a firm framework.

Nonetheless, being a physiological sensation, this 'self-enclosed individuality,' which could also be rephrased as 'mood (*kibun*),' has a more fragile foundation than 'social individuality' which one constructs via relationships with others. Because it is both illogical and physiological, it is difficult for it to have constancy.

In addition, the self's being based on the 'self' means that the situation could arise where one strayed into an endless paradox. If, for example, persons each seeking 'their real self' were to search for 'their real self' based not on their relation with others, but upon 'themself,' then even if they felt for an instant that 'their real self' had been found, this would instantly be recast by a new 'real self' that would arise due to stimulus coming from their mood and environment at those various times. Their pre-existing 'real self' would be easily dismissed, and their 'truly "real self"' would be elicited.

In turn, that 'truly "real self"' itself would be supplanted by a new 'self' arising through moods and feelings, spawning a 'really "truly 'real self'"' and so on, with the 'real self' being born in infinite regress. In a society without secure standards, a self that was based on the 'self' would be stimulated by all kinds of social norms in an unregulated manner, changing its form on every occasion. This could be called an extremely unstable self-existence (Doi 2003).

Where is differentiated communication heading?

Ubiquitous meta-differentiation

Up to this point, I have analysed the rhetoric of *CUTiE* girls, and have educed five targets to which they conform. In summary, they are as follows: 1) *ko-gyaru* (same-sex others); 2) males/lovers (opposite-sex others); 3) awareness that members of the opposite sex prefer *ko-gyaru*; 4) society in general (generalised others); and 5) themselves.

This kind of structure is one that applies not just to *CUTiE* girls, but can be extended to a society with 'horizontal differentiation' where 'vertical differentiation' does not function. Even among a diverse range of commodities, fashion launches new products in the most rapid of cycles, and its establishment is possible for the very reason that people are frequently aware of differentiating themselves from others, as in 1) to 4).

In the case of 5) conformity to themselves, however, not even 'horizontal differentiation' functions, and it becomes a matter of the physiological dimension. As there is not even any competition with others for differentiation, it is also a situation that is hard to call 'fashion' any more.

By way of example, the utilisation of second-hand clothes became generalised among *CUTiE* girls from about the late 1990s, to the extent that in a readers' questionnaire in the August 2005 issue, first place among 'brands of clothing often purchased' went to 'second-hand clothes.' Naturally, second-hand garments have no efficacy as trendy brands, and become things that call attention to the wearers' "individual" style through their manner of dressing (layering or combining items such as accessories). In the fashion world, which keeps the market humming by churning out styles of a new era one after another, this could also be dubbed 'fashion that is non-fashion.' Moreover, second-hand style, which enables the everyday minute adjustment of an individual's mood = individuality on each occasion, could perhaps be understood even as a manifestation caused by self-conformity.

Figure 7.4: Targets of conformity for CUTiE girls

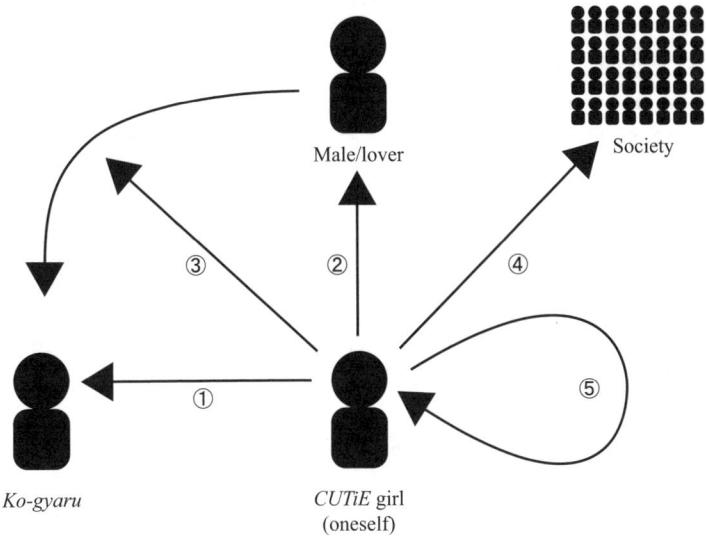

What is recalled in such circumstances is the prolific advertising copy and consumer-society discourse seen in the 1980s. For instance, in advertisements for Seibu Department Store, copy-writer Shigesato Itoi created such catch-phrases as: '*Fushigi, daisuki* (The mysterious – I love it)' (1981); '*Oishii seikatsu* (A delicious lifestyle)' (1982–83); and '*Hoshii mono ga, hoshii wa* (I want [there to be] things I want)' (1988). Representing neither a 'style that is a cut above,' nor 'style that is the same as everybody else's,' these were messages that worked on people's unreasoning sensibility.

Ultimately, that, too, was consumed as meta-differentiation, that is, 'the difference that constitutes "rejecting difference."' A good example of this would be the way 'Muji[rushi ryōhin] (No-brand quality goods),' which started business in the 1980s, continues to enjoy popularity as a 'no-brand brand.' This is because in the 1980s, when vertical differentiation was lost, negotiating horizontal differentiation on the presumption of a meta-agreement that 'this, that and everything represents difference' was one style, in itself.

In the early 1980s, Chizuko Ueno stated: 'The nightmare of endless differentiation in consumer society is not something that could be destroyed or avoided along with its mechanism. All we can do is just manage to choose "just a slightly better nightmare" from its midst, resisting the horizontal alignment of values' (Ueno [1982] 1992). It can certainly be said that her prediction hit the nail on the head, though only until the collapse of the economic bubble at the dawn of the 1990s.

Since the 1990s, as with the *CUTiE* girls, for example, there has come to the foreground a tendency to treasure one's own impulses (moods) more (self-enclosed individuality), not differentiation in comparison with others (social individuality). It is no longer meta-differentiation, but something quite similar to the undistorted, all-over materialisation of the advertising copy which Shigesato Itoi hammered out a whole twenty years previously: 'I want [there to be] things I want.'

The future course of differentiated communication

Having ended up at self-enclosed individuality, via unlimited horizontal differentiation, where might fashion head after this? Finally, I will cite one phenomenon that has deserved attention for the past few years – the reinstatement of vertical differentiation based on economic strata. This originated from the expansion of economic disparity in the long-continuing, post-Bubble recession, brought about by economic policy that further liberalised the market.

LEON, launched by Shufu-to-seikatsu sha in 2001, was a fashion magazine targeting middle-aged men with large disposable incomes. It caught the limelight with such catch copy as '*choi waru oyaji* (old guys that are a tad bad),' '*choi mote oyaji* (old guys that are a bit popular).' Its sister publication aimed at a similar female demographic, *NIKITA*, was also launched in 2004. In 2007, Ichirō Kishida, who was the chief editor of *LEON*, started up a new company, finally launching *ZINO*, which obviously targeted the well-heeled. An increase in the fashion-sensitive middle-aged cohort was one reason for the establishment of these magazines, but on the other hand, it was probably also due to the present consciousness of an economic disparity between strata, to the extent that 'rich' is becoming established as a status.

The thing that worked to make this kind of awareness spread widely among the general public was a book called *Karyū shakai* (Low society) by the marketeer Atsushi Miura, which sold about a million copies (Miura 2005a). In that work, the stratum that has weak aspirations for economic improvement, and 'generally has low life ambitions' in reference to communication and the like, is defined as 'low (*karyū*).' Moreover, Miura analyses female fashion at this time, coining the expression '*kamayatsu onna*' for the so-called 'loose casuals' that include *CUTiE* girls, and concluding that they are 'vocationally-oriented,' with 'no great desire to improve themselves, nor aspiration to climb,' in short, that they are 'low.'[3] Regardless of the appropriateness of this analysis, Miura has actively attempted to give a close reading to the connection between social strata and fashion.

Then again, it would not do to forget the 'celebrity' boom, either. In Japan, the term 'celeb (*serebu*)' is used with the implication of 'well-off' or 'high-class,' or else '*nouveau riche*,' and so on. The Kanō Sisters who attracted attention as readers' models in *25 ans*, or Marie, who was a model in such magazines as *ViVi*, became 'talents' who appeared frequently on television. In the early 2000s, the catchy word 'celeb' often danced across the pages of fashion magazines.

In contrast to the 1990s, when horizontal differentiation was rife, economic vertical differentiation was progressively introduced in this manner in the 2000s. It is certain, though, that it has not shown as much concrete movement as the topic would suggest. The keyword of '*choi waru* (a tad bad)' and celebrity talents are consumed half as material for gags, and the like. Moreover, about six months after its launch, the company managing *ZINO* was bought out, and *NIKITA*, too, suspended publication upon its March 2008 issue. The '*kamayatsu onna*' so named by Miura show no indication of wide penetration, either.

What I recall at this time is the disparity discourse seen in the mid-1980s. Kazuhiro Watanabe's *Kinkonkan*, for example, which was released in 1984 and became a best-seller, was a book that classified thirty-one types of popular occupations in an engaging and amusing manner, comparing and contrasting them in terms of '*maru-kin* (rich)' or '*maru-bi* (poor)' (Watanabe 1984). In 1985, the next year, Masako Ozawa, who had been in charge of economic analysis at the Long-Term Credit Bank of Japan, published *Shin, kaisō shōhi no jidai* (New [edition], The age of stratified consumption). Her analysis using sophisticated data, which concluded that the expansion of income disparity exerts a large impact upon consumption, became a hot topic (Ozawa [1985] 1989). The era in question was the heyday of the DC brand boom, when young people were preoccupied with minute differences.

As the social situation is different now from what it was then, one cannot state categorically, but if we consider previous cases such as this, then even if the introduction of vertical differentiation were treated as proof, as well, this would also appear to signify the social expectation of breaking away from horizontal differentiation. This means, in short, that the differentiation strategy against horizontal differentiation (the differentiation of difference) is vertical differentiation.

The aspiration for self-enclosed individuality that would seem to invalidate horizontal differentiation, and the restoration of vertical differentiation in counter to horizontal differentiation: these two phenomena might be said to be the cutting edge of present-day differentiated communication.

Notes

1 Nanba (2007) points out that in recent years, the '-*zoku*' denomination has changed to '-*kei*.' While '-*zoku*' was a name for (people under) certain circumstances of coexistence, '-*kei*,' by contrast, has spread as a 'web consisting of bodies and things represented by the media,' and Nanba supposes it to be 'an option whether to access it or not, more than a question of whether to become a member or not.'
2 See Matsutani (2004a) for the classification from around summer 2004, and a more detailed explanation of each genre.
3 The author of this chapter was responsible for part of the surveys analysed in this *Karyū shakai* (Low society) and a previous work of Miura's, '*Kamayatsu onna*' *no jidai* (The age of women [who prefer] 'cheap-and-cheerful' fashion) (Miura 2005b). For his analysis of '*kamayatsu onna*,' see Matsutani (2004b).

8 Why make e-*moe*-tional attachments to fictional characters?: the cultural sociology of the postmodern

Yoshimasa Kijima

Few, if any, readers in Japan would not have heard of the word '*moe*.' While there are various views as to its definition, it is an expression which indicates 'having affection for a character that does not exist in reality' (Sasakibara 2004); and, thanks in part to a work called *Densha otoko* (Train man) becoming a hit in its diverse media permutations, *otaku*-related subculture, which had conventionally been seen as an 'obscure hobby,' leapt out of the shadows into the light of day in a single bound. There are surely many who have gained something of a grasp of the image of *moe* from the media reportage that has been unfolding day after day, while alternatively there might also be some who get a vague sense of 'creepiness' from it.

Here, let us think about the connection between *otaku* and '*moe*' from a proper face-on perspective. What is novel about the '*moe*' phenomenon, and in what way is it new? How do *otaku* youth become so completely absorbed in '*bishōjo* (beautiful girls)' who do not actually exist? Through analysis of the above questions, in this chapter I will make it clear that the behaviour called '*kyara-moe* (emotional attachment to fictional characters)' has social characteristics that cannot be ignored, not only in people who themselves are self-acknowledged as '*otaku*-like,' of course, but also in those who are not. What will become obvious from this is a huge transformation in our way of thinking vis-à-vis 'human-ness' and 'reality,' which we have been used to regarding as self-evident.

The attitude of loving 'beautiful girls'

The onslaught of the *'moe* character'

Anime- and game-type characters, having transcended a stage called the '*moe* bubble' in the early 2000s, are thought to have now thoroughly permeated our everyday lives. '*Moe*' was nominated for the 2005 grand prize for buzzword of the year, and beautiful girl characters which had hitherto been regarded as the monopoly of *otaku* youth even came to be employed as mascots by places that could be considered unconnected with them, such as local government bodies.

> In Minabe Town in Wakayama Prefecture, the production area for Kishū Binchō charcoal (*Binchō tan*), the Minabegawa Forestry Cooperative made into its mascot character a girl dubbed 'Binchō-tan' ['-*tan*' not referring to 'charcoal' here, but being a childish equivalent of the suffix '-*san*' after a personal name], wearing a stick of Binchō charcoal on her head. Its producer, the game software company 'Alchemist' (Tokyo), suggested an alliance to the cooperative in 2004, saying they wished the character to be used for the dissemination of Binchō charcoal...The company's spokesperson, Mr Kazuhisa Nagata (33), himself from Wakayama Prefecture, commented: 'It has turned into an opportunity for us to have a wide range of people other than conventional *anime* fans get to know a *moe* character, as well' (*Asahi shinbun*, evening edition, 3 March 2007).

This not only shows simply that *otaku* culture has spread, but also suggests a transformation on the part of other phenomena. Indeed, lovable three-dimensional *bishōjo* characters are now to be found dotted all over town, and have become commonplace, everyday culture. Seen from this perspective, *otaku*-style subculture no longer even needs to be tagged as 'subculture,' and perhaps could be considered to have settled into being a cultural phenomenon not particularly worth discussing. How about focusing on the activities of people who adore those characters, though? From that point of view, it is rather precisely because *otaku*-style subculture has permeated the everyday that the surfacing of crucial questions can be acknowledged. What might that mean? In order to deepen

Figure 8.1: A signboard bearing Minabe Town's mascot character, Binchō-tan. © Alchemist; © Minabe Town.

our understanding, from here on let me first roughly identify the changes in the '*bishōjo*' who have so captivated *otaku* youth.

The objectification of people

The 1980s, when '*otaku*' were socially discovered,[1] saw an unprecedented 'idol boom,' and the *bishōjo* in whom those *otaku* were engrossed displayed different features from those in earlier times. According to sociologist Tatsuo Inamasu, this decade can be summarised as a period when female idols rapidly lost their 'sense of everyday living (*seikatsukan*) = sense of being alive (*seimeikan*)' (Inamasu [1989] 1993, pp. 243–44).

The singer Seiko Matsuda's theatrical behaviour symbolises this. Seiko, who made her debut in 1980, is a presence typifying the 'second-generation idols' whose way of acting on television was greatly divergent from that of 'first-generation idols,' namely Momoe Yamaguchi and her ilk, who won popularity in the 1970s. Momoe presented even the raw circumstances of her own upbringing and so on (= her genuine side) without pretense, but Seiko conversely behaved so as not to impart a sense of being human, consistently putting across overblown acting dubbed '*burikko* (cutesy-cutesy)' (= her 'public face'), by such means as wearing frilly skirts and flouncing around like a princess.

Figure 8.2: The single, 'Hoshizora no pasupōto (Starlight passport)'.
© *Sony Music Entertainment (Japan), Inc.*

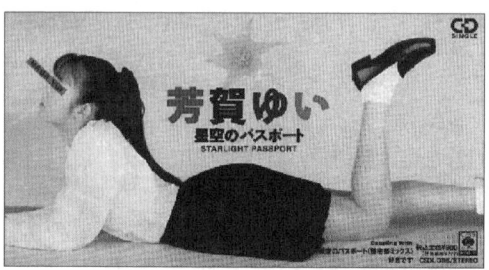

In the background, there was a change in people's acceptance of media. Seiko's popularity was only established upon viewers' understanding that an idol is nothing more than a 'doll' in televisionland. In other words, fans loved Seiko with a more 'sophisticated' gaze than before, and her apparently fake acting which previously would probably have been rejected as 'phony-smelling' was now accepted as a 'mutual agreement (*o-yakusoku*)' with the audience in the realm of television. Nowadays, the style of enjoying events in the media as 'joke material (*neta*)' rather than taking them in a 'straight (*beta*)' manner has become established, and Seiko's popularity is thought to be one factor that precipitated the formation of this kind of viewing attitude.

Moreover, at the end of the 1980s, after the attitude of regarding idols as 'live/characters/products' had taken shape (Ogawa 1988, p. 121), an idol that did not possess a flesh-and-blood body finally made an appearance. 'She,' named Yui Haga (or Haga Yui, if following Japanese word order with the surname first), was born from a trivial joke on late-night radio. During the broadcast of a programme called 'All Night Nippon,' radio personality Hikaru Ijūin remarked that it would be nice if there were an idol with a comical combination of syllables in her name, as in 'Haga Yui = *hagayui* (irritated/vexed).' Listeners then jumped on the bandwagon, too, continuing to send in fabricated accounts of sightings, which resulted in the setting up of a Yui Haga corner in the programme, and the fleshing out of a concrete image of the character.

What is of deep interest is the fact that 'she,' by rights nothing more than the product of fantasy, actually expanded 'her' entertainment activities. When CBS Sony, having learned of the programme's growing momentum, had Yui Haga make her recording debut as a 'masked idol' (with an anonymous female singer providing the vocals), the single 'Hoshizora no pasupōto (Starlight passport)' which went on sale in 1990 reached as high as fifty-first place on the Oricon chart, selling 20,000 units. Moreover, events such as live performances and handshaking sessions were also held frequently – with multiple Yui Hagas (performers playing her part) appearing at the venues in order to preserve the image of 'her' that each fan held – and fans loved that actually non-existent idol just as if she did really exist, even while knowing full well that she did not.

The anthropomorphising of objects

Though Yui Haga was something conjured into being by the imaginative power of radio listeners who mused that if she were an actually-existing idol, she would do such-and-such, ultimately she was modelled on a human being. By the mid-1990s, however, a fictitious *bishōjo* not modelled on a real live human started to gain the same kind of popularity as if she really existed.

Her origins can be found in game software called 'Tokimeki Memorial' which manufacturer Konami launched in 1994. It is a game where the player, who has enrolled in a school called 'Tokimeki Gakuen,' nurtures friendship with multiple *bishōjo* characters while engaging in life at that fictitious upper-secondary institution, with the object of hearing a confession of love from one of his favourite girls 'under the fabled cherry tree' on the day of the graduation ceremony. This work, which enables a simulated experience of ideal romantic love which would be difficult to savour in reality, was transplanted to multiple game consoles and recorded a cumulative total of one million hits, becoming the impetus for the spreading of a game genre called the 'dating sim[ulation].'

Among the game's idols, the popularity of the principal heroine, Shiori Fujisaki, was enormous, and in 1996 she made her 'singing debut,' with her single 'Oshiete Mr Sky (Tell me, Mr Sky)' reaching a high of number two on the Oricon chart, and selling 200,000 units. After that, methods for marketing *anime* or game characters in an 'idol-like' manner were refined, and the musical numbers which characters in the work were supposed to be singing – called

Figure 8.3: 'Binchō-tan' inside an electric rice cooker © Alchemist.

'*kyara-son* (chara[cter] son[gs])' – began often to enliven the upper ranks of the music charts.

Moreover, as an extension of this trend, anthropomorphised *bishōjo* characters that did not even require an original work to inspire them became active.[2] 'Binchō-tan,' introduced at the beginning of the section, is a typical example. 'She' originally was nothing more than a single illustration posted on the Web, but due to the unexpected reaction that received, commercial development was undertaken and 'her' fan cohort rapidly expanded. 'Binchō-tan' was adopted as Minabe Town's official mascot, two million dolls of the character and 100,000 comics featuring her were sold, and in 2005–06, she even secured her own television *anime* series.

This does not mean that 'Binchō-tan' had been equipped with traits qualifying her to be called a character from the beginning. The popularity of the design took off by itself, with data such as

Why make e-moe-tional attachments to fictional characters?

a personal history and a personality being added in the meantime, and 'she' progressively acquired a presence.

So humans are now redundant?

As seen above, with around 1990 as a turning-point, the vogue for '*bishōjo*' that absorb *otaku* youth has shifted from the 'objectification of persons,' in which actually-existing humans lost their sense of everyday living, to the 'anthropomorphising of objects,' in which fictitious characters gained a presence (Figure 8.4). As each age passed, humans were deemed less and less necessary, and in the end, the attitude of loving even objects that could not possibly be regarded as human as '*bishōjo*' became conspicuous.

In light of this, it will be appreciated that the novelty of the '*moe*' phenomenon lies in the fact that '*bishōjo*' with no material existence began to have a realistic influence which more or less surpassed that of humans. Actually, even for readers with scant familiarity with *otaku* culture, this is by no means somebody else's problem. The reason for many scholars' focus on *otaku* in recent years is their idea that *otaku* manifest the characteristics of Japanese society in a radical form. Accordingly, in the next section, let us examine the major debates relating to present-day *otaku* culture, and explore the social backdrop against which the attitude called 'character *moe*' arose.

Figure 8.4: Transformations in the 'bishōjo (beautiful girl)' in otaku culture

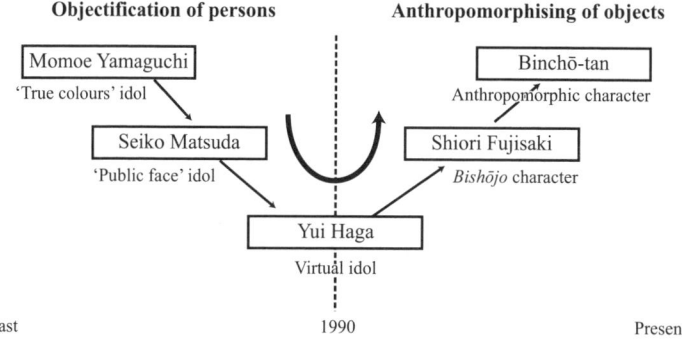

Methods of consuming works

Consumption that extracts fragments

First, let us get a grip on the way the consumption style of *otaku* youth engrossed in *anime* and games has changed. The thinker Hiroki Azuma (2002) cites the example of the difference between two giant robot *anime* series which typify Japanese television history, 'Neon Genesis Evangelion' (1995) and 'Mobile Suit Gundam' (1979), to explain the great change taking place at the juncture of the 1990s in the state of cultures which were all too easily lumped together as being '*otaku*-like.'

One difference is the totalisation of 'simulacra.' This is a notion from the French sociologist Baudrillard ([1981] 1994) indicating a state where an intermediate form that can be described neither as an 'original' nor a 'copy' is rampant. According to Baudrillard, the supposition that consumer goods of some sort are being produced purely from zero no longer holds true in contemporary society. In other words, we have entered an age where we do not say one thing is the 'original,' and another its 'copy,' but where everything circulates as a 'copy of a copy.' 'Sampling' in club music, 'cut-up' in contemporary art, and so on, are typical examples, and the situation in which new 'works' are thus born through the combination of existing works was likened by Baudrillard to the way light endlessly continues to reflect itself in a hall of mirrors. In terms of this simile, everything in a situation where each thing references (copies) the other constitutes a 'simulacrum.'

Azuma, in turn, argues that this 'simulacrum' has come to be strongly identified in *otaku* culture, also. According to Azuma, ever since the initial work in the Gundam series, telecast in 1979 (called 'First Gundam'), numerous sequels have been made, but most of those have been conceived in alignment with the same fictitious history (dubbed the 'Universal Century'), and that history has also been respected in 'derivative works' created by fans (parodies based on the original work). In the case of Evangelion, though, from the time of its first television showing in 1995, there was no intention to depict a single history – a parallel world that seemed to parody the main plot would be inserted during telecasts, for example, and after its first telecast, the same work would be remade several times in alternative versions. In short, in that features which might be called derivations of the original work are observed, the *anime* 'Neon Genesis Evangelion' is no longer a privileged 'original.'

Now, another difference is the rise of 'character *moe*.' Many Gundam fans scrutinise the mechanical data and chronological tables, feeling elation at having a deeper understanding the world of the work. In the case of 'Neon Genesis Evangelion,' however, the younger the fans, the more they 'require finely-detailed settings for the sole purpose of empathising with the setting of the main characters, drawing erotic illustrations of the heroines, making giant robot models, and so on,' and, 'for that reason, they show a paranoid concern, but seldom immerse themselves further in the world of the work' (Azuma 2002, pp. 59–60).

To sum up the above, Azuma understands the change in *otaku* youth's consumption style as being a transition from 'story consumption' (Ōtsuka [1989] 2002) to 'database consumption.' In other words, this is a transition from a mode of enjoyment through reading a work's worldview to one of having fun by extracting its settings and suchlike; and while *otaku* of the previous generation tended to be fixated on the specific logic of a work's world and the profundity of that world, new-generation *otaku*, by contrast, are not so preoccupied with such aspects, but rather sever the characters at will from the chain of reasoning in the work-world, and enjoy them in a fragmentary manner – that mode of enjoyment, it is argued, became the mainstream.

The spread of RPGs

Why, then, did such a change of mode arise? The thing that people at the site of production emphasise – especially the novelist Kazuma Shinjō (2006) and the original author of *manga*, Eiji Ōtsuka (2003) – is the impact of role-playing games (RPGs).

RPGs, as their name suggests, refer to games in which people act out (play) roles. Many of the roles played are pretend ones such as 'sorcerer' or 'warrior,' and these typically were inspired by an adventure fantasy worldview of 'swords and magic' with their origin in classic novels such as *Lord of the Rings*. As they emerged as a kind of card game in their country of birth, the United States, with several members playing around a table, RPGs are often referred to as 'pen-and-paper RPGs' in English, or as 'Tabletalk RPGs (TRPGs)' in Japanese.[3] In Japan, though, due to the popularity of video games, typified by 'Dragon Quest I' (1986), having preceded them, the image has become established of RPGs as 'games to play against a computer.'

Though such dissimilarities in ways of acceptance do exist, RPGs popularised a new way of enjoying stories which differed from a 'novelistic' way of amusement. Of particular significance is the point that players themselves have the right to decide how the story unfolds. In a novel, the development of the story is the prerogative of the author, but in the case of an RPG, it is the player that determines its development, and at least she or he can freely choose the story's evolution not by gazing at it from 'the outside,' but by acting it from 'the inside.' This, moreover, fosters a recognition that grasps the story in a multilinear manner. This is because the characters who appear in a novel are based on the idea that they 'only live once' in the world of the work which has a fixed conclusion, but game characters live 'multiple lives,' changing according to who is playing, or every time the game is played (Azuma 2007).

In this way, in RPGs, the charm of the story as a setting retreats into the background, while the attraction of the characters who play their roles in it come to the fore, but what is important is that this 'game-like' way of enjoyment spread like wildfire to other cultural genres. From the late 1980s, especially, novels that incorporated RPG-like techniques appeared on the market and began to gather explosive support, led by the young. The actualisation of ways of creating and enjoying novels which prioritise the establishment of characters rather than story-development, on the momentum of the hits of *Record of Lodoss War* (1988), the novelisation of play records of a 'Tabletalk RPG,' and *Slayers* (1990), which incorporated a 'Dragon Quest'-like work-world, is what Ōtsuka terms the establishment of the 'character novel,' or Shinjō calls the 'light novel (in the narrow sense).'

The dissemination of the 'mutual agreement'

As such, what kind of conditions does enjoying novels and *anime* in a 'game-like' manner indicate? Social philosopher Shin'ichirō Inaba (2006) focuses upon the point that, in order for a story to be understood by a large number of people, prerequisite knowledge has to be shared between the creator and receiver. Employing the term '*o-yakusoku* (mutual agreement),' he explains the differences between what are called 'novel-like' and 'game-like' methods here.

According to Inaba, conventional 'novel-like' methods basically depend on the 'common sense' of real society. This refers to the hypothesis that people who are born in the same times, actually sharing the same language and similar skills and lifestyles, share a considerable degree of knowledge, way of thinking, and values; and 'common sense' in this light – as a 'mutual agreement' that is neither perceived nor needs to be perceived as such (Inaba 2006, p. 56) – has been deemed to be a precondition when enjoying a story in which humans appear, from pure literature to the 'genre novel' (science fiction, mysteries, and the like).

Yet 'game-like' methods are not preoccupied with such 'common sense' from the real world. In other words, the characters in a work might suddenly use magic, or do a time-slip and travel to a past age, but there is no questioning of why such episodes could occur, they being enjoyed in terms of 'that is just the way things are.' What constitutes a precondition instead is 'mutual agreement' in the work-world – in short, the science-fiction or fantasy-like 'gadgets of the fictional world' (Inaba 2006, p. 74); and, due to the media-mix-like evolution of cultural works which thrived from the 1990s – the simultaneous market entry of groups of works in different media formats (comics, *anime*, games, and so on) which loosely shared the same worldview – 'data bases' made up of an accumulation of these things apparently came to be easily learnable by anybody.

Transcending macro-scale situational analysis

To organise the above, 'chara(cter) *moe*,' which involves loving beautiful girls who do not actually exist, can be thought to symbolise the 'data-base consumption' seen in *otaku* culture nowadays, and to have permeated with two social conditions at its core: namely, the spread of RPGs and the expansion of media-mixing. In other words, because a way of enjoyment which emphasised the characters more than the story became widespread, and an environment that facilitated the learning of the 'mutual agreements' of the work-world was put into place, the hypothesis holds true that a consumption style came to prominence in which characters were extracted in a fragmentary manner, without concern over consistency with the real world.

This may, however, still be puzzling to readers with no interest in *otaku* culture, regardless of how much it is explained in this way. This is because as the discussion so far has been geared to a macro-scale situational analysis focusing upon social moves and generational differences, ultimately such readers will have no understanding at all of how *otaku* youth come to have 'e-*moe*-tional attachments' to *bishōjo* characters.

Useful in this case are the qualitative approaches examined in Chapter Four. Among these, the life-history approach, which focuses upon the sequence (changes occurring in succession) in which a certain individual changes his or her awareness or behaviour, 'demonstrates greater effectiveness when one is trying to understand one's object – a different culture – from the inside, tracing back to the motivation for human behaviour' (Tani 1996, p. iii). That is to say, by the analyst's reconstituting and showing the 'internal' transformation in the survey targets, it will become possible even for readers with little familiarity with that culture to relive the concrete sequence. In the next section, therefore, let us examine the path of one *otaku* youth that led to him becoming engrossed in *bishōjo* characters.

The path to emotional attachment to fictional characters

Focusing on an extreme example

Here, I will introduce an interview survey which I conducted from May to September, 2007. The survey target was Jun Yamada (pseudonym), a bookshop employee living in Osaka Prefecture, born in 1972. Being thirty-five years old at the time of the survey, he was already approaching the age when one would hesitate somewhat to call him a 'youth.' If we follow Azuma's classification seen in the previous section, Jun would correspond to the previous generation in *otaku* culture, and by rights it would not be unusual if he were to enjoy 'story consumption' in which he would peruse the works' worldview. Jun's way of enjoyment, however, was rather of the 'data-base-consumption' type, and though one would expect him to have been born in the previous generation, his being equipped with new-generation-type consumption style marked him out.

The decision to take up Jun's case was due to his display of marked 'contrast' in a dual sense. One refers to an age-related contrast – that an 'upstanding adult' would become absorbed in *bishōjo* characters; while the other to a contrast in interest – that he, who once had not had any interest in *otaku* culture, did an about-turn and fully embraced an interest in it. As was confirmed in Chapter Four, the qualitative approach is suited not so much to taking a bird's-eye view of the average traits of a group (= looking at a forest), but rather to taking a worm's-eye view of individual features (= looking at a single tree). Through our examination of an extreme case, the path that people take towards becoming engrossed in *otaku* culture will rise more vividly to the surface.

We can divide Jun's life history roughly into three stages according to his degree of immersion in *otaku* culture, these being, in other words, the 'first stage' (from infancy until the age of twenty-eight), during which he had no interest in *otaku* culture; the 'second stage' in which he crossed the threshold into *otaku* culture (from twenty-nine to thirty-one); and the 'third stage' when he become engrossed in *otaku* culture in earnest (from thirty-two onwards). Below, I will examine these in order, while weaving his profile into the text. The quotes in inverted commas are Jun's own account (his actual voice) obtained in interviews.

Jun's *otaku* life history

The first stage (infancy to age twenty-eight)
Jun has not been in constant contact with *manga* and *anime* all his life hitherto. When he was a child, he enjoyed them 'in an ordinary way,' but from about his second year in lower secondary school, he gradually lost interest, and from then on became immersed in such 'realistic things' as history and geography. Jun calls this period his 'long frozen period.' What was it that drew Jun's interest within this 'frozen period'? One of the recollections remaining in his memory is of the activities of his geography club during his university days. This was quite a 'serious' academic club which conducted scrupulous interviews with the local Chamber of Commerce and Industry and residents, based on concern as to the question of 'whether the construction of a freeway had enhanced the region's economy,' and summarised their views in a survey report.

Another of his recollections is of 'travelling on a shoe-string budget' after university graduation. His impetus was a book entitled *Go! Go! Asia* by travel writer Jin'ichi Kuramae. At that very time, the comedy duo Saruganseki had begun their 1996 'transcontinental hitchhike' in a television programme called 'Susume! Denpa shōnen (Advance! Electric-wave youth),' and backpackers who travelled through all kinds of countries with their packs on their backs were in vogue. Since his first trip through India at the age of twenty-three, Jun roamed Thailand, Italy and Turkey, setting off each time he saved up enough money from his part-time job.

Accordingly, even after he began working at a bookshop at the age of twenty-eight, the cultural works that Jun preferred centred upon television documentaries such as TBS network's 'Sekai isan (World heritage)' and tv asahi's 'Sekai no shasō kara (See the world by train).' Of course, he knew that there were many people who enjoyed *manga* and *anime* even in adulthood, but this was perceived by Jun as being unconnected to himself, 'something like a war happening in distant Africa.'

The 'second stage' (twenty-nine to thirty-one)

After he had worked for just over a year at the bookshop, however, Jun once more began to take an interest in 'the imaginary,' triggered by being placed in charge of comics at the bookshop. Being unable to answer customers' questions would mean being 'a failure as a bookseller,' and having been assigned the job, he thus had to equip himself with a broad knowledge relating to *manga* – in short, he was bolstered by a sense of professional ethics.

Jun therefore searched among the comics that were selling well in the bookshop for the sort of works that he, too, might be able to read, and purchased them at random. Apart from the 'classic boys' *manga*' carried in the *manga* magazine, *Shōnen janpu* (Boys' jump), he also extended his hand to all kinds of girls' *manga*, 'full-on (*koi*)' *manga* popularly called '*gangan-kei* (action-fantasy-type),'[4] and, in addition, light novels that adjoined the comic section. Though he had hitherto been mystified as to why they were selling so well, the works he bought 'hit the bull's-eye' in terms of his own preferences, and Jun came to rethink his previous 'biased view.'

Though the works he enjoyed around this time were mainly ones with a 'strong story-line,' and he did feel affection for the characters at that point, this was not much different from the 'feeling akin to empathising with Tsubasa in *Captain Tsubasa* and [the Monkey King] Son Gokū, in *Dragon Ball*,' in his boyhood. On the other hand, however, around this time, Jun gained an understanding of *'moe'* for *bishōjo* characters. His motivation was the four-panel *manga*, *Azumanga daiō* (Great King Azumanga)[5] (2002), which depicted a slice of the unremarkable everyday lives of high-school girls. Jun distinguished such 'strongly symbolic' works from those designed for appreciation of the story, enjoying the former at bedtime for a change of pace, 'sort of like munching on snack food.'

The 'third stage' (thirty-two to the present)
In this manner, Jun increasingly deepened his attachment to *bishōjo* characters, but there was a big 'brick wall' there, as well. This was because the works with which Jun had previously come into contact were mainly light novels, and he had not been able to harbour affection for *bishōjo* characters in *anime* or games. Jun especially felt 'resistance to the voices' that the voice-actors provided.

Nonetheless, this 'brick wall' collapsed due to the film adaptation of works to which Jun had a strong emotional attachment. The turning point was the 2004 conversion into a television *anime* of the light novel, *Maria-sama ga miteru* (The Virgin Mary is watching you), which assiduously described interpersonal relationships in an old-fashioned girls' school. As Jun, living with his parents, 'was too embarrassed to ask them to record it,' he purchased a hard-disk (HDD) recorder for his own exclusive use and watched it. Though 'not always completely satisfying in its execution,' this *anime* marked the start of his subsequent appreciation of other '*bishōjo anime*,' as well, and one year later, Jun had already bought his second hard-disk recorder, enabling double recording, and in parallel, he became involved in so-called '*bishōjo* games' such as 'dating simulations.'

Following the collapse of his 'brick wall,' Jun stopped making as much of a distinction as previously between works in which he enjoyed the story and those where the pleasure resided in the symbols. For Jun, both of these were 'like the two wheels of a vehicle,' and each mutually operated to enhance the other's attraction within one work. Moreover, the scope for enjoyment of a work broadened, and he became able to enjoy it with the feeling that 'it just needed to have something that was strongly appealing,' from story-like features such as the *bishōjo* characters,' a 'destiny they had to bear' or 'moving scenes,' to symbolic features such as 'personality' or 'physical appearance.'

Expansion of the range of acceptance

As seen above, Jun's *otaku* life history can be summarised as a pathway – having lost his interest in 'imaginary things' in the first stage, he rediscovered the charm of stories in the second, and became enlightened as to the nature of diverse 'character *moe*' in the third. The especially important turning point *en route* was the collapse of the 'brick wall' in the third stage. By means of this, the cultural genres with which Jun came into contact changed from a stage focusing on a paper medium (*manga* or light novels) to one which also extended a forefinger at an image medium (*anime* or games); and, in concert with this, Jun's way of enjoyment transformed from one that placed emphasis on the story to one that relished the story along with symbolic attraction. Jun expresses this change as a 'feeling that the story and characters melt together.'

Table 8.1 is a consolidation, relying on Jun's memory, of what it was about *bishōjo* characters that provoked his e-*moe*-tional attachment prior to acquiring this 'feeling that the story and characters melt together' (the second stage), and after that (the third stage). As is common knowledge, in the *otaku* culture of recent years, the trait of '*moeru* (becoming emotionally attached)' to characters – this corresponds to what Azuma calls 'data bases' – is clearly expressed in such a term as 'attributes (*zokusei*)' or 'elements (*yōso*),' and is in popular use. The '*moe* elements' shown in the lower portion of the table are its characteristics, and here, for the time being, 'well-bred young lady (*o-jōsama*),' 'hot-and-cold (*tsundere*)' and the like can be considered to indicate characters' personality-like traits, while 'blonde hair,' 'knee-high socks' and so on to indicate external features.

Now, what can be apprehended from a look at this table is that not only those features which are likely to exist in reality, but also those unlikely to do so, have made their appearance during the transition from the second to the third stage. By way of example, one often encounters females 'in uniform' or who are 'self-assured,' while one could hardly see the sight of women dressed as 'maids' (except, perhaps, in Tokyo's Akihabara) or wearing 'cat's ears.' To sum up, by embracing image-based media and enjoying works in a cross-media way, Jun learned what Inaba calls the 'mutual agreement' of the work-world, and gradually became able to feel '*moe*' towards incredible *bishōjo*, as well.

Table 8.1: Differences in ways of enjoyment in the second and third stages

	'Objectification of persons'		'Anthropomorphising of objects'	
Stage	Second Stage (2001–2003)		Third Stage (2004–present)	
Consumption characteristics	Contact mainly with paper-based media		Contact also with image-based media	
	Story-centric consumption		Consumption incorporates symbolic elements	
Age	29	30–31	32	≥33
Moe elements discovered	'self-assured' 'spectacles' 'blonde hair' 'in uniform' Indian 'silver hair'	'black hair' 'well-bred young lady'	'spiked hair' 'knee-high socks' 'maids'	'cats' ears' *tsundere* (hot-and-cold)'

The age of choosing 'reality'

As we have seen above, today's *otaku* culture has an environment in place where it is easy to love characters that do not actually exist, and the *otaku* youth of today are well-versed in how to appreciate them. If we rearrange this in different terms, the picture should make it understandable – namely that the necessity for someone's opposite number in communication to be human speedily weakened as a result of the dissemination of methods of 'mutual agreement' symbolised by '*moe*,' to be replaced by the rise to prominence of communication vis-à-vis objects (works).

If this be the case, a lifestyle in which communication with nothing but objects was thoroughly implemented could also be considered as a final destination for such circumstances. The 'happy married life with the "girlfriend in one's brain (*nōnai kanojo*)"' proposed by novelist Tōru Honda is just that. In the author's profile in Honda's 2005 book, *Denpa otoko* (Electric-wave man), his 'family' is introduced, as follows: 'Wife: Misaki Kawana; younger sister: Yū Honda; younger sister: Akane Suzumiya; younger sister: Kana Tōdō; maid: Nagisa.' These are all *bishōjo* characters displayed on PC (personal computer) monitors. According to Honda, if one flirts

Figure 8.5: Tōru Honda and his 'family' © *Sansai Books*

with 'two-dimensional' *bishōjo*, then there will no longer be any need to engage in romantic love with actually-existing humans.

He is joking, of course, yet it cannot necessarily be flatly declared a joke. What is important is that 'freedom of choice' has expanded to the extent that such a joke could be seriously considered plausible. It is this point, precisely, that can be seen as a contemporary feature of Japanese society, manifest in a radical form in *otaku* culture. What might this signify?

The multiplication of 'reality'

One individual who has made a deeply interesting observation relating to this point is Yoshihiko Kihara, a scholar of English literature (Kihara 2006). Kihara has analysed the unique topic of changes in the social acceptance of myths about UFOs and aliens, and states that contemporary Japanese society transitioned from the 'age of fiction' (Ōsawa 1996) to the 'age of reality,' with 1995 as the turning point.

> What is important, however, is that the reality when we say the 'age of reality' diverges from the sort of thing we could call a single 'reality with a capital R' which everyone would unanimously acknowledge, the former meaning something that could have a multiple existence, something that could be conceived in opposing pairs, namely 'one reality and another reality,' or 'my reality and someone else's reality.'...

> Previously, there was a 'reality' upon which the majority of people's opinions agreed, and 'ideals' and 'fiction' existed as its opposites. At present, though, ways of apprehending reality itself have diversified, and, moreover, this situation has come to be regarded not as abnormal, but as something natural (Kihara 2006, pp. 186–7).

What Kihara is demonstrating is that an age has arrived in which people each can choose their preferred 'reality,' based on individual values. This will be readily understood if we grasp it in terms of a transition from the 'age of television' to the 'age of the Internet.' In that the mass media at its 'heart' conveyed information unilaterally to viewers in the 'periphery,' the 'television age' can be apprehended by means of a tree-shaped model. The age when the 'reality with a capital R' beyond the picture-tube was simultaneously accepted in living rooms all over the country was certainly one that deserved to be called the 'age of fiction.' By contrast, in 'the age of the Internet,' the dominance of that kind of transmission model crumbles, and 'reality with a capital R' in which everyone can uniformly believe loses currency, too. The situation in which individuals can transmit information freely in blogs, and can efficiently receive only the information of interest to those individuals by means of search engines, is one that can be grasped by a web-shaped model where networks lacking a 'heart' intertwine in a complex manner.

Pointing to such situational changes, many of the advocates introduced in this chapter locate today's Japanese society in an age where the 'big story' has expired – in short, in a stage that is 'post-modern' through and through.[6] As Kihara states, this does not merely mean a situation where there is 'truth' (as in: that is a lie/that is true). We now have the ability to choose even our 'opposite number' in communication at will, by means of a 'brutal' (Azuma 2002) feeling such as pleasant/unpleasant. The completeness of the 'post-modern' is another name for a 'free-choice society,' so to speak.

The trap in 'free-choice society'

Of course, this 'free-choice society' is a society which has both merits and demerits. While on the one hand there are no bounds to one's freedom to choose a 'reality' that suits oneself, if one selects nothing but lopsided 'realities,' then this will be an obstacle to one's social activities in some cases. These are two sides of the same coin, but for that very reason, reactions to them tend to split into two extremes, in the form of 'total affirmation/total rejection.' Moreover, the social focus on *otaku* youth can also be seen to be due to the ready visibility of their pros and cons, all the more because their 'free' consumption style is so conspicuous.

If this be the case, then how have you understood the presence that is *otaku* youth? In fact, your very way of understanding is likely to constitute a clear confirmation showing how you are living through the 'age of reality.' One person to have made a suggestive comment on this point is the novelist Masaya Nakahara (Nakahara et al. 2006), who posits as follows on his irritation vis-à-vis the '*moe* bubble' of recent years.

> NAKAHARA: ...I cannot bear the situation where [they] fortify [their] vicinity with nothing but [their] favourite things, and somehow make do with that. I really detest it. It is nothing more than a simple emotional argument, but the world will not become any more interesting that way, after all.
> SARASHINA: I interpret works not as 'education' but as 'tools,' like, 'when I want to cry, this *anime* [would do the trick],' 'when I am jerking off, this game [would be good].' Would you say that the works are not comprehensive drugs, but supplements?
> NAKAHARA: That issue in the end is influencing all the no-good parts of society now – for example, the comment which made me laugh the most out of those arriving at the editorial division of [the movie magazine] *Eiga hihō* (Cinema's hidden treasure) was the criticism that said: 'Everything apart from what I already knew was boring' (Nakahara et al. 2006, p. 190).

> NAKAHARA: Ultimately, the mentality on which *otaku* are grounded is just the same as ordinary people's mentality, and that makes me feel angry. *Otaku* think that they are special human beings, but in my opinion, they are actually extremely similar to regular people (Nakahara et al. 2006, p. 191).

What is important here is Nakahara's highlighting that a disposition which involves 'fortifying one's vicinity with nothing but one's favourite things' is not one unique to *otaku* youth, but is perhaps close to a commonplace 'ordinary people's' attitude – believing only what one wants to believe, not seeking knowledge beyond what one knows, and associating only with 'others' with whom one wants to associate. 'Free-choice society,' to borrow Nakahara's expression, is a society that enables people to live by excluding 'heterogeneous noise,' and we currently are living through an age where, by such exclusion, each of us is able to create 'our individual reality' with extreme efficiency.

On that assumption, what is most risky in this case is by no means 'being *otaku*.' In contrast to the vulgar image of *otaku* as 'confusing fiction and reality,' the example I have introduced in this chapter has been the figure of a young man who, on the basis that the work-world constitutes a 'mutual agreement,' progressively equips himself with the attitude of enjoying fiction as fiction. Of course, this is only a single example, and if one actually associates with *otaku*, one will find that they, too, include diverse types. It is not a matter of them being 'good/bad because they are *otaku*.' It simply means that there are 'good *otaku*' and 'bad *otaku*.'

The greater risk probably lies rather with the 'ordinary people' who dislike *otaku*, and can simplistically spit out the word 'creepy (*kimochi warui*)' to describe them. An attitude which makes no attempt to understand human beings in terms of anything but a stereotyped image,[7] or to correct distasteful preconceptions, is precisely what constitutes the trap in 'free-choice society' in an 'age of reality.' One of the reasons why a micro-scale survey method such as the life-history approach (= analysis that looks at a single tree) is thought necessary in sociology, which deals with the macro-scale object (a forest-like thing) that is 'society,' lies in the fact that the former makes us aware of the danger of this 'trap.'

If you were not prejudiced against *otaku*, no more needs to be said. If, however, you had made up your mind that *otaku* were 'creepy,' then it might be you who is that 'creepy' kind of human being. That is, the '*otaku*' might be you, yourself.

Notes

1 Columnist Akio Nakamori's 1983 employment of the expression '*otaku-zoku* (*otaku* tribe)' as a term indicating a personality type, in *Manga burikko* (Comics [with] cutesy-cutesy girls), the soft-core porn *manga* magazine he edited, is taken to be the first instance of its use. At that point, *otaku* still had low social recognition, only becoming the focus of attention in earnest around the time when it was reported that the perpetrator of the so-called 'serial killings of young girls,' Tsutomu Miyazaki, owned an enormous number of *anime* videos.

2 Attempts to convert inorganic objects into adorable *bishōjo* like 'Binchō-tan' are called '*moe* anthropomorphism.' It was Internet-based collaborative activity that propelled these attempts, which are taken to have already existed from the 1980s in the coterie market, into major amusements. Endeavours to change all manner of things into *bishōjo* characters, touched off in earnest from about 2000, have now progressed to game consoles (Nintendo DS, et cetera), the operating systems of personal computers (Windows Vista and so on), convenience stores (ampm and the like), and extending even to the names of chemical elements (Natrium, et cetera) (Gijinka Tanpakusho Seisaku iinkai 2006).

3 The expression 'Tabletalk RPG (TRPG)' is a hybrid term coined in Japan. Its representative work is 'Dungeons and Dragons.' It is well-known that a scene in which children play a TRPG appears in the 1983 film, 'E.T.,' directed by Steven Spielberg.

4 '*Gangan-kei* (*gangan*-style)' refers to *manga* magazines (and their works) published by game manufacturer Square Enix and launched at the beginning of the 1990s. A representative work is *Hagane no renkinjutsushi* (Fullmetal alchemist). According to *manga* critic Gō Itō (2005), its characteristic is found in the development of works within *manga* culture that have a strongly character-based nature. Moreover, Itō has made a very interesting proposal which distinguishes the notion of '*kyarakutā* (character)' from its abbreviated form, '*kyara*,' and his explanation is worth a read as a topic relevant to this chapter.

5 This is a monumental work which popularised the genre commonly known as '*moe yon-koma* (*moe* four-panel [comic strip]).' Tamaki Saitō, famed as a psychoanalyst with expert knowledge of *otaku*, states that 'this made me understood *moe*.'

6 Since its very establishment, one of the missions it has been deemed that sociology should undertake constitutes 'diagnosing the times.' In other words, this is the task of observing contemporary social phenomena, showing what kind of an age we currently inhabit, and trying to provide an appropriate prescription. Among these attempts, the type which aims to diagnose the times by focusing upon trends in *otaku*-like subculture has grown dramatically in the past decade, and the sociologist Masato Hase has named this 'the sociology of the post-modern' (Hase 2005). As Hase also points out, it is not only academic researchers that are taking charge of this, but people active in the critical realm, such as in trade magazines, including critics well-versed in the scene, as well.

7 By way of example, *otaku* youth tend to be taken up by the mass media as 'ones who like sexual depiction,' but this is not necessarily so. In Jun's case, he treated *bishōjo* characters with a modest attitude akin to gently gazing at sweet flowers blooming by the roadside and admiring them, and he says he has a strong resistance to their 'being sexually assaulted' in coterie magazines and so on. In this way, there is certainly no dearth of *otaku* who want their favourite characters to remain unsullied, and, just as the architect Kaichirō Morikawa has situated it in the expression, '*wabi, sabi, moe*,' which links *moe* to the Japanese ideal of rustic and imperfect beauty (*wabi-sabi*), there are also advocates who do not regard '*moe*' as mere pedophilia (a sexual taste for young children), but read into it a unique aesthetic.

9 Why do people gather at rock festivals?: communication mediated by music

Jun'ichi Nagai

The season that music fans have eagerly awaited [is coming] – we will introduce all kinds of high-profile fests: [their] venues, locations, and performing artists, as well. People who want to make noise, those who want to dance, and those who want to listen to music in a relaxed way, too, surely should find a fest that suits them perfectly (*Pia*, 2007).

The above text is one published in a special feature article in an entertainment information magazine. Lately, such articles can be seen with increasing frequency along with the advent of summer, and posters for rock festivals (forthwith abbreviated to 'rock-fests' or 'fests') meet the eye everywhere, such as at convenience stores. Many people, even if they have yet to experience rock-fests, would probably acknowledge their existence. So, what are rock-fests, anyway?

'A lot of artists appear all at once, in the open air...' But is that all there is to fests?

They have the kind of enjoyment that cannot be expressed in a single phrase, nor savoured from compact discs (CDs) or concerts. Moreover, the majority of people who have experienced them have succumbed to their attraction and become repeat participants, or 'repeaters.' In this chapter, I wish to shine a spotlight upon that experience, and think about why rock-fests cast their spell upon people.

Let's go to a rock-fest!

It is probably impossible to avoid the existence of rock festivals when discussing the popular music of today's Japan. Starting with the Fuji Rock Festival in 1997, the Rising Sun Rock Festival in Ezo was launched in 1999, and the Rock in Japan Festival and Summer Sonic in 2000. These festivals, called the Big Four, each average more than

Figure 9.1: Magazines and free newspapers reporting festival scenes

30,000 visitors daily, and their numbers of entrants have continued to rise until the present day. In addition, various music events have come to be held before and after them all around the country, these numbering over fifty Japan-wide even in just the three months from July to September. Moreover, recently there has been an increase in 'spring fests' and 'autumn fests,' and 'winter fests' which are held indoors have come onto the scene, as well. Throughout the year, Japan takes on the appearance of a 'rock-festival archipelago,' and one even can hear the expression 'fest bubble.'[1]

The frequency with which fests are featured in media such as magazines has also risen. Figure 9.1 shows magazines and so-called 'free papers' relating to fests published in 2007. Music magazines and information magazines carry reports which convey wild enthusiasm for fests, and these publications naturally include special features such as 'how to' guides aimed at novices. Moreover, recently fests have been discussed from all angles, with outdoor magazines giving instruction on outdoor life at fests, women's fashion magazines reporting on the 'latest fest fashions,' and so on. Though the doldrums in the music industry have been in the news of late, there are extremely large numbers of people enjoying music at rock festivals.

What sort of people come along to such fests, then? Are they passionate music fans? Or is a fest a rally for people who have some kind of intention or thought? Music events held in the past indeed had such aspects.² This is not necessarily the case with fests nowadays, however. These days, when many festivals are held and the threshold is comparatively low, there are also plenty of people who declare that they like fests, even if they have little detailed knowledge about music. They enjoy this kind of music festival with just the same feeling as any festive occasion, as something akin to a type of leisure activity involving travel. Today's fests are ones in which any individuals can participate if they have a little energy and financial resources. And people who have experienced them will be entranced by their enjoyment, and become repeaters.

A new mode of listening to music

So, why has the popularity of fests grown to this extent? Above, I described contemporary fests as being akin to leisure, but if I delve a little more deeply, I can describe them as a new mode of musical reception – in other words, a new style for listening to music.

There are many different methods of listening to music in our daily lives. If, for example, we have a vague desire to hear hit tunes, we might listen to the radio, while we would probably listen to a CD if we wanted to hear specific music. However, sales of CDs, which have constituted the mainstream mode of music-listening up till now, have been following a downward trajectory over the past decade. On the other hand, though, in complete contrast, attendance numbers at fests have been rising, as shown in Figure 9.2. Such a trend can be considered strikingly to demonstrate a change in the way of listening to and enjoying music. In actual fact, at fests, audiences have an experience which differs from listening to CDs at home, and they also engage in behaviour dissimilar to that at ordinary concerts.

Moreover, at the same time, companions who share the fests become an important presence. The existence of these buddies, who not only watch the concerts but travel together, and sleep and eat together, as well, are a vital factor for the enjoyment of fests and the enrichment of the fest experience. The fest experience, in this manner, also constitutes communication mediated by music. In addition, participants' way of connecting – by the medium of fests which were composite things to begin with – is one that differs from existing fan culture. By scrutinising fests from such a perspective, we will be able to explore the nature of a new music culture.

Figure 9.2: Shifts in CD sales and audience mobilisation numbers at the four major rock festivals, 2006–2007 financial year

CD sales: 290,252,000 units[a]
Audience numbers at 4 major festivals: 452,000[b]

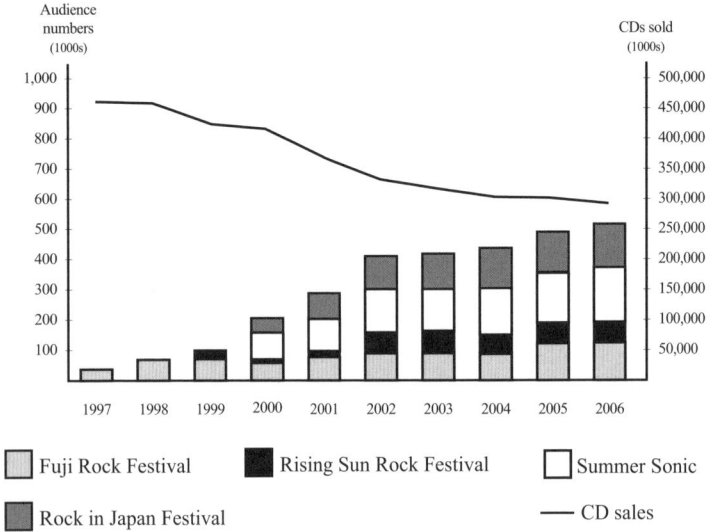

Notes.
a: CD sales figures from Recording Industry of Japan (RIAJ) survey.
b: Festival attendee numbers represent gross numbers for event duration as published by promoters.

In this chapter, after I have set out my points of argument below, let us consider audience behaviour at fests, and the related interpersonal communication which is mediated by that behaviour, based on insights gained through my fieldwork and interview surveys.

Concert and live-performance audiences

Before launching into the main topic, let us first think here about concerts and live performances prior to the advent of fests. What sort of presence is the audience at a concert or live performance? What kind of image comes to your mind?

Why do people gather at rock festivals? 175

If it is a concert of art music (classical music), you might imagine people sitting in seats, listening quietly and intently to the playing, while if it is a live performance of rock, you might envision a pumped-up crowd jumping around in time to the music, or singing along. The word 'audience' covers quite a broad range. Such listening styles which we feel are natural nowadays have actually not been the same in every age. While there have been times when listeners shouted their appreciation to art music performers, there have also been times when audiences sat on chairs and listened keenly to hard rock. The nature of music audiences at concerts has been diverse in different ages and societies.

Rock festivals have also generated a novel listening style. Their audiences are often taken to be a more active presence that differs from that of ordinary concerts, and are called 'participants' (forthwith, in this chapter, also, I will specifically call fest audience members 'participants'). In order to shed light on their listening styles, let us for the time being think about audiences at concerts and live performances as their objects of comparison.

The audience for art music

According to Hiroshi Watanabe, the present-day 'kind of concert where [the audience] listens intently and wholeheartedly to famous pieces of music in silent concert halls' is something that arose in the nineteenth century, concerts previously having been held in a fairly chaotic atmosphere, accompanied by such activities as eating, drinking or chatter, and even occasionally with dogs running about (Watanabe 1989). Of course, there were probably also some people who came to listen to the music with serious intent, but the character of concerts in those times, which drew the lavishly-attired aristocracy in great numbers, was more that of a hub for social interaction than nowadays.

Later, when the bourgeoisie started to come along to concerts, the situation changed. Due to the increase in audiences, concerts expanded, became commercialised, and their entertainment qualities intensified. Accordingly, musicians came to be treated as stars, and there was a stampede of die-hard fans. On the other hand, however, the broadening of the base meant a steady growth in audiences eager to listen to music 'seriously.'

By listening to musical works in a structural manner, such 'serious' audiences aimed to approach music as art, and the spirit of the great masters inscribed within it. To that end, one must not go wild over a single phrase or motif, but understand how it is situated within the entire musical piece. This is why it is necessary to listen intently in silence to music.

Theodor W. Adorno named this mode of conduct 'structural hearing.' This was not the kind of conduct of which every listener was capable, but one that only a handful of 'experts' who had equipped themselves with education and knowledge relating to music could manifest (Adorno 1962, p. 5). Later, this way of thinking became connected with the principle of 'cultivation,' and it became the dominant one in concerts, leading to the establishment of a concert style like that of the present day.

The popular music audience

On the other hand, how would the audience be in the case of popular music, including rock? The figure which might be conjured is of an audience 'really into it (*norinori*),' in contrast with one for classical music. Naturally, it is not possible to treat classical and popular music equally, given the dissimilar significance and social background against which each is, and has been, created.[3] What is important in popular music is that it presupposes the existence of mechanical reproduction techniques (media).[4] Concerts, also, have different implications according to this precondition.

Generally speaking, many of the opportunities we have to hear music in our daily lives are through media such as CDs, radio or television. If they present pieces of music or artists that we like, then we will turn our steps to concerts or live performances. In other words, this means that the places we go in order to confirm the images constructed through the media are concerts and live performances. It is there that carnivality and the aura held by musicians are added. An aura is the special quality of 'being present here and now' that works of art essentially possessed, and this provided artistic works with mystery and tension, but Walter Benjamin ([1936] 2008) has pointed out that this has been lost due to the emergence of techniques of mechanical reproduction. If we are talking about music, in principle it is a one-off thing, it being impossible to repeat a performance in exactly the same way, but since the advent of mechanical reproduction techniques, it has been possible to hear exactly the same performance any number of times on records or CDs. In such an environment, it is live performances which enable listeners to feel an aura, and it may be argued that in the current age, concerts and live performances are given relatively high appraisals for that very reason.

Hiroshi Ogawa is of the opinion that the element which controls concerts in such a media society is '*nori* (being "into it"; "rocking").' Most of the audience that attends popular music concert venues nowadays can be said to come for the *nori*. For that reason, too, 'prior study' becomes necessary. Audiences do not unconsciously rise to their feet because the playing is superb, but in order to 'get rockin'.' Rather than standing up *after* getting into 'into it,' they stand *in order to* be 'into it' (Ogawa 1988, p. 87–8; emphasis added).

In order to 'rock' at concerts, it is important for attendees to gain a solid prior knowledge of the artists, and to 'read up' on the musical numbers. What is more, feeling the music directly with the body – physicality rather than spirituality – looks to be the aim there. At its core lies not a structural understanding, but a response to fragments which presupposes getting 'into it.' We can call such a way of listening 'fragmentary hearing,' in contraposition to 'structural hearing.'

The difference between fests and concerts

From past theory, whether in relation to art music or popular music, and whether aspiring to spirituality or physicality, it is understood that concerts have their respective styles, or what one ought to call etiquette.

Generally, fests are supposed to differ from concerts in their ordinary form that feature solo artists, of course, but also from omnibus concerts in which multiple artists simply perform. Music critic Dai Onojima has summarised the unique features of fests as follows, taking as his example the Fuji Rock Festival, deemed to be the model of present-day fests (Onojima 2002, pp. 24–5):

[1] [Participants] set out to stay overnight by camping or suchlike;
[2] fests are held over a long period of time, stretching over multiple days, [or] from one morning through to the early hours of the next morning;

[3] multiple stages proceed simultaneously;
[4] lineups have a mixture of Japanese/imported music, mainstream/indie, rock/jazz-club-type music;
[5] venues have no partitions or block divisions;
[6] the presence of attractions other than music

This does not mean that all fests comprise conditions such as these, but most fests nowadays either satisfy several of the conditions from the list, or forge their respective characteristics by a combination of them.

If we look at Onojima's analysis, it will be seen that the only description relating to live performance is [4], while weight is placed on the other terms. Fests nowadays are not simple pastiches of live performances: rather, the other elements create the atmosphere unique to fests. In addition, the presence of these elements becomes a trigger to unleash the audience's activeness, and produces a space with a high degree of freedom in comparison with ordinary concerts.

At an omnibus-type of event in which performances recur in sequence on a single stage, for instance, the period during which an attendee's desired artist does not appear becomes 'dead time,' but as fests offer many amusements apart from live performances, this does not occur. Moreover, this leads not to enjoyment of the live performances *per se*, but to an attitude of enjoying the atmosphere of the venue as a whole.

Let me reiterate that what I wish to confirm here is that the listening style at concerts and live performances, which tends to be regarded as something self-evident, is actually not always universal. In light of the above theory, in the next section let us look at the manner in which fest participants actually enjoy fests.

The 'fest' experience

In this section, let us think about what constitutes the 'fest' experience, based on insights gained from fieldwork. First, I will give an overview of the fieldwork that I myself conducted.

After several preliminary surveys, I have participated continuously in rock-fests since 2004 as a member of the audience and of the backstage crew, and have carried out participant observation in the form of conducting interviews with ordinary participants encountered there. In the interviews, I did not ask many questions, but tried to have interviewees speak in as natural a flow as possible, making efforts to collect participants' 'live voices' and 'vocabulary for talking about fests.'[5] The interviews were often conducted at venues while the fests were in progress. There were some that I implemented at a later time and place, or where I interviewed the same person multiple times, but in those below, I will note the sex, age and fest at which I first met each respective informant.

'Participation' in fests

The fest participants I have also already mentioned can be situated as a more active presence than audiences at concerts and live performances where they simply 'watch a live performance.' When the participants arrive at the venue, they first exchange their ticket for a wristband. This wristband becomes their proof of entry, and they can enter and exit any number of times while the event is going on. Once they are done with entry, while fully enjoying the feeling of freedom from being in the open air, as well as the scenic aspects of the venue, they simultaneously scrutinise the programme and plan the day's schedule. This means making up their own individual programme, so to speak, by way of choosing the acts they want to see from among multiple stages that will proceed simultaneously. Being able to see many live performances in one day is one of the pleasures of a fest.

After having their fill of their desired live performances, participants utilise the various in-between times to take breaks or meals. In the concessions area, businesses selling local specialties or famous establishments set up numerous stalls. At fests in recent years, it has been usual for not simple fare, but elaborately-contrived menus, to be arrayed; and there are also many exclusive menu items that can only be tasted at fests. If participants and their friends each contribute one dish they have chosen to share and they all have a merry meal together, smiles will naturally result.

When stomachs are full, it will be time for a short break, but here, too, the participants are never bored, because various attractions are provided at each fest. Participants can cast an eye over giant *objets* or artworks, be soothed by such relaxing services as foot-spas or massages, play at a casino, ride a Ferris wheel, or enjoy street performers or comedy shows. It would also be nice to lie down on the grass with a drink of beer and take an afternoon nap. The existence of these attractions enhances the pleasure of fests, to the extent that one could enjoy oneself all day without even watching a live music performance.

In this way, participants are pressed for choice on all sides at fests. This has become a trigger to their activeness, and the very enjoyment of the atmosphere of the venue, including these things, is what is demanded of the participants.

Of course, this does not mean that everyone engages in 'participation' such as this. Many participants become repeaters, and in the process of participating in many other fests, they progressively learn such ways of enjoying fests, and acquire the appropriate listening style. The following statements from participants vividly illustrate this.

> In short, I used to think that concerts were all the same, whether I saw them at Club Quattro, or Osakajo Hall, or Osaka Dome, or anywhere. I thought that it was only a matter of whether the distance between the players and me was near or far. [Then] I sort of came to see that they were enjoyable because of the 'sound plus something else' that made them fun. I realised that they weren't all the same no matter where I heard them.
>
> In terms of the senses, [they involve] not only hearing, but sometimes taste, or sight, or smell, holistically – to sound pompous, that's what they involve, I guess.
>
> If you really want to hear a particular person's sound, you simply need to listen to the sound source, right? If you just want to hear their sound, of course it would be better to do it in a hall like those where they play classical music (Male/early thirties/Fuji Rock Festival).

> As I attend more and more times, I come to realise that it is fun even if I am not so greedy for the live performances – I learn a different sort of enjoyment. If I want to see my favourite artist, I should go to a solo live performance, because somehow, with a fest, the whole thing is fun (Female/late twenties/Arabaki Rock Fest).

They are talking about the changes in their way of enjoying fests between the first time they attended and subsequent times, and it can be seen from their statements that they recognise fests and ordinary live performances as being different experiences.

In the beginning, they participate in fests with the idea that they are no different from ordinary concerts, but through contact with the location and atmosphere of the venues and the music streaming there, they come to appreciate fests' unique brand of enjoyment for the first time. At fests where numerous famous artists appear, it is not always the case that participants will stroll from stage to stage and watch the live performances one after another. Rather, they will only catch a few live shows, and will enjoy meals, alcohol, chatting with their companions, or taking naps, savouring to the full an environment resounding with music in every quarter.

Attitudes towards live performances

People with a liking for fests are not necessarily avid devotees of specific artists. As evidence of this, there is always a fierce scramble for the highly-sought-after 'early-bird discount tickets' that each fest employs, which go on sale at a stage prior to any publication of the names of performers whatsoever. Repeaters absolutely adore their fests.[6]

Rather, fixation upon specific artists and live performances sometimes becomes the target of criticism. The 'reserving of a place' in front of the stage by avid fans of popular artists often comes under fire. The sight of such individuals who save a spot with a good view of the artists from one or two live shows prior to that of the acts they want to see, and show no interest in the live performance being played out before their very eyes in the meantime, courts ill-will from many participants. Moreover, not only fans, but artists themselves who boast an enthusiastic following, are the object of criticism, with people saying they do not want those artists to appear. In short, this means that fans and artists who dampen the fest atmosphere in their obsession with live performances are ill-suited to fests. The atmosphere is all-important.

Given this kind of attitude, the 'prior study→confirmation' schema such as Ogawa illustrates does not always apply. For a start, at fests where multiple stages proceed simultaneously, it is physically impossible to see all of the artists, but in addition, the more that participants endeavour to enjoy the atmosphere of the venue, the less their obsession with live performances becomes. Naturally, setting up a rough schedule while scrutinising the timetable which is published in advance is something that many participants do, and starting to discuss various aspects from prior to the holding of the event is also one of the joys of fests. However, participants who have learned by experience that things 'do not go as planned' stop being fixated upon live performances as they are carried away by the 'laid-back' atmosphere. Though there are differences of degree, spending the day by deciding only on a few live shows to see and relaxing for the remainder of the time is the listening style often observed at fests in recent years.

As a result, what naturally becomes more frequent is encounter with artists that one did not previously know. While there are all sorts of triggers: 'When I happened to pass by, they were playing,' 'My friends were going to watch, so I went with them,' or 'When I was dozing, the performance started up there,' and so on, such encounters are also one of the pleasures of fests.

> I heard 'Hanaregumi' for the first time in the flesh, and thought he was good. There was 'Caravan' and so on, as well. I knew Caravan's name, but I heard him in the flesh and thought he was good, so I then went to his live shows (Female/late twenties/Arabaki Rock Fest).

Here, a process arises that is the reverse of the one ordinarily conceived, in which people go to live performances of artists of whom they have become fans, or attend live performances after listening to a recording. They get to know artists at fests and then become fans, listening to recordings after they have experienced a live show. Rather, it is precisely because ignorance of the artists and musical numbers is presupposed that the physical sensitivity for responding immediately to the music becomes all the more important at live performances at fests. It is a form that is a development of fragmentary hearing, and through it, a way of enjoyment that involves crossing from one *nori* to another becomes possible. Moreover, a review-type of enjoyment method which means confirming those artists at a later date through CDs or live shows, rather than a prior-study type, is on the increase.[7]

The group called 'fest buddies'

As we have already seen, at fests nowadays more importance is placed upon enjoying the fest and its atmosphere rather than enjoying individual live shows, and upon 'being' at the venue rather than 'seeing' the live performances.[8] Moreover, networks are built in a variety of forms and communication frequently conducted with the aim of enjoying the fest in the above manner. I reiterate that their characteristic feature lies in the fact that participants are not music maniacs well-versed in all performers, nor rabid devotees of specific artists, nor followers of a genre, but people who have gathered in order to enjoy the fest itself on its own terms.

If they feel a sense of unity at fests, it is a kind of sympathy towards the atmosphere of the venue. The engaging thing about fests is that though participants each watch different live shows and indulge in disparate activities, they share one memory.

Even if, for example, they think that it would be all right to watch actual live performances by themselves, many participants wish to participate in a group in order to fill in the rest of the time. They proactively strive to secure 'fest buddies.' Of course, there are also some participants who watch one live show after another by themselves, carrying their ready-made food in one hand, without taking anyone else into consideration, but in the majority of cases, attendees participate in groups of several people.

> It would sort of be okay to be alone, but I guess it would be more fun in a big group when [your taste in artists] overlaps with somebody else (Female/late twenties/ Arabaki Rock Fest).

> Well, it's lonely being all by myself. It's long, after all. If it were an ordinary live performance, I'd be able to concentrate, but [at] fests there are times for meals and stuff, yeah? There is the fact that I can feel at ease if others are there.
> I don't mind watching live shows alone, but in between times... (Male, late thirties/Summer Sonic Osaka).

Here can be seen an intentionality unique to fests which differs from previous concerts and live performances. It constitutes a shift from an 'artist–audience' solidarity to a loose 'audience–audience' solidarity. For the latter, live shows and fests are clearly different things, and the presence of companions with whom to spend time occupies an extremely important position. Accordingly, the kind of discourse that says 'the attendees are the protagonists at fests' and 'it is the participants that make fests' gains credibility. This is because for the participants, fest buddies are at least as important a presence as the performers that appear, or even a more important one, in terms of making fests an even better experience.

For that reason, participating in groups is what they seek. Groups can be classified into several patterns in their process of formation. Here, I will dub these 'snowballing,' 'off-line' and 'sharing,' and examine each pattern forthwith.

The formation of human networks

Snowballing

The most orthodox case is that in which people who have experienced fests play the role of cultural mediators, conveying the pleasure and attraction of fests when they become 'repeaters.' A cultural mediator is someone who connects enterprises and consumers, or artists and audiences; and by employing this concept, Keith Negus emphasises that it is not that the music industry produces music in one-way assembly-line fashion and audiences consume it, but that audiences contribute to meaning-creation in works, and to the formation of artists' images (Negus 1996, pp. 95–8). Moreover, while it is mainly people involved in the music industry that Negus has in mind at this time, here it could be argued that 'repeaters' are fulfilling a similar role.

Their presence is important in putting across such things as the atmosphere of venues which cannot be fully conveyed by such means as the mass media, and even fests that feel somehow inapproachable can seem familiar by friends' mention of them. Especially in the case of regional fests that receive little press, this kind of word-of-mouth publicity functions effectively. It is not difficult to imagine 'repeaters' inviting along friends, lovers and the like, and that this has contributed to the present-day increase in the fest population.

It means that they actually gather the members who go to fests, and it is often the case that friends of friends, and their friends, too, get together, leading to the formation of small groups of between about five and under ten members. The groups grow in size just like snowballs.

> Last year, I came in a group of five. It was so much fun! So I thought it might be enjoyable if we increased the number of people. This time I got tickets for eight, so I thought we'd need three more to add to last

Why do people gather at rock festivals?

> year's five. I invited people who couldn't come last year, and so on (Male/early twenties/Arabaki Rock Fest).

> [The reason why I didn't go last year was that] it was a long distance away, and there was like, 'Are you really going to go?' After I heard talk of last year from the members that went, I already was intending to go [the next time] (Male/early twenties/Arabaki Rock Fest).

While there are some cases of members having been friends from the start, there are also cases where they become acquainted through other friends, and actually meet for the first time at the site. Then again, there are also cases of them meeting beforehand if they live near each other. Some groups involved compile mailing lists and introduce themselves beforehand, or swap and share information relating to the fest. Whatever the case, such encounters become yet another of the pleasures of fests. Participants who become the central figures in that process are mediators who not only connect fests with people, but connect people with other people, as well.

There are also cases where this configuration arises in the form of the agglutination of originally small groups. Groups which each used to participate in different fests, and those which used to participate in the same fest in isolation, develop into a comparatively large group through mediators.

In the cases I introduce here, two groups were participating in a fest in a conjoined manner. While it was actually at another fest that they met, on the impetus of having hit it off there, they then came to participate in a series of fests.

> At the time of this year's spring Arabaki, I went with some of these members and some others, and because they were good members, when it came time for us to want to go again, it was decided that we would go and immerse ourselves in a fest we'd never visited before. Well, I hadn't been to Rock in Japan Festival so I went with some of these members and some other members, in a group of seven. So we went to Rock in Japan, but 'cos it was like we'd go to Rising Sun Rock Festival in Ezo, as well, it was these members that agreed (Male/late twenties/Rising Sun Rock Festival in Ezo).

Though they have hit it off with each other, these members who reside in different areas do not meet frequently. They are literally fest buddies who only meet at fests. From the statement of this informant who desires continuity, however, it can be appreciated that they find positive value in such relationships.

Though this group continues, it often happens that its constituents are not static. When another opportunity comes along, they will recruit participants from their number and take part in the next fest. Naturally, there are also times where new members enter the group. They move from one fest to another while repeatedly changing members in a fluid manner, and repeatedly dividing and agglutinating like amoebae.

Off-line

There are also cases in which people find members to accompany them by recruiting fest buddies through the Internet and suchlike, in order to participate when they cannot find companions close at hand. The examples I introduce below are cases where companions got together at an off-line meeting on the impetus of posts on a certain Bulletin Board System (BBS).

> The first year I went, I went alone, but the next year I wanted to go with someone, that's why. It so happened that when the 2001 [Fuji Rock Festival] finished, there was a post saying 'Let's hold this year's after-fest party in Kyoto.' Because there were still only small numbers of people going from Kansai in those days, I thought it would be nice if I could find people to go with the next year. It's not as if going together means being together all the time for three days – I thought, 'Oh well, it would be good if we could share the travel expenses and so on' (Male/early thirties/Fuji Rock Festival).

This off-line meeting later expanded into the form of a DJ event at a rock bar, and began to be held continuously. A type of community was moulded there: there was no dearth of people who participated in the Fuji Rock Festival after having built relationships on the impetus of having actually become acquainted at this event; and there were even some who found a partner in real life. Moreover, this event is held in a form that interlocks with websites relating to Fuji Rock Festival. Immediately following the start of the event (2002), when fest information was less prolific than it is now, there were diverse responses to sites and events, and, in particular, they functioned as points of contact for novices. In recent years, though, the main organisers keenly sense that responses to the sites and events have shrunk.

> I guess everyone can go [under their own steam] now. I think that people who go for the first time would have quite a bit of trouble, but I feel that there are fewer people like that now. Before, people would search on the Net and recruit companions because they didn't know what to do, but I think that as everyone has become used to [fests], that sort of thing might not be needed anymore (Male/early thirties/Fuji Rock Festival).

Sharing

On the other hand, a trend which has become popular recently is one called sharing. Typical examples are the recruitment of companions to stay in lodgings together, dividing up travel expenses among the members, and sharing camping space.

> Even with accommodation, recently my way of thinking has changed a bit. I got the feeling that if I booked for four or five [persons] to begin with, and then if people couldn't make it, I would start recruiting, and it would be okay even if I collected complete strangers. I suppose fests might have that kind of atmosphere. Even with total strangers, the fest we share becomes a unifying force, and so they can blend in (Male/late thirties/Fuji Rock Festival).

Such trends had existed since previous times, but recently they have come to be seen extremely frequently. Two major background factors can be considered here, the first being the ticket situation at today's fests. Firstly, participation in fests held over multiple days makes overnight accommodation necessary. For that reason, participants need to stay in lodgings or to set up camp. In the case of camping, at many fests campers have to buy a camping ticket. In addition, a parking-lot ticket also becomes necessary in order to come to the venue by car. In other words, there is a necessity to purchase an entrance ticket, campsite ticket and parking-lot ticket in combination, but as different fests have different methods of purchase, things are quite complicated. What is more, due to the popularity of fests in recent years, tickets have become hard to obtain. In cases where participants stay in lodgings, they have to finalise their arrangements as early as possible for accommodation close to the venue, and also have to secure their means of transportation.

Under such circumstances, there are numerous cases where people cannot buy tickets as they wish, or are forced into a manner of participation different from their original plans. In such cases, they will find participants that fit their various conditions and share them.

Sharing has become a lively practice. Other grounds for it have been the popularity of SNS[9] in recent years. The shrinkage in influence of websites is something that many participants point out, but this does not mean that actual interchange via the Internet has collapsed, but that it has virtually shifted to SNS. This is probably because a sense of security can be obtained more from semi-anonymous communication than from absolute anonymity. Based on such grounds, 'sharing' has been enlivened. Let me present one example of this below.

A certain informant (female) decided to participate in a fest by herself, and bought an entry ticket and campsite ticket. However, there were elements of anxiety such as her participating as a solitary female, it being her first fest, and her being unaccustomed to camping, and so she utilised SNS (mixi community), calling for someone to share with her, and succeeded in making contact with a group of three. She reports that the trio invited a further person who was going to participate alone, and in the end the five of them camped together. The items which each respective constituent contributed are as follows:

- 1 female→tent, sleeping bag, campsite ticket
- Mixed group of 3→car, tent, sleeping bags, barbecue set
- 1 female→campsite ticket

From this, one can see that the vested interests are clear-cut. In other words, by each party contributing something that was lacking, they alleviate the risk. The informant claims that she watched nearly all of the live shows by herself, but says that in hindsight, she is glad she 'shared.'

> What was good, after all, was feeling secure, and feeling confident. When I did something alone at night I was really scared. They put up the tent for me, too. It would have been absolutely impossible if I had done it alone. And then, it was also great to be able to exchange

information like: 'This live show was good,' in real time. It was good to be able to swap information even on the toilet problem[10] and it was fun (Female/early twenties/Rising Sun Rock Festival).

This female participant also said: 'It might just have been that the people I met happened to be nice.' 'Sharing' was just a way of getting her foot in the door, and the subsequently deepened interaction led to her satisfaction.

The pleasure of fragments

The communication called fests

Let me summarise the theory up to this point. The rock festivals which have spread in the past decade or so could be described as events that have provided us with a new musical experience. This does not, however, refer to the experience of understanding music by listening to it in a structured manner or responding to a known piece and getting 'into it' at ordinary concerts or live performances. Rather than digesting a pre-determined programme from beginning to end, it means enjoying the atmosphere in circumstances where live performances are present as an environment (music reaching one's ears wherever one might be). The style of enjoying live shows one after another at fests is akin to spinning numerous experiences (fragments) into one thread, and being 'into it,' such as by reading the mood of the occasion and synchronising oneself with it, becomes important. This could be said to be one of the forms that evolved from the fragmentary hearing seen in live performances of popular music. This very 'pleasure from fragments' is the attraction of fests.[11]

The fragments in fests consist of each of the live shows, as well as the diverse elements which add colour to fests apart from the live performances. Though the sight of participants relaxing without watching the live shows might seem at a glance to belie the fact, they enjoy fests with a positive attitude. Without having a particular style thrust upon them, they are savouring a sense of freedom, and each individual shares the same fest with a unique way of enjoyment.

Moreover, such a way of enjoyment subsequently links with aspirations towards relationality. The communication that takes place there also is a reflection of fests. While sharing the same set of values (fests) in certain aspects, in other aspects participants are accepting of dissimilar values (various artists and music and their respective fans). The relationships there are not as 'dense'[12] as in traditional fan culture but represent an ad-hoc solidarity that respects individual will. Zygmunt Bauman dubs such groupings of people 'cloakroom communities' or 'carnival communities' (Bauman 2000, pp. 199–201). According to Bauman, these 'do not fuse and blend individual concerns into 'group interest' (2000, p. 200), but fest participants do find positive values in them. One of the attractions of fests is the pleasure and comfort of the kind of relationships that share the *nori* of each different occasion, seeming to diffuse even while participants gather in one place. The act of taking part not with friends but solo, and finding 'fest buddies,' could be called a typical example of this.

Why do they gather?

As we have seen hitherto, in the musical field nowadays, fests have a strong unifying force. People with truly diverse occupations and personalities come along to fests. They tend to be considered as young people's events, but there are many adults in their thirties and into their forties, and numerous participants can also be seen accompanied by children. The hitherto commonly-observed pattern had been for people to distance themselves from music upon finding a job or getting married, but people have now come to be able to enjoy music endlessly through fests. When they grow older, fests will perhaps become places where an even greater variety of people gather, because everyone equitably enjoys music there and shares the possession of fests.

It is also necessary, however, to note that they are not a mirror reflecting society. In fact, the main attendee cohort differs according to fest, and the venue atmosphere and ways of enjoyment also differ.[13] Compartmentalisation is accomplished by people's choice of a fest that suits themselves. In fieldwork that I conducted, for example, many informants were in an environment where they could use the Internet, and were also SNS users. Nowadays, much of the information on fests is published on the Internet, and it is also likely that the presence or absence of Internet use is related to fest participation. This is because filtering occurs unwittingly at that point, and there could be the great possibility that people with similar tendencies are gathering together.

Fest buddies that have congregated in this way are contiguous with daily life in some cases, but not in others. Such an idea gives rise anew to the following sort of questions. To start with, why do they gather at fests, one wonders? Who constitutes 'the other' in that context? In this way, fests might become the trigger for thinking about groups and society, and the individual.

Notes

1 There is no clear-cut definition of '*fesu* (fest),' but in the media and suchlike, it is used as a blanket term for a music event held outdoors. For now, in this paper, in light of such circumstances, I will interpret the word 'fest' in its broad sense and employ it as such from here onwards.
2 Woodstock, for example, which was held in 1969, and the Nakatsugawa Folk Jamborees held from 1969 to 1971 in Japan, are deemed to be highlights of the counterculture that had its heyday at the time.
3 For a definition of popular music, see, for instance, Tagg 1982.
4 'Audience (*chōshū*)' originally was a concept indicating listeners to music as a whole, including those listening to media, and not only listeners to concerts. I omitted them due to page limitations, but Negus (1996) details the series of audience theories, starting with that of Adorno.
5 In such interview surveys, the impression that the researcher gives to the interviewee is also important. It is advisable to employ different approaches as appropriate to different times and circumstances: a formal versus a casual way of speaking; formal versus casual attire; and so on.
6 The festival which shows this most markedly is Asagiri Jam. Its tickets are sold without any disclosure whatsoever of the names of artists who are to perform. In spite of this, it boasts high popularity.
7 In actuality, since the 1990s there has been an extremely large number of musicians who have made names for themselves at festivals. For artists, festivals are an arena for calling the attention of people other than their own fans to their music, as well; while for the music industry, they are a supreme opportunity for promotion.
8 This is something which the Fuji Rock Festival upheld as their banner. See Hidaka 2003, p. 199.
9 An abbreviation of Social Networking Service, SNS, as its name suggests, is an Internet service oriented towards connecting people with each other. Until now, much of the communication on the Net was anonymous, but SNS requires users to register their profiles.
10 At the 2007 Rising Sun Rock Festival, there were insufficient toilets for the number of entrants, and ultimately the situation worsened to the extent that all of the toilets inside the venue became unusable.
11 Minamida 2006 details the quality of music-listening at festivals.

12 Izumi Tsuji, for one, points out that the relationships of Johnny's fans is oriented towards 'feelings of closeness (*shinkinkan*),' and for that reason, they 'become unstable at the slightest impetus' (Tsuji 2007, p. 280).
13 Kōsuke Okada, for example, positions the Fuji Rock Festival and its participants as 'trying to distance themselves from the 'J-pop' discourse – in other words, [as] aspiring to be "alternative" vis-à-vis 'mainstream'" (Okada 2007).

Part III: Immediate Everyday Life

10 What are contemporary aspects of the parent/child relationship?: mother/daughter friendship and its social context

Yasuko Nakanishi

Nowadays, the parent/child relationship is said to have developed into an intimate connection of equals who seem just 'like friends,' unlike the clear-cut hierarchical relationship of old; and the pros and cons of this phenomenon, called 'parent/child friendship,' have been debated repeatedly since the 1970s. In contrast to this lively debate, however, there has been little attempt to grasp the actual situation of intimacy between parents and children. Many discussants, having each conjured diverse images of the 'friend-like parent/child dyad,' have severally pointed out its merits and demerits. What is more, their discussion has been tied to a normative argument, namely: 'Essentially, how should the parent/child relationship be? Can the present closeness between parents and children be called the form that ought to exist?'

In order to judge its pros and cons, though, there is probably a necessity first to apprehend its actual situation. What kind of social conditions lie behind parents and children being connected not only by their role-relation but also by emotional intimacy, and their building of the sort of relationship sometimes described as 'friend-like?' In addition, what kinds of people have established an intimate relationship with their parents, and in what form?

As such, in this chapter I will deal with the mother/daughter relationship, which is said to represent an especially close connection among parent/child relationships, and will use a statistical method to elucidate the social background of that intimacy. Through data analysis, I will show how intimacy between parent and child, which appears in a simple sense to be an extremely private and individual phenomenon, is being swayed by such macro social circumstances as the economic situation and diversification of the female life-course.

Contemporary aspects of the parent/child relationship

In this chapter, I will explore how the extremely private phenomenon that constitutes intimacy between parent and child has been socially prescribed. Why do I focus upon such an individual emotional matter as parent/child closeness? It is because the bond between parent and child in modern times has developed into one supported not by an institution, but by emotional ties.[1] Furthermore, there is said to have been a quest for a 'pure relationship' (Giddens 1992) in the contemporary family, centring upon those emotional ties.

The 'pure relationship' is the conceptualisation by British sociologist Anthony Giddens of a form of human relationship in modern times. The term indicates the discovery of meaning in the very connection with another person. In other words, it 'relates to a situation where a social relation is entered into for its own sake, for what can be derived by each person from a sustained association with another' (Giddens 1992, p. 58). In addition, the continuation of that relationship is swayed by whether each party is able to obtain sufficient satisfaction from the tie with the other, in itself. The term 'pure relationship' is one which refers to the nature of such a connection. In many cases, the relationship between friends or lovers has their mutual connection as an end in itself. For that precise reason, if there is expectation of some other merit from that tie, then the relationship could court the criticism that it is 'not pure.' Moreover, if one of the parties ceases to feel satisfied with the connection itself, then it will become difficult to continue that relationship. Accordingly, relationships between friends and between lovers could be said to be ones in which a pure relationship is the aim.

This form of tie is said to be now permeating into family relationships. Vis-à-vis the quest for a 'pure relationship' in the family, Giddens points out that after first having taken hold between husband and wife, such an aspect has started to appear next in the parent/child relationship, as well. 'It is the quality of the relationship which comes to the fore, with a stress upon intimacy replacing that of [the] parental authoritativeness [of the past],' he argues (1992, p. 98).

Particularly in a parent/adult child relationship, the mutual connection between the parent's and child's roles is ambiguous, and

What are contemporary aspects of the parent/child relationship? 197

this therefore facilitates the emergence of ties which connect parent and child for the sake of their mutual emotional satisfaction. Among the combinations of the parent/child relationship, it is mothers and daughters, especially, who are thought to be proactively building such ties. Rather than daughters leaving their parents and going their separate ways once they have grown up to a certain extent, one can now see the sight of mothers and daughters cementing a friend-like connection with each other once more. As one example, let us examine the situation of mother/daughter pals depicted in a special feature in an information magazine.

> This relationship that has been fun, lately! 'How about going to take a breather with your mum, who is more than a friend?'
>
> We who have a busy time every day listening to long meetings and the impossible demands of our bosses – now, when we decide we want to go somewhere for a break, even if we ask a boyfriend or friend to go with us, often our schedules just don't mesh, and we end up saying, 'Next time, then.'
>
> At times like those, haven't you ever thought how nice it would be if there were somebody you could lightheartedly invite who would adjust their schedule to yours?
>
> Actually, it might be her mum close at hand who would listen to the self-serving, selfish things that such a daughter had to say. In fact, our mums are just as busy as we are, and could be expected occasionally to want to forget their housework, too, without any fuss, and take it easy (OZmagazine, no. 419, 2007).

The expression 'more than a friend' manifests a sense of the reason being that the respective parties are 'on the same wavelength' rather than 'because they are parent and child.' Here, not only the 'vertical' relationship that is parent and child, but a 'horizontal' relationship between two adults, is constructed afresh, and a parent/child relationship that is selectively and consciously constructed with emphasis on the 'quality of the connection' can be found. 'This relationship that has been fun, lately' could be called a way of being which embodies the contemporary nature of the parent and child.

What merits attention here, however, is that just because the parent/child relationship and the 'quality of the connection' are given weight, it does not follow that all parents and children will be 'good pals' and be 'close.' This emphasis on the relationship means rather that a difference of opinion on the emotional front also becomes a big problem between parent and child. Might there not be potential for subjects such as disparities in values and feelings of discomfort or empathy vis-à-vis aspects of the other party's personality, which used to become problems in the past within selectively-formed relationships such as friendships and partner relationships, to inhibit intimacy between parent and child, and invite conflict? By way of example, let us take a look at scenes from *manga* (comics) which deal with discord between a mother and daughter.

Firstly, in Scene I, a parent/child conflict situation between a daughter who is continuing to work and has no marriage prospects, and her mother, a full-time housewife, is pictured.

Figure 10.1: Scene II, on the other hand, depicts conflict between a career-woman mother and a daughter who desires a life in which she considers her family first, in reverse of Scene I.

Scenes I and II, respectively, depict how a value-gap between mother and daughter in regard to how to live as a 'woman' has given rise to conflict in the mother/daughter relationship. Nowadays, though importance has come to be attached to emotional ties in children's connection with their parents, that intimacy is specified by a variety of factors. This does not mean that those factors are determined merely by 'individual issues' like personal preference or compatibility, however. In fact, they are also prescribed by such social factors as economic circumstances. In the *manga* scenes cited above, it can be seen that a macro social situation – the diversification of women's life-courses – is influencing each separate mother/daughter connection (micro-situation).

Strong feelings on the part of each individual are involved in the parent/child relationship. With the parent/child relationship as a 'social phenomenon,' grasping its general tendencies might be considered somewhat difficult for that reason. Perhaps it might be in the spirit of 'nobody else could understand about our family, or anything like our feelings towards the family, either.' When viewed from a sociological perspective, though, some common social patterns can be found within configurations of the family and its relationships, which look to be individually different.

What is more, when a line is drawn between the public and private domains, the family is treated as belonging to the private domain – in other words, as a private matter. Yet the private and public domains actually are extremely closely interrelated. While

What are contemporary aspects of the parent/child relationship? 199

Figure 10.1: Manga scenes of parent/child relationships

Note.
Scene 1 © Nanae Haruno. Scene 2 © Satoru Makimura.

such public-domain institutions as the legal system, education system and economic situation strongly prescribe the nature of each separate family, matters which arise within each individual family also exert a great influence upon social circumstances outside the family.

For that reason, intimacy between parents and children: 1) is not limited to various individual matters, but has definite social patterns; and 2) such patterns are further related to all manner of social situations outside of the family. From here on, having first briefly organised the theory relating to parent/child intimacy, I will empirically clarify the abovementioned 'patterns' and their structure.

The absence of a framework for apprehending parent/child intimacy

Parent/child intimacy, which has been assumed

In order to understand the nature of the contemporary parent/child relationship, it has become absolutely essential to grasp the actual circumstances of intimacy in the parent/child relationship, and the factors which impact upon it. In spite of this, intimacy in the parent/child relationship itself has not been sufficiently taken up as an object of inquiry.

Though research has been conducted into family role structure and power structure in past family sociology studies, the family's emotional structure is said to have received scant handling. Commenting on such a tendency, Yamada (1999) points out that family sociology hitherto has taken as a natural assumption the proposition that 'the family is a site of affection,' and, as a result, its characteristics – which deserve explanation – have not become a target of analysis. Such a tendency can be said to be especially obvious in studies of the parent/child relationship. Within the family relationship, there have been attempts at apprehending the intimacy between husband and wife in terms of degrees of satisfaction, and progress has been made in verification of various promoting or inhibiting factors that affect the relationship. Nevertheless, there has been extremely little research that made any such attempt towards understanding or confirming the parent/child relationship.

This does not mean, though, that the intimacy between parents and children has received no attention whatsoever. 'Parent/child friendship,' for example, has been taken up since the 1970s as a term expressing a feature of the modern parent and child (Shōji 1997). There has been little research that has endeavoured to make clear what that intimacy comprises in concrete terms, or what kind of social context supports it, however, and hardly any light has been shed on its general characteristics. In Japan, one often hears such expressions as '*maza-kon* (mother complex),' or '*faza-kon* (father complex),' but in actuality even their definitions are hazy, and empirically nothing is known as to the ratios in which they might exist, whether there have been any changes along with the times, and so on (Kinoshita, 1996, p. 149). With such ambiguity of definition, and almost no clarification of the actual situation, the merits and demerits of that manner of relationship were debated; and, in consequence, critical indications that it constituted '*amae* (indulgence)' and 'dependency' occupied the mainstream.

The dearth of research on the middle-phase parent/child relationship and its importance

Due to the steep rise in post-war average life expectancy, a unique situation has arisen in which the parent/child relationship presently spans a period of more than five decades. Of those fifty-plus years, in children's early-phase parent/child relationship in infancy, and the late-phase parent/child relationship after the parents reach old age, there can be a functionally mutually-supportive relationship of unilateral care and dependence. In the other period (the middle-phase parent/child relationship), however, the kind of relationship is sought in which the parties are functionally mutually independent, and deepen their emotional interaction with each other (Masaoka 1993). 'But we still do not sufficiently understand what kind of social relationship parents and children should develop as adults, and how to achieve it' (Masaoka 1993, p. 67). In one sense, it is the middle phase of the parent/child relationship spanning the longest term, but the parent/child relationship of that period has not been made clear, and it is deemed necessary to grasp the actual situation.

Moreover, the ties in the middle phase of the parent/child relationship also establish the supportive relationship between parent and child in the late phase. According to Giddens, '[k]inship relations once used to be a taken for granted basis for trust; now trust has to be negotiated and bargained for' (1992, p. 96). Moreover, it is said that 'the clear trend of development is for [material and social] support [of ageing parents] to depend upon the quality of the relationships forged' (Giddens 1992, p. 97).

As an easily-understandable example, let us think about the care of aged parents. It used to be institutionally established that the care of parents was the 'role' of their children. Now, however, there is a strong tendency for the question of whether children will undertake the care of their parents to depend on the quality of the parent/child relationship. Is it perhaps more readily acceptable now to say: 'I *want to* care for my parents myself *because I am close* to them,' rather than: 'I *ought to* look after them *because they are my parents*'? The need to elucidate the relationship between adult children and their parents, and its background, could also be indicated from the fact that these can become the principal motivations for acceptance of support between parent and child.

Intimacy in the mother/daughter relationship and its social background

'Friendship intensifies in the relationship between mothers and daughters. The intimate mother/daughter connection in Japan is very strong' (Yamada 1997). As these words reflect, the mother/daughter relationship is pointed out as being the result of emphasis on the quality of the connection. This is because in the current situation where importance is placed on the quality of the relationship between parent and child, and a pure relationship is being sought, the most applicable relationship is considered to be that between mother and daughter.

In concrete terms, then, what factors could be conceived as the social background for such intimacy in the mother/daughter relationship? The most frequent explanation is that the psychological distance between parent and child is close, and they build an intimate connection because the mother and daughter are of the same sex.[2] It is explained that mothers and daughters come to be chums because the mother raises her daughter as her own 'alter ego' (Yamada 1997). What happens to that relationship, though, in cases where the alter ego has chosen a different way of living from the mother?

In the *manga* (Scenes I and II) shown at the beginning of the chapter, situations in which conflict arose in the parent/child relationship due to the daughter desiring a different lifestyle from her mother were depicted. Having different aspirations relating to a woman's way of living, so to speak, constitutes a factor that inhibits mother/daughter intimacy. With a focus on the conflict between daughters who reject a way of life resembling that of their mothers who have devoted themselves to their family role, and the mothers themselves, it has been pointed out in Western studies of the mother/daughter relationship that confrontation between women over women's happiness and desirable lifestyles also has a great impact upon the mother/daughter relationship.[3] In recent years, women's life-course has diversified, and there are now many cases of daughters not choosing the same sort of life-course as their mothers. Iwakami argues: 'The pattern that consisted of [children] becoming adults by emulating their parents began to crumble from the mid-1960s. The emotional impact aside, parents lost the ability to be a guideline for the way to live, in the sense of being a model to follow' (2003, p. 122). This impact is especially striking in the case of women, because a tendency for women to be more highly educated, changes in configurations of marriage such as the switch to non-marriage or delayed marriage, changes in employment behaviour such as the rise in the female labour force participation rate, and the like, have emerged since the 1980s, and women's life-course has diversified. The female way of life which was mainstream in the mothers' and daughters' generation, respectively, is vastly different, and there is thought to be high potential for that gap to have exerted an influence on the closeness of the mother/daughter relationship.

That being said, even in the current situation where women's life-course has diversified, and a values-gap is assumed to exist between mothers and daughters, the focus in Japan at present is more upon the 'intimacy' of the mother/daughter relationship rather than on its 'conflict.' Grounds envisioned for this include the parents' economic power and the mother's having time to spare (the presence of a mother who is a full-time housewife). It has been pointed out, for example, that 'a friend-like parent and child appear at a glance to be equals, but are actually in a dependent relationship consisting of uni-directional supply and consumption' (Miyamoto 2004, p. 149). Moreover, the observation that 'the expression "*ichiransei oyako* (monozygotic mother-and-daughter)" was used to indicate a mother (a full-time housewife, of course) and daughter like two peas in a pod, holding hands as they shopped at a department store in the daytime on a weekday' (Natsume 2005, p. 345) embodies the assumption that it is the full-time-housewife type of mother who becomes close to her daughter. Just as the mother who is a full-time housewife is also envisioned in the magazine excerpt cited at the beginning of this chapter, it seems that the image of the non-working mother is assumed as the background to chummy mothers and daughters.

Is the mother/daughter relationship in contemporary Japan one that is prompted by the parent's leeway in economic and time-wise terms, without regard to the shape of her life-course? In actuality, it is accepted as natural that a daughter will find it hard to mimic her mother's life-course in the first place, and the view that changes in a mother and daughter's way of living influence their intimacy has reportedly ceased to apply (Eliacheff and Heinich, 2002).

So, in the face of the impact of environmental factors such as the parent and child's respective economic situation, or their residential configuration, that is, whether they reside together or apart, are similarities and differences in their way of life no longer an issue? Or else, does the gap between their life-courses exert an influence upon the mother/daughter connection in a form that is hard to discern? From here on, in order to answer these questions, I shall conduct analysis using statistical data, and elucidate the social background of the modern mother/daughter relationship with the results.

Intimacy in the modern mother/daughter relationship and its social background, seen through data analysis

Explaining the data: the target of analysis and its characteristics

In this section, by statistically analysing quantitative data collected from a questionnaire survey, I will verify the kind of factors by which intimacy between adult unmarried females and their mothers is prescribed. Additionally, I will focus especially upon similarity in life-course aspiration[4] between mother and daughter, as a factor influencing the mother/daughter relationship.

Accordingly, in this chapter let us particularly examine and try to analyse unmarried females in their twenties, who seem often to be discussed in terms of 'mothers and daughters as friends.' For unmarried women in their twenties, the connection with parents is said to be a condition of 'semi-dependence/semi-autonomy' (Miyamoto 2004). In this period, translating prospects for the life-course they are about to follow into reality becomes a huge issue. At the same time, this issue makes them aware of the similarity or difference between the mother's life-course and the daughter's own life-course aspirations, and is thought to exert a strengthening or weakening influence upon the closeness of the mother/daughter relationship in this period. According to whether the mother has already pursued the life-course that the daughter herself considers desirable, or has followed a completely different one, differences might arise in the daughter's way of relating to her mother, might they not?

The survey data used for analysis derives from part of a series of surveys entitled *Shōshi/kōreika shakai ni okeru seijin oyako kankei no raifukōsuteki kenkyū: nijūdai–gojūdai chōsa* (Life-course research on adult parent/child relationships in a society with low fertility and an ageing population: a survey of [people in their] twenties to fifties).[5] The data is taken from a survey conducted in 2001, targeting males and females aged twenty to twenty-nine years residing in Fuchū City in metropolitan Tokyo.[6] Fuchū City is a medium-sized municipality with a population of about 200,000, and was chosen as the kind of place that would represent a residential area in the so-called suburbs of Tokyo. Out of the data as a whole, females are the sole object of actual analysis here, and I have also excluded students on the rationale that they would complicate our grasp of economic circumstances. In short, I take 217 women aged twenty to twenty-nine years, excluding students, as my target sample for analysis.

Prior to the analysis, let us confirm what manner of life-course was the mainstream in the targets' mothers' generation, and how it has changed since then. The birth year of the unmarried women in their twenties who comprise the current target was between 1972 and 1981, with the birth year of approximately sixty percent of their mothers falling between 1940 and 1949, and about forty percent in 1950 or later. Many in the mothers' generation were Japan's so-called 'baby boomers' (born between 1947 and 1950), a generation in which 'housewifisation' advanced to the greatest degree. Presumably, 'the bottom of the M-curve became deeper and deeper until the baby-boomer generation, then has risen in the subsequent generations,' (Ochiai 2001, p. 18). Moreover, if we look at life-courses involving employment, while the career-interruption-and-re-employment type has become the general rule, the continuous-employment type, also, has increased little by little (Andō 2003). On the other hand, the life-course deemed ideal by women has also changed dramatically since the beginning of the 1990s. The re-employment aspiration persists, but the aspiration to become a full-time housewife, which had the highest ratio in the late 1980s, has fallen to bottom place, while the continuous-employment ratio is on an upward trend (Kokuritsu Shakai Hoshō/Jinkō Mondai Kenkyūjo 2004). In such circumstances, it should be clear that it is by no means rare for daughters' preferred life-course to diverge from that of their mothers.

How close are mothers and daughters?

The initial problematic issue when verifying the factors that prescribe intimacy in the mother/daughter relationship is the question of how to measure 'intimacy' and apprehend its degree, in the first place. Though it is a tricky problem, let us first try to understand intimacy in the mother/daughter relationship from the perspective of 'interaction,' namely the frequency of communication between mother and daughter.

In the following description, which sketches the image of a close parent/child relationship between an unmarried adult woman and her mother, two configurations of interaction are cited as manifestations of intimacy.

> Reciprocal confidences on the most intimate subjects, mutual advice and assistance of the utmost seriousness or triviality, the maintenance of contact on an everyday basis (or even more often...) without any hidden secrets, going on shopping trips together and swapping clothes: nowadays, these mothers and daughters appear to be permanent accomplices, progressively erasing all generational differences (Eliacheff and Heinich 2002, p. 386).

If we look at this description, companionate activity centring upon consumption behaviour, and dependency in emotional and informational aspects, are taken up as manifestations of intimacy. These two kinds of interaction have been adopted as indicators showing the intimacy of relationships in research into social support and the like (including Nishimura et al. 2000). In the analysis in this chapter, taking these prior studies into account, I measure the intimacy of mother/daughter relationships from the two aspects of 1) frequency of synchronous action[7] and 2) emotional closeness.

Firstly, in the case of 1) frequency of synchronous action, I employ the total frequency of the five categories of action with the mother: 'conversation (including on the telephone),' 'shopping,' 'eating out,' 'travel' and 'hobbies.' I score the responses 'never,' 'rarely,' 'sometimes' and 'often' in order from zero to three. Moreover, with the current data, when I divided the results of scoring into a low group with less than the mean value, and a high group with greater than the mean, I found that 52.1 percent corresponded to the high group.

Next, in regard to 2) emotional closeness, I ascertained whether each of the following was applicable to the mother, giving a zero for 'No' or one for 'Yes' for each item, and used the total score of the five categories: 'She is someone who listens to my worries,' 'She is someone who understands my feelings and thoughts,' 'She is someone who values my ability and effort,' 'She is someone with whom I can have an enjoyable time,' and 'She is someone who gives me suggestions and advice.' When I again tried dividing those with a score lower than the mean value into the low group, and those with a higher score into the high group, 45.1 percent corresponded to the latter in regard to emotional closeness.

Factors that can influence mother/daughter intimacy

Similarity or difference in life-course
The most important factor (explanatory variable) that exerts an impact upon intimacy is the intergenerational gap between mothers and daughters surrounding the female way of life. I apprehend this by means of the similarity or difference between the daughter's life-course aspirations and the life-course actually followed by her mother. In concrete terms, I ascertain it by combining questions[8] about the ideal life-course and the mother's life-course. I understood the life-course that women in their twenties deemed ideal in future in terms of four types, as follows: 'Non-married employment (continuing work all their lives without marrying),' 'DINKS (marrying, but not having children, and continuing work all their lives),' 'Continuous-employment type (marrying and having children, but continuing work all their lives),' 'Re-employment type (marrying and having children, but retiring temporarily upon marriage or childbirth, and having a job again after child-rearing),' and 'Full-time-housewife type (marrying and having children, retiring upon marriage or childbirth, and not having a job thereafter).' I further

ascertained the life-course actually pursued by the mother by means of the three types: 'Continuous-employment type,' 'Re-employment type' and 'Full-time-housewife type,' and apprehended both in combination. The combinations are as in Table 10.1.

Environmental factors
In addition to variables relating to the life-course, I take up the following five environmental factors as factors (explanatory variables) that can influence intimacy: 'Annual income of the individual in question (under 300 million yen/ ≥ 300 million yen),' 'Parental life circumstances (1 Very badly-off; 2 Somewhat badly-off; 3 Average; 4 Comparatively well-off; 5 Extremely well-off,' 'Living with parents or not (1 living apart; 2 living with parents),' 'Mother's current occupation full-time housewife or not (1 full-time housewife; 0 not),' and 'Age[9] of the individual in question.'

What specifies intimacy?
Next, in order to see which out of all the factor variables has strong impact, I carried out analysis using a method of multivariate analysis called logistic regression analysis,[10] the results being as in Table 10.2. That table shows which kind of variable exerts an influence upon synchronous action and emotional intimacy, respectively. Moreover, the numeric value shown beside each factor variable is its 'odds ratio.' When the odds ratio is greater than one, it expresses a positive effect, but a negative effect when less than one. In other words, when it is greater than one, it indicates that synchronous acts and emotional intimacy intensify according to the applicable variable. This means that the nearer the odds ratio is to one, the smaller the influence of the relevant variable will be.

In the above Table 10.2, firstly, in Model 1, I have examined the impact of various factors such as whether the child resides with parents or apart, or the parents' economic circumstances, which constitute environmental factors. Next, in Model 2, I verify not only the environmental factors, but also the influence exerted by a match or mismatch between a daughter's life-course aspirations and her mother's life-course, as well. Further, in Models 3 and 4, I am looking at the impact exerted not only by a simple life-course match or mismatch, but by combinations within them. In Model 3, I have confirmed which of the combinations among the matches has the most impact, and which one out of the mismatches in Model 4.

Table 10.1: Combinations of daughters' ideal life-course and mother's life-course (% of total)

	Daughter's ideal life-course			
	Non-married & DINKS	Continuous-employment type	Re-employment type	Full-time-housewife type
Mother's life-course				
Continuous-employment type	1.3	12.7	9.1	2.0
Re-employment type	3.0	16.2	24.4	7.1
Full-time-housewife type	3.6	5.6	11.7	3.0

Shading represents congruence (Sum total 40.1%)

Non-shading represents non-congruence (Sum total 59.9%)

Table 10.3 is a summary paraphrasing the results of the analysis in Table 10.2.

What could be indicated from the above analysis results? Firstly, in the current analysis, it was shown that the relationship differs according to what is employed to measure intimacy. The relevance of the intergenerational gap in regard to women's way of life to the closeness of the mother/daughter relationship has been construed in various ways, but the social background differed according to the aspect from which intimacy was measured.

When intimacy was measured in terms of synchronous acts, similarity with the mother in life-course aspirations had no relevance. Of relevance were environmental factors such as the economic situation on the part of both parent and child, and whether the child lived together with parents, or separately. Furthermore, in addition to physical distance from parents, when there was leeway in parental life circumstances, or when the daughter's annual income was low, connections through synchronous acts had strengthened. In other words, the economic circumstances of both parent and child had an influence on the frequency of synchronous acts. If we limit ourselves to the aspect of synchronous acts, it can be argued that the situation of children's economic dependency upon their parents surely is supporting mother/daughter intimacy.

On the other hand, emotional closeness between mother and daughter is scarcely affected by whether they live together or apart, or their economic background. What greatly prescribed emotional intimacy was similarity or difference between mother and daughter

Table 10.2: Determining factors in synchronous action and emotional intimacy

	Synchronous action				Emotional intimacy			
	Model 1 Exp(B)	Model 2 Exp(B)	Model 3 Exp(B)	Model 4 Exp(B)	Model 1 Exp(B)	Model 2 Exp(B)	Model 3 Exp(B)	Model 4 Exp(B)
Environmental factors								
Age	1.25[b]	1.26[b]	1.26[b]	1.27[b]	1.04ns	1.06ns	1.06ns	1.07ns
Individual's annual income (<¥3 mill. = 0; ≥ = 1)	0.48[d]	0.45[c]	0.45[c]	0.43[c]	0.64ns	0.64ns	0.64ns	0.61ns
Parent(s) life circumstances	1.60[c]	1.65[b]	1.70[b]	1.72[c]	1.62[c]	1.47[d]	1.51[d]	1.54[c]
Living with parent(s)	2.49[b]	2.52[b]	2.62[b]	2.68[b]	1.19ns	1.46ns	1.45ns	1.54ns
Mother's occupation: full-time housewife dummy	0.89ns				0.50[c]			
Ideal life-course and mother's life-course								
Ideal life-course same as mother's (Same = 1; diff. = 0)		1.33ns				3.18[a]		
Both continuous-employment type			1.52ns				2.39[d]	
Both re-employment type			1.40ns				3.66[b]	
Both full-time housewife type			0.58ns				2.85ns	
(Reference: both continuous-employment)								
Only mother full-time housewife type				0.54ns				0.17[a]
Only mother re-employment type				1.16ns				0.34[b]
Only mother continuous-employment type				0.52[b]				0.57ns
(Reference: same as mother's life-course)								
Model chi-square	22.21[b]	23.03[b]	24.00[b]	26.64[b]	10.41[d]	19.64[b]	20.24[b]	24.693[b]
–2 log likelihood	232.517	235.943	234.966	232.333	243.271	239.617	239.020	234.567
N	184	187	187	187	184	188	188	188

Note. a: < 0.001; b: < 0.01; c: < 0.05; d: < 0.1.

Table 10.3: Summary of results of analysis

	Synchronous action	**Emotional intimacy**
Parental financial leeway	Frequency increases commensurate with improvement in parental life circumstances	Intimacy increases commensurate with improvement in parental life circumstances
Child's own state of economic dependence	Frequency rises the lower the child's annual income	No connection
Mother's amount of free time	No connection	Intimacy weakens in cases where mother is a full-time housewife
Living together or apart from parent(s)	Frequency high if living together with parent(s).	No connection
Affinity between life-course aspiration and mother's life-course	No connection	Intimacy increases in cases of affinity with mother's life-course

in life-course aspirations. The result obtained was that when a daughter's life-course aspirations were the same as her mother's life-course, emotional intimacy intensified.

Frequent shared engagement in shopping trips or travel are often pointed out as indications of mother/daughter intimacy. In short, as their closeness is often apprehended by the frequency of their synchronous acts, even if a situation should arise in which it would be hard to make the mother into a life-course model, mother/daughter intimacy appears not to have been influenced at all. When intimacy is grasped from the aspect of emotional closeness, however, it will be understood that intergenerational similarity or difference around the life-course certainly does exert an impact upon the intimacy of the mother/daughter relationship. In order also to avoid falling into a stereotyped interpretation, there is arguably a necessity to clarify which aspects of the relationship are influenced by the various factors.

Similarity between mother and daughter in life-course aspirations and emotional intimacy

Why might similarity with the mother in terms of life-course aspirations fortify emotional intimacy? The fact that the mother has already pursued a life-course that the daughter regards as ideal leads to a commonality of values with the mother, and her proving dependable as a guide. It could be understood that emotional intimacy rises as a result. When a daughter's aspirations and her mother's life-course are both of the continuous-employment or re-employment type, emotional intimacy is strong in comparison to other cases.[11]

On the other hand, when a daughter is thinking she does not want to be like her mother, it is envisioned that she will harbour negative feelings towards her mother. When we look at the impact which a gap between the mother's life-course and her daughter's life-course aspirations exerts upon emotional intimacy, intimacy is seen to weaken when the mother alone is the full-time-housewife or re-employment type. When only the mother is of the continuous-employment type, no connection is seen with emotional intimacy. It tends to be thought that mothers who are full-time housewives readily become close to their children, and their children, too, easily become dependent upon their mother, due to the time the mother has to spare. In the analysis in this chapter, however, a completely opposite result was obtained. In cases where only the mother was the full-time-housewife or re-employment type, the situation is considered to have arisen where the daughter whose ideal is continuing to work has difficulty in making her mother her model, or mentally relying upon her, because the mother quit or interrupted her job.[12]

By contrast, even in similar cases where life-course aspirations diverge from the mother's life-course, when combined with the mother alone being the continuous-employment type, that difference did not have a weakening influence upon intimacy. A plausible reason for this could be that the figure of a mother who continues to work is likely to be positively appraised by her adult daughter. Even if she does not become a life-course model, a mother who has taken on a workforce role is probably a reliable presence for her daughter. This is a result which implies that a mother who is continuing to play a role in the workforce is more readily felt to be dependable in both emotional and informational aspects than one who, in the absence of a workforce role, devotes herself to her role within the home – in short, to looking after her own children, their father, and others. In the case where only the mother is the re-employment type, it can also be said that she is taking on a workforce role, unlike the full-time-housewife type. Nonetheless, the way she shoulders her workforce role can be considered perhaps to lack the positive appraisal given to the continuous-employment type. With the re-employment type of mother, it often happens that her employment status upon re-employment is an unstable one such as contract worker, despatch worker or part-timer. Fujiwara (1981) states that when the mother has a part-time job or similar, she cannot expect to try to improve herself, equip herself with a sense of responsibility or confidence, or find joy through working. For that reason, Fujiwara argues, it is hard for the figure of a mother who is exhausted every day, pursued by housework, to be an affirmative model vis-à-vis social advancement as far as her daughter is concerned. From a daughter's perspective, the continuous-employment type and re-employment type are life-courses of a different nature, and for a daughter who aspires to be a continuous-employment type, the life-course of a mother of re-employment type is unlikely to appear to be a desirable way of working.

The point which must be noted, however, is that when the daughter herself is also of the re-employment type, even if her mother is following a re-employment type of life-course, their emotional intimacy is robust. The reason that comes to mind for this kind of discrepancy to arise is that there are different frameworks for acknowledgement and appraisal of a mother's re-employment type of life-course depending on whether the daughter also has re-employment aspirations.

Various aspects of the mother/daughter relationship: for consideration of current and future parent/child relations

The 'pure relationship' which has the sole aim of an emotional tie with another, rather than connecting for the sake of fulfilment of some sort of role, has traditionally been thought to be one applicable only to friendships formed by choice, and the like. The parent/child relationship, on the other hand, is a non-selective relation systematically established by blood ties or by law. For that reason, it has been recognised as a relationship in which the mutual fulfilment of set roles is vital. As such, in the traditional view of the family, the emotional tie between parent and child was an incidental one. In the present day, however, the formation of the parent/child relationship is also centred on an emotional connection, giving rise to selective aspects based on the quality of such a connection. This point is particularly obvious after the child reaches adulthood, when the role relation becomes ambiguous, and we are confronted by the hitherto non-existent issue of 'how to build the parent/child relationship as mature adults.'

Even so, the actual situation of intimacy between parent and child has scarcely been elucidated. Even in the 'parent/child friendship' discourse, which encouraged lively debate focusing on parent/child intimacy, a strange situation continued in which judgement on its pros and cons was made without the actual state of affairs being made clear, as stated in Yamada (1997):

> People each imagine something different when they hear the expression 'parent/child friendship.' One person might bring to mind the figure of a father playing catch-ball with his primary-school-aged son, while someone else might imagine a grownup daughter and her mother going shopping together, clad in matching outfits. As for its evaluation, while there are some people who welcome [such friendship], interpreting it as liberation from the authoritarian parent/child relationship of old, there are also some who lament, citing it as evidence that parents have grown irresponsible, having themselves become infantilised.

A parent/child relationship which emphasises the emotional tie with the other party breeds a friend-like intimacy. Yet this also gives rise to conflict stemming from a difference in values. The pursuit of a 'pure relationship' in a husband-and-wife relationship, while enhancing the affectionate connection between wife and husband on the one hand, is said to have 'brought on the social phenomenon of divorce among the middle-aged and older, and the practice of *de facto* marriage' (Miyasaka 2000). Likewise, the parent/child relationship, while carrying the risk of relationship breakdown, is thought to be building intimacy.

In order to ponder the future of the parent/child relationship, it is first necessary to grasp what kind of social background supports the emotional connection comprising intimacy between parents and children, and how it influences that connection. As part of that research, in this chapter, I examined the social background of intimacy in the mother/daughter relationship. The results imply that the parent's and child's economic circumstances are an underlying factor in parent/child intimacy, and that intergenerational differences to do with the female life-course contribute to the inhibition of intimacy.

Women's life-course has diversified, and women have become able to choose their own life. Might that have caused conflict to arise due to variation in life-courses among different women, though? One often hears tales of full-time housewives and single career women feeling that they are at cross-purposes in their friendship. This is probably because acknowledging the happiness of a woman who has chosen a life different from one's own can shake one's confidence in one's own choice.

This kind of thing can also emerge between a mother and daughter. There may be some people who think that such conflict is unlikely to occur even between friends, let alone between parent and child. The relationship between parent and child tends to be considered a robust one that would not change under any circumstances. In Japan, in particular, as there is a strong tendency to regard the affection between parent and child as sacred, there arguably would be a reluctance to acknowledge that the parent/child relationship would change due to the social situation, and at times be burdened with discord.

In addition, it might be difficult to accept that the parent/child connection is influenced by such so-called pragmatic conditions as women's working environment or the economic power of parent and child. If we think on the basis of the results of the current analysis, however, synchronous action that included consumption behaviour outside the home was impacted by the financial situation of both mother and daughter, and so on. In other words, if there is a change in socio-economic circumstances – especially those of the parent's generation – then the relationship can be expected to change in response. As a result, a class disparity might also influence the intimacy between parent and child, for example. Moreover, changes in the working environment for women are anticipated to have an impact upon each individual mother/daughter relationship. To sum up, there is call for a renewed understanding of the contemporary parent/child relationship from the perspectives of what kind of influence macro social circumstances exert upon parent-and-child intimacy, and what sort of risk and potential can be envisioned.

Notes

1 E. W. Burgess and H. J. Locke have offered the following explanation for the family as having moved 'from institution to companionship': 'The family in historical times has been in transition from an institution with family behaviour controlled by the mores, public opinion, and law to a

companionship with family behaviour arising from the mutual affection and consensus of its members' (1945, p. 22).

2 This assertion is made based on Freud's psychoanalytic theory. One work which developed its argument with focus on the distinctiveness of the mother/daughter relationship is Nancy Chodorow's *The Reproduction of Mothering* (1978).

3 This is also dealt with in Japanese feminism studies (such as Mizuta), but, perhaps due to a lack of familiarity with psychoanalysis used as a methodology, it appears generally not well-known.

4 When analysing life-course awareness in terms of the kind of life-course women consider desirable, either the 'ideal' or the 'anticipated' life-course, or both, are frequently employed. Iwasawa (1999) calls these two types of life-course awareness by the generic term of 'life-course projection.' In this chapter, as I deal only with the life-course deemed 'ideal,' I use the expression 'life-course aspiration' to differentiate the term from Iwasawa's. Forthwith, in this chapter, I will call the 'ideal' life-course 'life-course aspiration.'

5 This survey, as representative of studies by Professor Mami Iwakami of Seishin (Sacred Heart) Women's University, forms part of survey research made possible by receipt of a 2001–2004 Fiscal Year Monbukagakushō (Ministry of Education, Culture, Sports, Science and Technology) Grant-in-Aid for Scientific Research (Basic Research Project no. 13410062). The survey research constituting its matrix, which aimed to elucidate the actual condition of separation and dependence between unmarried adult children and their parents, involved sampling surveys in both Fuchū City and Matsumoto City, targeting unmarried males and females in their twenties, and males and females in their fifties who were assumed to represent the parents' generation, as well as interview surveys targeting females and males in their fifties in both districts.

6 The sampling involved carrying out stratified sub-sampling by means of the Basic Resident Register, and selecting 1500 samples. The survey was conducted by a structured questionnaire, using the householder method of delivery and collection, over the period from 19 September to 2 October 2001. Completed surveys numbered 620, and the response rate was 41.3 percent.

7 In the survey, the term 'synchronous action' was employed to mean action which shared the same time, space and interests.

8 The question posed in regard to the ideal life-course was: 'What type of life do you think is ideal?' and that relating to the mother's life-course was: 'What type of life is your mother's?'

9 As there is a tendency for a subject's annual income to rise in tandem with age, even supposing it were to emerge that the subject's annual income affected intimacy, it would be difficult to discern whether that was the result of the annual income *per se*, or that the effect of age had appeared indirectly. Accordingly, in order to make the direct effect of the subject's annual income more visible, we control subjects' age when carrying out analysis.

10 Multivariate analysis refers to a method which enables the simultaneous analysis of the influence of three or more variables. There are several variations, but in this case I employ one called logistic regression analysis,

a statistical method for estimating the likelihood that an event constituting a result (an explained variable) will occur. In this chapter's analysis, by clarifying the influence of the respective primary factor variables, namely, to what extent they increase or decrease the probability of intimacy with the mother, I statistically examine the primary factors which exert an influence upon mother/daughter intimacy.

11 Perhaps because there was an extremely small number of cases in which the ideal life-course and mother's life-course were both 'full-time housewife,' it is considered that no influence was recognised.

12 This includes cases of combinations in which only the mother was of the re-employment type, and the daughter was of the full-time-housewife type, but this kind of interpretation is possible because the proportion of daughters with full-time-housewife aspirations where their mothers were of the re-employment type was less than one tenth (of the total percentage), as shown in Figure 10.2.

11 Is 'poverty' or 'affluence' the reality?: towards consideration of 'living in the regions'

Hisashi Fujii

Japanese people do not live solely in 'Tokyo' or the 'Metropolitan Area (*shutoken*).' If we view everywhere apart from the Metropolitan Area' as being 'regional,' then more than half of the total population of Japan will be living in 'the regions (*chihō*).' Yet whatever does it mean to 'live in the regions'? Though 'the regions' are sometimes used in conventional sociology as material with which to interrogate the 'centre' and the 'whole,' 'an existence lived in the regions' has not directly been made an issue. In this chapter, while taking up two works by the *manga* writer Naoki Yamamoto, *Furagumentsu* (Fragments) and *YOUNG & FINE*, which depict the diverse feelings of people who live in provincial areas, I endeavour to consider 'what it is to live one's existence in the regions.' The key to this will be the question of whether people with a regional livelihood can employ the 'poverty' or 'affluence' they find as a resource for living vis-à-vis the reality they confront. Moreover, I wish to show readers four basic structural patterns for 'an existence lived in the regions,' pivoting around ways of responding to that issue.

'Living in the regions'

Whatever does it mean to 'live in the regions'? This is altogether too vague a question. Is it not true, though, that not enough direct consideration has been given in sociology to the facts of 'living in the regions' to prompt the posing of such a question? At least, that is how it appears to me, someone who has lived for two-thirds of his life in a regional area, including at the present moment. Of course, there are likely to be counter-arguments to this assertion, saying that sociology has an abundant accumulation of research that has been conducted on regional culture and local culture.

However, even when I look through a book straightforwardly entitled *The Sociology of Regional Culture* (Aiba ed. 1998), for example, I get the impression that the content somehow misses the point, based on what I perceive daily in my life in a provincial area. By way of experiment, let me cite part of the 'Preface' from the same volume.

> The regions still have the leeway to function severally as sites for various cultures to exist. Even supposing they have changed in the direction of uniformity in modes of living, that tendency, further hampered by diverse lifestyles, has not been strong enough to tear regional cultural values from their roots. Conversely, one could argue that a situation where culture has been unilaterally disseminated is an opportunity for the regions to adopt it in a positive manner, using it to their advantage for the creation of an open cultural system, in order to shape it in a direction useful to the invigoration of their locality. One might add that, having made full use of that chance as a task for generating a unique culture, regions harbour the potential to become competitive and transform it into an opportunity to transmit culture to counteract the centre. Research that delves into the burgeoning of 'cultural transmission from the regions to the centre' ultimately arrives at the issue of re-interrogating the state of the whole from the periphery, namely, 'what is central culture?' (Aiba ed. 1998, pp. ii–iii).

In this book, a number of sociologists are indeed seeking material in 'the regions,' but their objective lies in 're-interrogating the state of the whole from the periphery.' Moreover, for that reason, analysis has been conducted by sociologists from such various angles as 'government and regional culture,' 'life in rural villages and regional culture,' 'development of leisure/sports and regional culture,' or 'regional culture and local government,' to name a few examples. Naturally, this does not mean that there is anything wrong with such writings, yet I feel dissatisfied with their lack of perspective on what people think, and what problems they face due to their dwelling in 'the regions,' in a place that is 'different' from 'Tokyo,' for instance – in other words, a perspective relating to the 'existence' of people who live in 'the regions.'

At the present point in time, it is difficult to find a connection between drawing up what people living in 'the regions' vaguely or deeply feel amid their lives day to day, and trying to 're-question the state of Japan as a whole,' using 'the regions' seen from the viewpoint of 'the city (more or less Tokyo)' as material. I suggest, however, that the majority of conventional sociological discourse belongs to the latter category, to a greater or lesser extent.

Are the regions 'affluent' or 'poor'?

Regional 'poverty'

Under such circumstances, a book entitled *Fasuto fūdoka suru Nihon: kōgaika to sono byōri* (Japan attuning to a 'fast-food-like' culture: suburbanisation and its pathology) was published in autumn 2004, attracting much comment. Its author was Atsushi Miura, a critic with such best-sellers as *Low Society*, and whose career also includes having been the chief editor of a marketing information magazine in the past. Let me first introduce the drift of the argument in its concluding portion, below.

> Originally, there were numerous cities and rural villages which, though small, had individuality. Those cities and rural villages had traditions, merchants, artisans and farmers, and had real livelihoods. For the past twenty years, however, regional cities have been clamouring to make a Tokyo-like commercial environment. For that reason, in every corner of the regions, while on the one hand farmland which is cheap and has simple rights-relations has undergone development and the central business districts have decayed, roadsides have conversely started to bristle with commercial facilities. Now, the scene is more thoroughly suburban than the Tokyo suburbs. However, though there are objects in roadside commercial facilities, there is no life. Colourless and transparent consumer society, which has no connection with daily life, overflows with excessively mass-produced goods, and the sense of something being unique and irreplaceable is lost. As such, streets and jobs and lives, too – all that ought to be real – have become virtual reality, and love for real things, or real love for things, is hard to cultivate. If one looks at the things overflowing within such a virtual space, even life itself will be perceived as a thing that will be discarded when there is an excess of it, in the same way as a mass-produced article. It is imperative to halt the progress of suburbanisation which foments crime, to sense the real as real; and the site of daily life that

we experience must be reinstated. That is an issue for people, and an issue for children, too (Miura 2004, pp. 205–7).

The reason for my focus on Miura's book is that I think it touches upon one fragment of something the inhabitants probably sense from the dreary 'regional' landscape spreading before their eyes, typified by commercial facilities lining the roadsides and a decaying central business district. While Miura's argument itself is crude, its rarity has far from trivial significance in that it deals face-on with issues relating to the existence of people who live in 'the regions.'

As can also be understood from the above book's subtitle, 'Suburbanisation and its Pathology,' the wellspring of the argument to be seen here was the 'suburban discourse (*kōgai ron*)' which came to be discussed prolifically from the mid-1990s onwards.[1] *Fasuto fūdoka suru Nihon* directly extends the various points of argument in the suburban discourse to 'the regions,' such as the homogenisation of landscape, loss of the concrete feel of unique local qualities and lifestyles, and unruly roadside development; and it stands on the recognition that under the economic principles blanketing Japan today, there is no qualitative disparity between 'the suburbs' and 'the regions.' For Miura, the 'suburbs = regions' are already a site where arbitrary development that follows economic principles and the undesirable effects it causes become problematic, and, frankly speaking, they are 'poor' places which have lost things that could be discussed in their own terms (of course, what is meant here by 'poor' is not an issue of economics, but refers consistently to those provincial circumstances expounded by Miura as lacking what in his mind are positive elements). In addition, albeit imperfectly, Miura has gone so far as to address the issue of what kind of impact such a 'poor' place exerts upon the existence of the people who live there, though there is arguably a conspicuous simplification with an eye to marketing. By means of the volume in question, a perspective that problematised 'human existence lived in the place called the regions' perhaps achieved wide social recognition at long last.

Regional 'affluence'

This is not to suggest that the aforementioned perspective had not been present in and around sociology prior to *Fasuto fūdoka suru Nihon*. As far as I can see, one of the rare discussants to have presented an argument with a similarly extensive scope was Shinji Miyadai, though it could be said that his assertions did not have the same universality as *Fasuto fūdo*. Next, let me introduce below a summary of the points made in a text entitled 'The telephone-dating-club girls of Aomori,' contained in Miyadai's *Maboroshi no kōgai* (The illusionary suburbs), published in 1997.

> A man in his thirties whom I interviewed in Aomori told me the following story. When he summoned a girl from a telephone-based dating club, one from a certain university-entrance-oriented high school turned up, and as she said she was 'in a foul mood,' they then enjoyed 'relations like romantic lovers' in accordance with her wishes. Just as they were parting, when he asked: 'What are you going to do now?' the girl replied: 'I'm going to study for exams until dawn.' When he handed her five thousand yen, saying: 'It's tough to be taking the entrance exams for a university in Tokyo. Buy yourself some supper or something with this,' the girl reportedly left him with the final words: 'I'll be able to knuckle down now because I feel refreshed. Thanks hugely. See you again somewhere!' This kind of experience seems not to be unusual in Aomori. Simply because the two of them are persevering in the same Aomori, something that 'resonates' with the high-school girl recurs in the heart of the middle-aged fellow. In that manner, soon after the pair of strangers have met, even without any weighty conversation, they share 'quality time' and say a cheery farewell – in telephone-dating clubs in the Tokyo vicinity, where there is no longer anything that strangers can share without the mediation of words, such communication has of course become extinct (Miyadai 1997, pp. 43–5).

According to Miyadai, 'This is not something unique to Aomori, but can be said of any regional city.' In such a place, because 'what people share from the start is large, even without words,' everyone appears with 'their face unadorned.' If it were Tokyo, as the other person would be a 'dangerous being' whose identity was unknown, each of them would cloak themselves in a package labelled 'high-school girl' or 'cute sugar-daddy,' and 'meet only within a "symbolic" fantasy.' Miyadai states that he 'feels it is a fairly bizarre thing,' in an utterly different realm from moral rights and wrongs (1997, p. 45).

What I focus upon here is not a phenomenon as highly likely to arouse curiosity as a 'provincial telephone-dating service' or an 'Aomori high-school girl.' Rather, it is the fact that by using a telephone-dating club and high-school girls as clues, Miyadai has divined that there is some kind of heterogeneity lying between 'an existence lived in Tokyo' and 'an existence lived in the regions,' and moreover that this seems to derive from the effect of the very place called 'the regions.' In *Fasuto fūdoka suru Nihon*, Miura showed 'the regions' as a 'poor' place with nothing that could be discussed in terms other than of unregulated development and the negative impact it caused. On the other hand, in 'The telephone-dating-club girls of Aomori,' Miyadai suggests in regard to 'the regions' that it is sometimes possible for 'mutual strangers to share "quality time" not long after they meet, even without conversation of any importance' – in other words, for Miyadai, there exists some kind of desirability that is qualitatively different from both 'Tokyo' and 'the suburbs' – one might venture to say the soil to support some kind of 'affluence.'[2] Of course, that indeterminate 'affluence' is merely one that just happened to be observed by Miyadai from the window comprising a 'telephone-dating club,' and has no direct connection either with telephone-dating clubs themselves, nor high-school girls.

What needs to be questioned?

The disparity between Miura and Miyadai, at the most basic level, concerns whether there is some kind of uniqueness about the place called 'the regions.' Miura concludes that in the current circumstances, there is no such thing; and, further, gives a negative assessment to its 'non-existence.' Miyadai, on the other hand, finds a kind of uniqueness peculiar to 'the regions,' and refers to it in positive terms. To me, actually living in a regional area, however, feelings come to mind that clash with both Miura and Miyadai, but which I frequently encounter, namely that 'no uniqueness exists any more, and that in itself is desirable,' and/or 'there certainly is some sort of uniqueness, but it is something disagreeable.'

In the actual regions, it is doubtless still often the case that no positive meaning is perceived in the 'real lifestyle' underpinned by their native history, the situation where the living environment becoming 'more suburban than the Tokyo suburbs' (Miura 2004,

p. 26) in itself is being felt to be the attainment of affluence. What is more, there is definitely the feeling in regional areas that having no choice but to meet on a one-to-one basis as flesh-and-blood human beings, without the ability to cloak oneself airily in a 'fantasy package' as in Tokyo, is not something that leads to what Miyadai terms '*nōmitsu-na jikan* (quality time),' but to the hopeless poverty and barrenness of the rural areas. There is nothing special about the perception that the very uniqueness which lingers in 'the regions' is an unpleasant 'poverty,' and that losing it, and various scenes in everyday life being encoded to Tokyo standard or even higher, means heading in the direction of 'affluence.'

If this is the case, then even in Miura's and Miyadai's arguments, there are only limited points of contact for the people who actually inhabit 'the regions' – at least, one must admit that there is no common ground except for certain people who share the same value judgement.[3] Ultimately, especially if that represents the spread that is 'the regions,' then it means merely that there are enormous numbers of people who are by turns dissatisfied or satisfied with the various circumstances confronting them. If we are to attempt to think of an argument that has broader and deeper relevance to 'an existence lived in the regions,' which is the topic of this chapter, then it will be necessary to depart from the type of problem-setting that restricts the points of contact, such as 'indications of (a lack of) uniqueness' or 'evaluation of the same,' and to raise the level of abstraction.

For that purpose, in this chapter I wish to adopt the perspective of questioning whether the reality faced by people living in provincial areas is 'projected' in their field of vision as 'something poor,' or as 'something affluent.'

Taking up some phenomenon in the regions and assessing somebody as 'affluent/poor' is basically a different matter from people living their lives in regional areas 'seeing' 'affluence/poverty' in regard to the reality before their very eyes. The former depends upon the discussant's choice of examples and the presence or absence of empathy towards value judgements – what will be deemed 'affluent/poor,' by what criterion – but 'seeing' 'affluence/poverty' in a reality is not something unrelated, as far as anyone is concerned. Rather, perceiving reality positively ('seeing affluence') or perceiving it negatively ('seeing poverty') is the most fundamental activity in giving direction to the state of one's own existence. Moreover, with that basic activity as a starting-point, certain behaviours are triggered in response to conditions. That being the case, one thinks of what kind of patterns these have – if one sets such questions, then it will become possible, I suggest, to achieve some distance from specific choices of example and value judgements that rely on theorists, and have a more general discussion.

As such, from the next section onwards, as material which exemplifies patterns of behaviour that 'living in the regions' establishes in response to immediate reality, I would like to take up two works by the *manga* artist Naoki Yamamoto, set in a 'regional area' (Hokkaido): the first volume of *Fragments* (hereafter denoted as *Fragments I*) (Yamamoto 1997) and *YOUNG & FINE: umibe no machi de bokura wa nakayoshi datta ka* (Were we pals in the seaside town?) (Yamamoto [1992] 1997). Below are the two reasons for my choice.

Naoki Yamamoto is a *manga* artist born in 1960, who hails from Fukushima (unrelated to the *tsunami*-affected Fukushima, on Honshu) in Matsumae County, Hokkaido, a town with a population of only just over five thousand, at the tip of the Oshima Peninsula. Apart from 'Naoki Yamamoto,' Yamamoto also has the pen names of 'Tō Moriyama' and 'Mori Tōyama.' After graduating from lower secondary school, he attended upper secondary in Hakodate, and went on to a university in Tokyo. Since then, he has continued his creative activities in Tokyo.

From his early works to his current newest work, *Red* (Yamamoto 2007–), a feature which frequently appears in his *manga* is that his characters harbour some sort of 'excessive feelings.' These include, for example, sexual desire, destructive urges, vague feelings of emptiness, mixtures of reality and delusion, the notion of 'revolution,' and so on, or sometimes compounds of these. Furthermore, in several works, including his *Fragments I* and *YOUNG & FINE*, characters do not stop merely at 'harbouring excessive feelings,' but personally end up having a reflexive viewpoint towards an existence that has embraced that excessiveness. In concrete terms, this means that within the *manga*, the characters themselves make an issue of 'how "they themselves, with their excessive feelings that XX," will live,' and this becomes the driving force for the story. Here, what would replace XX would be, for example, 'the immediate reality of the regions is poor' (*YOUNG & FINE, Fragments I*); 'family ties ought to be absolute' (*Arigatō* (Thanks)); or 'delusions are more realistic than reality' (*Believers*).[4]

It is not direct outpourings of the heart or the manifestation of behaviour, but this recursiveness inherent in several Yamamoto works that matches the level of perspective this chapter is endeavouring to establish. *Manga* in which 'provincial life' is a vital element of the work are not rare (Fusako Kuramochi's *Tennen kokekkō* (Natural cock-a-doodle-doo), for instance); nor is Naoki Yamamoto the only *manga* artist to depict the way characters who have a certain excessiveness struggle with that 'self which harbours excess' by trial-and-error (Minoru Furuya, in *Shigatera* (Ciguatera), for one). As far as I know, however, no similar examples are to be seen of works set in 'the regions,' and, moreover, where people have the idea that 'their immediate reality is poor/affluent,' and which also illustrate 'how they behave for that reason,' as in *Fragments I* and *YOUNG & FINE*. In that aspect, these two works are a rarely-procurable subject for this chapter.

One more reason for addressing the above-mentioned two works is precisely because they constitute a medium called '*manga*.' As well as 'it being easy to share the same scene with other people' (Miyahara and Ogino eds, 2001, p. 29) through the development and refinement of expressive techniques exclusive to the medium,[5] *manga* have the characteristic of being able to provide an opportunity to trigger readers' thoughts and imagination even from a single scene, which is something that cannot be reduced simply to the magnitude of their information content due to their 'being composed of pictures and text.'

By using scenes from *Fragments I* and *YOUNG & FINE*, this chapter anticipates that these will not be ancillary material for the purpose of reading the discussion below, but a starting-point for expanding people's thinking, each in their respective ways, about 'living in the regions.' To put it differently, this chapter is not something that strives to deepen people's understanding of sociological concepts by means of the raw material called *manga*. Rather, through contact with *manga*, readers themselves will head in the direction of enriching their thought – regardless of whether it is 'sociological' or not.[6] The idea of 'opening up new thinking, when making a particular expressive realm into an object of inquiry in sociology, by means of suggestion from the object, instead of trying to force it into an established framework' had already been expressed at the beginning of the 1980s, in the attempts at 'literary sociology' by Kei'ichi Sakuta et al., for instance.[7] However, given the above-mentioned characteristic possessed by the medium called *manga*, making *manga* an object perhaps can have an independent significance that differs from such a sphere as literature or film, for example.

From here on, then, let us look at the two works by Naoki Yamamoto, in line with the perspective described above. This will, in other words, at least be an attempt that will provide a clue for a deeper consideration of 'an existence lived in the regions,' which was hardly visible in conventional discourse around sociology, while readers will simultaneously also start making that attempt, themselves.

Several patterns for 'living in the regions'

Fragments I

I would like you to imagine, for example, a country town left behind both by the time that flows through Tokyo, and even by the wave of suburbanisation which brings about 'fast-food-like acculturation,' and where no such change is going to occur. For no small number of people that live there, such a reality will no doubt often be perceived as 'poor.' From an opposite perspective, however, thinking that the reality surrounding oneself is 'poor' also means it is the yet-to-be-realised, diverse possibilities encircling the poor-looking reality that have assumed a more intense brilliance.

In 'Tokyo,' for example, though the possible variations of reality are so numerous as to defy comparison with regional areas, in every case, the range of possibility for brilliance which each properly should have assumed is compressed into bland symbols that compose a kind of reality seen somewhere before. In Tokyo, the type of potential that looks to people to hold promise of realisation often is felt to have already been attained by someone somewhere else, in a less-attractive form than envisaged; and, for that reason, people are forced into abandoning it, thinking: 'speaking of possibilities, though they might look beautiful at a glance, they will only end up in a reality that is not much different from any other, at any rate.' In Tokyo, it is the range of possibilities, rather than the realities, that are excessively regulated, and this conversely causes a decline in the imagination of possibilities, as well.

By contrast, in the regions, even supposing that the reality appears poor, instead, possibilities buzz around the periphery of reality, while maintaining a density proper to things which are not completely regulated. Imagination, daydreams, fantasy, delusion, reverie – though there are many ways of expression, whatever the case, provincial areas are better-endowed than Tokyo with the imaginary affluence that contemplates still-unrealised 'potential,'[8] and, for people for who have become aware of it, a path leading from there to a certain kind of spiritual 'freedom' is open – arguably, it is not necessarily impossible to think that way: to perceive the 'fertile land that comprises possibility' which is the reverse of 'the poverty of reality' as a value, and as a resource for surviving a poor reality; or, to put it differently, to counter-exploit a reality that could only be considered as poor, and raise the intensity of affluence in an imaginary domain high enough to surpass the unpleasantness of a reality tasting like sawdust. In fact, it is nothing absurd – if one is living a provincial reality, then would it not be a life activity which would appear comparatively naturally, or else unconsciously?

In several of the short stories in the collection entitled *Fragments I*, which was serially written by Naoki Yamamoto from 1995 to 1996,[9] the mayor of a fictitious town called 'Kaiba (Seahorse) Town'[10] appears as a defender and controller who embodies the above-mentioned so-called 'difficult freedom' (Yamamoto 1997, p. 14 [Scene A]). 'Kaiba' is a little town sandwiched between mountains and sea, reminiscent of somewhere on the Oshima Peninsula, on the coast opposite Aomori Prefecture. The town spreads out as if clinging to the slopes; and the office of mayor is inherited by heads of the 'Kaiba family' each of whom inherits the name of 'Tarō Kaiba' from his predecessor, generation after generation, as his material heritage. According to comments by a character called 'Saba,' whom I will describe later, Kaiba is a town that 'has not changed in fifteen years,' where 'it is as if time has stood still' (Yamamoto 1997, p. 75 [Scene B]).

In this Kaiba Town, there is no sign that the mayor, Tarō Kaiba, is enthusiastically committed to his duties. Far from it – it is not unusual for him to be away from home for days at a time without reason, and in the past, there were even occasions when he did not

Is 'poverty' or 'affluence' the reality? 229

Figure 11.1: [Scene A] Fragments I (Yamamoto 1997, p. 14)

Figure 11.2: [Scene B] Fragments I (Yamamoto 1997, p. 75)

return for as long as six months. Instead, he metes out punishment in respective ways to those who delude themselves that a 'more affluent reality' actually exists, and try lightly to manifest possibilities, such as a student who attempts to make a sexual object out of Yukiko, the mayor's mistress, or the artist 'Saba' who, while temporarily back home from Tokyo, invites Yukiko to elope with him. The easy realisation of potential is nothing more than a repeated compounding of an already tasteless reality; and, conversely, what potential means is that as long as it does not become reality, it can be something surpassing reality. That is why, in order to make this mechanism work smoothly, it is necessary to risk remaining within a poor reality – indeed, Tarō Kaiba's behaviour seems to be conveying such a recognition.

By contrast, though becoming the object of another's forbidden desire, 'Yukiko,' who never seeks anything on her own part, appears as a symbol of 'possibility itself' that takes on an intense, unspecified attraction for the very reason that it is not realised. As such, Yukiko and Saba talk completely at cross purposes, in the following manner:

> SABA: When you became his mistress, didn't you feel any uncertainty?
> YUKIKO: Uncertainty?
> SABA: Like, 'Would it be all right if my life were to end with this?'
> YUKIKO: At that time, I thought only that it was the way things were. I don't think too deeply about things. Maybe I'm stupid.
> SABA: That won't do, will it? You have to cherish your own potential more...Maybe you could have become a singer. Or, if you hadn't become a mistress, you might have been able to be an academic. But you were forced by another's hand to choose the path of being a mistress. You ought to seize your own future yourself. Once, when I escaped from this town, I thought like that, too, like: 'Am I going to spend my whole life as the boss of an eating house in a country town?' And I thought there might be a more different 'real me' hidden inside myself, you know?
> YUKIKO: But you're a great restaurateur, aren't you?
> SABA: That's not what it's about (Yamamoto 1997, pp. 86–9).

Saba, who finds no meaning in 'nothing ever changing' in Kaiba Town, invites Yukiko to elope (probably to Tokyo), saying: 'You should get out of here, too, like me. A girl like you mustn't be in a place like this,' and 'Let's run away together, away from this town. We'll carve out a new life by our own efforts' (Yamamoto 1997, p. 90 [Scene C]).

The plan fails, however, and they are brought back by Tarō Kaiba. In the end, leaving behind only the possibility of 'another life/another place,' Saba is made to 'disappear' by Tarō Kaiba, and Kaiba Town again settles back into a daily routine where nothing ever happens. At this point, the story of Kaiba Town comes to an end, and *Fragments I* transitions to yet another story.

Is 'poverty' or 'affluence' the reality? 231

Figure 11.3: [Scene C] Fragments I (Yamamoto 1997, p. 90)

Let me also make brief reference to the work called 'Yūgata no otomodachi (Evening friends)' which begins after the Kaiba Town stories.[11] Here, Yamamoto's fixation on 'difficult freedom' is even more apparent. The setting is a provincial city by the sea called 'Iruka (Dolphin) City,' created two years earlier by the amalgamation of five towns and villages; and the main character is a severely masochistic man called 'Mr Yoshida,' a water bureau employee. By a particular coincidence, he discovers the fabled sadist, 'Queen Yukiko,' and, while in a moribund state after having indulged in night-long, extreme sadomasochistic play without concern for his life, is given the final 'punishment' of 'being abandoned for ever in this godforsaken town (Iruka).' Later, though having recovered physically, 'Mr Yoshida,' being unable to see 'Queen Yukiko' ever again, chooses neither to search for 'Queen Yukiko' nor to go somewhere else, but to 'stay put' (Yamamoto 1997, p. 209 [Scene D]). In so doing, a situation of 'the desire for possibilities becoming something intense for the very reason that they will never be realised,' or, in other words, 'the intensity of potential itself,' more than 'the attainment of potential' is positively chosen in 'Evening friends,' also.[12]

YOUNG & FINE

Naoki Yamamoto is also the author of a medium-length tale of around 200 pages entitled *YOUNG & FINE: umibe no machi de bokura wa nakayoshi datta ka* (Were we pals in the seaside town?),

Figure 11.4: [Scene D] Fragments I (Yamamoto 1997, p. 209)

published in 1992. This work, too, is set in a country town on the coast of Hokkaido.[13] The formal protagonist in this work is 'Haino,' a boy in his second-last year of upper secondary school who has been raised without a father. His girlfriend 'Reiko Arai,' rugby, alcohol and sushi account for most of his interests in life, and he enjoys his immediate existence according to the mantras of 'As long as I can eat sushi, I'm in heaven' and 'The good thing about me is that I never worry' (Yamamoto [1992] 1997, p. 98). By contrast, the qualitative main character is 'Sensei,' a newly-appointed female teacher of chemistry at his school, who takes lodgings in an annex at the Haino home. 'Sensei's' parental home is in 'H City' (probably Hakodate), but she was once raised in the same town as 'Haino' and graduated from the same high school. During her high school days, she apparently had some kind of relationship with 'Haino's big brother,' who was her classmate. That 'big brother,' who was a good student, graduated from a university in Tokyo and even now is working for a Tokyo company.

If one starts to read YOUNG & FINE, there is one feature that will instantly come to notice, namely that, of all of the characters that appear in it, the only one to feel that the reality before her very eyes is 'poor' is 'Sensei.' Apart from that of 'Sensei,' no storyline where a person feels uncomfortable with reality is to be seen. Both boys and girls at the high school are all lewd and without secrets; Haino's mother works resolutely and supports the family finances, just as a father would; while the 'big brother' who occasionally comes home to visit does not seem to have grown tired of Tokyo. That means, however, that the circumstances surrounding 'Sensei' bear all the heavier a burden. Her parents are close to divorcing, her father has gone off somewhere, and her mother is a 'kitchen drinker,' while 'Sensei' herself is about to become an alcoholic, 1.8 metres tall but skin-and-bones, with a perennial cold caused by malnutrition. She still carries a torch for 'Haino's big brother.' Moreover, she cannot come to terms with herself in that she will probably continue to live a dreary life in rural Hokkaido. The situation in which 'Sensei' is placed – she at the same time being unlikely to see the 'fertile plain called possibility' on the underside of reality – is a bitter one by far in comparison with the world of *Fragments I*.

Let me cite an example. In the middle section of the story, 'Haino' and 'Sensei' eat their evening meal at a cheap, tasty and familiar sushi restaurant, and while the two of them are on their way home on a single bicycle, 'Sensei,' who has had too much to drink, throws up what she has eaten. After that, standing on the seashore as the summer sun is setting, the two of them have the following conversation.

> SENSEI: Sometimes I wonder what on earth I've been doing up till now.
> HAINO: I've been having it off with Reiko Arai every day.
> SENSEI: Lucky for you. At times, I can't keep going unless I have a drink.
> HAINO: Talking like a grownup again, eh?
> SENSEI: When I think that being born, working, eating and dying is all there is...
> HAINO: Hey, just because you're a schoolmistress, you don't have to go all complicated on me again.
> SENSEI: It isn't complicated. Even you are about to face circumstances that won't be solved by pigging out on comfort food, like going on to further education or getting a job, after all.
> HAINO: I make a habit of thinking about those things when they actually happen.
> SENSEI: Lucky you! (Yamamoto [1992] 1997, pp. 104–6) [Scene E]

As you see, though this pair appears to be on familiar terms, there is a huge chasm between what each is saying to the other. Moreover,

Figure 11.5: [Scene E] YOUNG & FINE (Yamamoto [1992] 1997, p. 105)

though naturally it is by rights the adult, and a teacher to boot, who is quite painfully aware of that fact, it is still 'Sensei' who, after having drunk too much in front of 'Haino' to the point of vomiting, is the one that makes pretentious statements smacking of tedious repetition.

'Being born, working, eating and dying is all there is.' 'Sensei's' depression, from which there is no escape, is symbolised by this line. If it were 'Haino,' eating cheap sushi at a familiar sushi restaurant would constitute almost too ample an ingredient for reality to be affluent. On the other hand, even if she goes to a sushi place, 'Sensei,' who thinks in terms of the prosaic constituting 'all there is' to life, ends up drinking nothing but *sake* until she throws up (Yamamoto [1992] 1997, p. 98 [Scene F]). The gaze of 'Sensei,' for whom even birth and death are 'all there is,' is like a bird's-eye view from high in the sky, which compresses everything at ground level into a dreary flatness.

Earlier, I mentioned *Fragments I*, stating that in the regions, even supposing that the reality looks to be poor, there are possibilities astir in reality's environs – things not completely regulated, while maintaining the concentration and density that they by rights can hold. As a matter of fact, though, this is also something that only

Figure 11.6: [Scene F] YOUNG & FINE (Yamamoto [1992] 1997, p. 98)

becomes possible once the supposition that 'the reality here now is poor, but if it were another place/another time...' has meaning. As with 'Sensei,' if one's viewpoint for surveying reality ascends to the heights of 'being born, working, eating and dying is all there is...,' then the distinction between 'here, now' and 'somewhere not here (some other time)' loses its significance, and an escape route such as in *Fragments*, where the conditions of a 'poor reality' were turned to advantage, will also be lost.

It is easy to imagine, but aspects of life such as these are likely to be matters of personal concern for those who return to their provincial home after having left 'the regions' and getting to know 'Tokyo,' and simultaneously also having discovered the difficulties of a 'Tokyo-style' life – in other words, after having lost the contrast between 'here, now' and 'somewhere not here (some other time).' What *YOUNG & FINE* was showing in advance of *Fragments I* was that this is a realistic way of life, at least for the multitudes of people who cannot access *Fragments I*-like solutions because of their inability to utilise the 'resource called potential.'

In spite of this, in the world of *YOUNG & FINE*, not a single person has any empathy with or sympathy for 'Sensei.' *YOUNG & FINE* is in no small measure an 'artificial' work, in its lack of concern and coldness of the surrounding people towards the probably universal depression of 'Sensei.' In the eyes of 'Haino,' especially, 'Sensei' appears as a woman who is both physically and mentally 'ill.' Even given the reality of her intolerable family, when 'Sensei' poses the question: 'Do you understand this situation, Haino, of not having any place to go back to?' 'Haino' conversely retorts: 'What a melodrama! You're a whole twenty-four, so you don't need to feel down just because your parents say this and that, do you?' (Yamamoto [1992] 1997, p. 151).

In the world of *YOUNG & FINE*, any 'darkness' has been intentionally removed by the author. In Yamamoto's configuration, people are 'living in simple abundance' in the 'seaside town' where the story is set, and this does not mean that, as in the world of *Fragments*, they will pursue a 'difficult freedom' on the underside of their 'poor' reality. What the author shows, therefore, is 'simple freedom.' In the 'seaside town,' everyone except 'Sensei' behaves as if it is self-evident for unadulterated reality to be affluent. For the people who live there, the activities that occur in the world – the men, the women, the town and the material things, the sea, the mountains, the wind and the snow, and rugby, sushi and the like as well – are hardly likely to be poor. In the 'seaside town,' a quite 'ordinary' affluence is arrayed before everyone bar 'Sensei.'

Of course, ever since the above-mentioned chat on the seashore, 'Sensei,' too, is strongly aware of this. The day after the 'conversation on the seashore,' for example, making an appearance with her hair cut so short that it looks a little odd (having done it herself, moreover), she says to 'Haino': 'Maybe I, too, will aim at [being] healthy or something like that, yeah?' (Yamamoto [1992] 1997, p. 110 [Scene G]).

That being said, it does not mean that 'Sensei' has any idea as to how her 'alienation' from 'simple freedom' will be resolved. In that 'seaside town' in November, which has begun to be blanketed in snow, 'Sensei's' cold develops into pneumonia, and she is hospitalised in H City for combined treatment of her alcoholism. Yet 'Haino's' interest (superficially, at least) is on his rugby matches, given his aspirations towards the national championships at Hanazono Rugby Stadium in Osaka, and 'Sensei,' whose family has been broken from the beginning, ends up being abandoned by everyone for more than a month. 'Sensei' expresses her gratitude to 'Haino,' who has lost his rugby

Is 'poverty' or 'affluence' the reality? 237

Figure 11.7: [Scene G] YOUNG & FINE (Yamamoto [1992] 1997, p. 110)

match and finally come to visit her in hospital, but 'Haino' shrugs it off, telling her that if she is going to thank anyone, she should thank the friend who has brought him there. In spite of that, at this point 'Sensei' abruptly comes out with the words: 'But I like you, Haino,' and, after having hesitated to say anything for a while, further gives voice to these comments: 'I thought about all sorts of things for a long time.' 'Haino, do you know how time drags on when you're on a bed just doing nothing?' 'After you have a meal, it takes 100 years until the next meal comes along.'

These utterances by 'Sensei,' namely: 'After you have a meal, it takes 100 years until the next meal comes along,' and, 'time... when you're on a bed just doing nothing' – at this point, readers will readily imagine that these words are, for 'Sensei,' overlaid on her life in the 'seaside town' where she, the only one pointlessly embracing perverseness, cannot participate in a reality which 'ought to be' affluent. 'Haino's' answer to 'Sensei's' entreaty: 'I want *you*, Haino, who are like the symbol of "simple freedom," to understand that I have nowhere to go,' is vivid almost to the point of morality: 'Sensei, looks like you're not better after all' (Yamamoto [1992] 1997, pp. 185–6 [Scene H]).

Figure 11.8: [Scene H] *YOUNG & FINE* (Yamamoto [1992] 1997, p. 186)

Though 'Sensei' is thus in dire distress in the 'seaside town,' recovery from her alienation eventuates in an unexpected form. One day in December, a month after her discharge from hospital, 'Haino's big brother' suddenly comes home, bringing his 'bride-to-be.' The Haino family, the fiancée and 'Sensei' hold a celebration party at their usual sushi restaurant, but in her heart, 'Sensei' does not take the engagement of the person she once loved calmly. In the end, 'Sensei' becomes dead drunk again, and when she awakes, having fallen asleep on the spot, only 'Haino' is still present. He, too, is called away by fellow members of his rugby club, however, and 'Sensei' continues to drink alone with glazed eyes. At a drinking party with his club mates, 'Haino' is lost in thought about something. Abruptly he stands up, declares: 'I, Katsuhiko Haino, intend to go now and confess true love to my beloved Manabu Izawa Sensei!' and runs to the sushi restaurant, but around then, 'Sensei' has suddenly become physical with 'Gen-chan,' the young master of the sushi place who, being unable to bear watching her unnatural way of drinking, has intervened to stop her.

Ultimately, 'Sensei' enters her third month of pregnancy, and unceremoniously marries 'Gen-chan.' Though she is supposed to have been an alcoholic, she 'becomes a mother surprisingly without mishap,' and gives birth to a baby girl in October the following year. After high-school graduation, 'Haino,' on the other hand, parts also from his girlfriend who has entered a university in Tokyo, and he gets a job in the local municipal office. One day, he accidentally bumps into 'Sensei' on the deserted seashore, and the pair converse for the first time in ages.

> SENSEI: It's you, isn't it, Haino? Long time no see! Not since the wedding, maybe? ...You know, at first it was pure coincidence that I ended up lodging at your place. The real estate agency just happened to refer me. But like, though I wouldn't go so far as to say I was turning over a new leaf, I sort of felt that something might change because of that coincidence.
> HAINO: But it didn't do any good?
> SENSEI: I wouldn't say that. Having met you, Haino, I feel as if I *have* changed to a certain extent, thanks to encountering your irresponsible and haphazard personality!
> HAINO: I never imagined I'd influence anyone.
> SENSEI: I liked you, Haino.
> HAINO: Why did you get married, then?
> SENSEI: Well, that kind of thing's just going with the flow. Shall we have a fling or something, next time?
> HAINO: No way!
> SENSEI: But if I hadn't met you, I probably wouldn't have got married, either.
> HAINO: Yeah? (Yamamoto [1992] 1997, pp. 217–220 [Scene I]).

Through the dialogue and expression here, readers will see, from the figure of 'Sensei,' who once begged sympathy from 'Haino' at the hospital, that something has utterly changed. The depression which had cloaked 'Sensei' appears to have become entirely a thing of the past. At last, amid the 'simple freedom' of the 'town by the seaside,' she was permitted to go on living. That being said, what was the 'reason' for that? Was it marriage, or pregnancy, or the birth of her child? There is no particular answer to this, apart from her merely saying that meeting 'Haino' had influenced her. Yet having come thus far, what is conveyed to the reader is the clear-cut will of the author, namely that 'the "simple freedom" to live in the straightforward affluence of reality is not something that excludes anyone, but is something that people will have already

Figure 11.9: [Scene I] *YOUNG & FINE* (Yamamoto [1992] 1997, p. 218)

encountered when they realise it at some point.' The story takes on an allegorical tinge in its final episode, and, coupled also with the effect of the stage-setting of the 'seaside town' built up to this point, a resonance with the work-world and the resulting catharsis are generated in readers (albeit momentarily). Soon after this, the *manga* comes to an end.

How can one live in 'the regions'?

Let me pull together the contents of the previous section for a moment. In *Fragments I* and *YOUNG & FINE*, given a standard of 'seeing the affluence/poverty in the reality before one's eyes,' the main theme of the stories has become 'whether one can or cannot utilise that affluence/poverty as a resource for living.' The people living their lives in provincial areas are by no means only those who are satisfied with the reality directly confronting them, or those who want in some way or another to compensate for an unsatisfying reality (but have given up on that idea). Yamamoto additionally elucidates the situation of 'even while seeing poverty in reality, still making use of it,' or 'even while seeing affluence in reality, being alienated from it.'

Let us arrange this in concrete terms. Firstly, Yamamoto illustrates the pattern of behaviour which appears through 'seeing poverty in reality' by means of 'Tarō Kaiba,' 'Mr Yoshida,' 'Saba' and 'Sensei,' and, similarly, the pattern appearing through 'seeing affluence in reality' by means of 'Sensei' and 'Haino,' respectively. Of these, Tarō Kaiba and Mr Yoshida 'utilise the density of potential behind a poverty-stricken reality as a resource for living,' Saba 'escapes from a reality of poverty that deserved rejection, and aspires to the attainment of other possibilities,' and Haino ends up 'enjoying reality directly as something affluent.' The one who needs attention is 'Sensei,' as she displays three different forms in the work. If we make these 'Sensei A,' 'Sensei B' and 'Sensei C,' respectively, then the subsequent course is followed. 'Sensei A' (in the initial state of affairs): 'resignation that the reality is poverty, yet other possibilities represent not much change', 'Sensei B' (after cutting her hair short): 'though the reality ought to have been affluence, she herself was alienated, that is, she was unable to enjoy it', 'Sensei C' (after her marriage to 'Gen-chan'): 'enjoying reality as something rich, in the same way as Haino.' Of these, it is 'Sensei A' that is grounded upon 'seeing poverty in reality,' and 'Sensei B' and 'Sensei C' that are grounded upon 'seeing affluence.'

If we schematise the above content and commit it to paper, it will be as follows in Figure 11.10. This figure seems to show the fundamental divergence in the behaviour that emerges on the presupposition of 'seeing affluence/poverty in reality.' Of course, other configurations are also possible in regard to the horizontal axis, but for the time being this mapping could be said to interrogate one aspect of the basic composition of 'an existence lived in the regions.'

Now, what manner of things can we recognise and tease out from this? Let me cite several examples.

1. What I first want to reconfirm is that all of the quadrants, from one to four, do not rely upon a specific environment or landscape. In critiques of fast-food-like acculturation and the contexts of urban theory and suburban theory, the monotonous and disorderly scenery of roadside shopping strips that are pervading the regions and suburbs is seldom mentioned in

Figure 11.10: The structure of 'an existence lived in the regions'

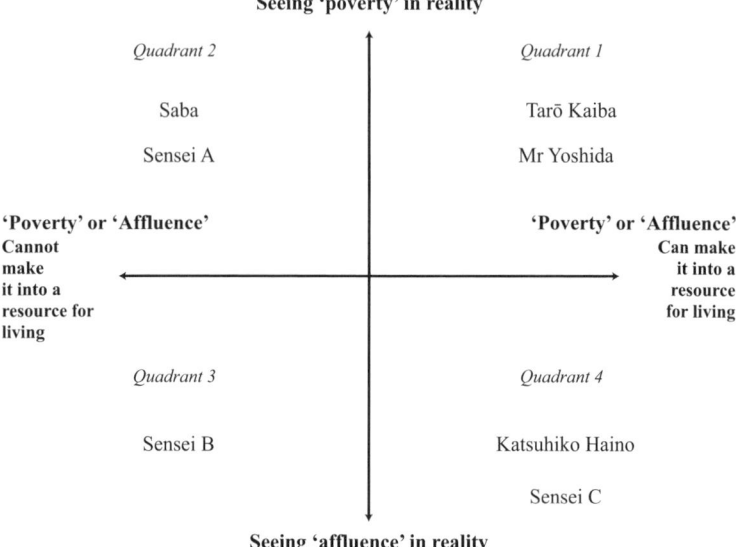

'Tarō Kaiba' and 'Mr Yoshida': utilise the intensity of possibility behind a poor reality as a resource for living

'Saba': escapes from a poor reality that he should reject, and aspires to the realisation of another reality

'Sensei A': though her reality is poor, other possibilities are not much different, either

'Sensei B': the alienation of not being able to enjoy reality herself, though it ought to be affluent

'Haino' and 'Sensei C': enjoy reality as something straightforwardly rich

positive terms. In Figure 11.10, however, it would not matter one iota even if, for example, the setting for the fourth quadrant were not a 'seaside town' but a provincial city that possessed a depressed central business district and roadside shopping strips proliferating in its environs. Accordingly, by way of example, it would also fall within the bounds of supposition for petty differences in the placement of chain stores to constitute the distinctiveness of a particular town; and the contrast between the glaring lighting on the roadside and the dark night sky, instead of lyrical scenery shaped by sea, wind and snow, and fast food in place of 'as long as I can eat sushi, I'm in heaven,' to be resources for procuring a palpable sense of being alive.

2. Furthermore, like the 'Sensei' sketched by Naoki Yamamoto, it would be conceivable for 'a person to move around among Quadrants 1 to 4 in occasional circumstances.' For instance, in the example of the high-school girl from Aomori that Miyadai introduced on an earlier page, a temporary shift from Quadrant 2 to Quadrant 4 appears, does it not? The high-school girl (Quadrant 2) using the telephone-dating club, who is 'in a foul mood' simply because she is in Aomori,[15] experiences an emotional 'resonance' with a middle-aged man merely because he, too, is alive in Aomori, and she shares 'quality time' with him, living in simple affluence (Quadrant 4). And her parting words are: 'I'll be able to knuckle down now because I feel refreshed. Thanks hugely. See you again somewhere!' This huge oscillation that appears in the level of existence, which is not visible from the outside, is probably of a different nature from life in 'Tokyo.' Moreover, if we are going to presuppose 'quadrant shift,' then it will also be possible to go one step further and ask: 'In the case where a certain person fluctuates among Quadrants 1 to 4 (or stays in one place), what reasons and grounds would there be for that?'
3. Finally, let me point out that the act of intentionally 'choosing' one or more from among Quadrants 1 to 4, oneself, is possible. If, for instance, while mainly being in Quadrant 2, one also made the hitherto-unconsciously-visited Quadrant 1 into a conscious choice, or, by venturing to engage in primary industry and committing oneself to local rituals and the like, attempts such as to approach Quadrant 4 asymptotically would also be conceivable.[16] In addition, there is also the option of blocking all but Quadrant 2 in order to realise one's desired possibility (though there is no guarantee that things will go as expected after this is attained).

I would like readers, also – especially if they happen to live in a provincial area – to try asking themselves what in their own minds constitutes the resources for procuring affluence; how many quadrants apply to themselves; and which quadrant they think they would choose. For my part, even if the chosen quadrants differ according to the individual, I think that it is preferable to have multiple quadrants applicable to oneself, rather than just a single one. In lieu of a conclusion, I would argue that it is precisely such self-questioning that will be the first step in pondering 'an existence lived in the regions = oneself,' and will also be the greatest recognised benefit that this chapter presents.

Notes

1 See, for example, Miyadai 1997, Matsubara 2002, Wakabayashi 2003, Yoshimi and Wakabayashi (eds) 2005, Wakabayashi 2007, Azuma and Kitada 2007.
2 Miyadai 1997 ultimately brings this back to a 'native sexuality in the regions' that contains pre-modern elements, but I consider that limiting the issue to the domain of sexuality has not fully exercised the potential which Miyadai himself discovered. Rather, I suggest that what Miyadai confronted amid his data collection in Aomori was an issue relating to the very state of communication in 'Tokyo' and 'the regions,' respectively.
3 It is symbolic that the words: 'A long seller with rave reviews from regional local government bodies [and] shopping arcades!' are printed on the wrapper band of *Fasuto fūdoka suru Nihon*. How would regional dwellers apart from 'regional local government bodies' or 'shopping arcades' have reacted?
4 In this connection, I would like to add a comment. The development of a strong consciousness of the difficulty that lay between people having fantasies and the latter's connection with reality, in a form symbolised by the 'Aum Supreme Truth poison gas incidents' and 'compensated dating (*enjo kōsai*),' could be cited as examples of the temporal context which made its marked appearance in Japanese society in the late 1990s, when Naoki Yamamoto published *Fragments* (I–III) and *Believers*.

It is tentatively possible to try to find a correspondence between this historical context and Naoki Yamamoto's works from the same period. The story in *Believers* (Yamamoto 2000), for instance, is one obviously reminiscent of the Aum Supreme Truth incidents, while the fixation upon 'not daring to turn potential into reality' in *Fragments I* (Yamamoto 1997), and *Arigatō* (Thanks) (Yamamoto 1995), which illustrates that the 'family' is nothing more than a disorderly crowd with disparate fantasies, can also be placed in this context.

One needs to be aware, however, that the very characteristics seen in the Yamamoto works described in the chapter did not undergo change around 1995, when, for example, 'compensated dating' excited the media, and police raids were carried out on the Aum Supreme Truth sect. Rather, in *Believers*, the Aum incidents were confined to being the inspiration for narrative ideas, and the theme of 'what action is taken by people with an excess of things they cannot handle' that appears in the same work, as well as in *Fragments I* and *Arigatō*, is something that Naoki Yamamoto had continuously sketched since before that time. Of course, it will not be completely unrelated to the historical context, regardless of the kind of person doing the expressing, but in my view, the argument that the historical background directly influences works is not applicable to Naoki Yamamoto, at least. There is, however, little doubt that the dramas which Yamamoto has drawn – brought about by such things as fruitless effort, dis-communication, rampage, resignation or choice due to the characters

Is 'poverty' or 'affluence' the reality? 245

harbouring some sort of excess – look to be a good match for conditions such as those in the late 1990s, especially.

5 Attempts to examine the 'appeal of *manga*' from such aspects as the dialogue or the panel layout include *Bessatsu Takara EX* 1995, Natsume 1997 and McCloud 1993. As an emergency that cannot be reduced to its elements appears not only in *manga* but in expressive behaviour in general, it is not possible to grasp *manga* from this aspect alone; but such attempts, represented by Fusanosuke Natsume, no doubt have produced results that cannot be offered elsewhere.

6 This description is based on the under-mentioned text by Shun Inoue:

> It is to be hoped that the course of enriching sociological thought – not by explaining the arts by existing concepts and theories in sociology at times as if wrestling them into submission, but rather through communion with them – will be duly acknowledged and further developed from here forward (Inoue 2000, p. 135).

While it might be splitting hairs, though I basically agree with Inoue's point, I am not entirely convinced as to why Inoue has to go out of his way to say 'enriching "sociological" thought.' By rights, it should matter not one jot whether the thought inspired by the arts (here, referring to *manga*) is consequently sociological or philosophical or literary, or else something that defies classification; rather, it would be preferable precisely for it to be 'something that defies classification' – or would making such a suggestion perhaps be going too far? Yet, at the very least, *manga* ought to constitute an expressive realm which is open wide to that kind of freedom of imagination. For now, let me cite Nagai 2000 as one example of philosophical thought which was inspired by *manga*.

7 See, for example, Sakuta 1981, and Sakuta and Tominaga (eds) 1984.

8 I might add that this is not necessarily a universal phenomenon. In post-war Japanese society, at least, for the regions, 'Tokyo' (or else Osaka, Nagoya, Sapporo, Fukuoka and the like, as its substitutes) has functioned until now as a destination that is 'somewhere that is not here, now/some time.' On the other hand, in the case of the real Tokyo, without a place corresponding to the 'Tokyo' that exists for the regions, the destination that was the functional equivalent of 'Tokyo' was not a geographical 'place,' but a 'brighter, more affluent future than at present.' This 'brighter, more affluent future' was something shining and indisputable until the wane of the age of high economic growth, but in the low-growth period of the 1970s, its existence began to be doubted, and since the collapse of the economic bubble at the beginning of the 1990s, its reality has been irrevocably lost.

9 The four stories in the first half of *Fragments I*, 'Yukiko,' 'Asagohan kara yūgohan made (From breakfast until the evening meal),' and 'Ryōriya no musuko (The restaurateur's son), parts I and II,' are narratives set in the town of Kaiba mentioned here.

10 At the same time, in Japanese, the town's 'seahorse' nomenclature also evokes the image of the hippocampus, the seahorse-shaped part of the human brain which controls spatial memory and navigation.

11 'Yūgata no otomodachi (Evening friends)' consists of three stories, and corresponds to the second half of *Fragments I*.

12 The magazine publication of 'Yūgata no otomodachi' extended from October to December 1995, while it was from February to July 1996 that the four stories about Kaiba Town were printed, the drawing of 'Yūgata no otomodachi' having been done first. From the order of their magazine publication, at least, I wish to note that 'Yūgata no otomodachi' clearly hammers out the idea of 'difficult freedom' prior to the 'Kaiba Town stories.'
13 According to Naoki Yamamoto, Esashi Town in Hokkaido's Hiyama County was the model for the 'seaside town' in which the tales are set. In a short essay newly added at the end of *YOUNG & FINE* on the occasion of its 1997 republication, entitled '*YOUNG & FINE* kankō annai (Tourist information for *YOUNG & FINE*),' Yamamoto comments as follows:

> Esashi is a split-level town divided by a coastal terrace into uphill and downhill parts. The view from the slope between them is also fine...The senior high school in Hakodate which I attended drew students from all of the communities in the region, but when I thought about it later, it was mystifying that I never encountered a single one from Esashi. It is not such a small town, nor is it especially poverty-stricken in comparison with others. I also sometimes mused that perhaps Esashi was a place where people felt so comfortable that they did not want to leave. That kind of Esashi in my imagination is the setting for *YOUNG & FINE* (Yamamoto [1992] 1997, pp. 228–9).

14 As there are no punctuation marks shown in the dialogue in *YOUNG & FINE*, I have added them as seems appropriate. This also applies to the parts cited from *YOUNG & FINE* below in the main text.
15 In 'Aomori no terekura shōjotachi (The telephone-dating-club girls of Aomori),' it is stated how 'irritating a place' Aomori was at the time. According to Miyadai, the irritation of 'there being nothing in Aomori, and [locals] having no money themselves, either,' around the time that Tokyo was enjoying the bubble economy, Aomori inhabitants somehow managed to absorb the hope of 'getting to Tokyo some day,' but the bad economic situation made that impossible, too. Nonetheless, the media was overflowing with Tokyo information, fueling the idea of 'us, too,' as could be expected. Though Aomori people can no longer think of 'getting to Tokyo some day,' the circumstance that Tokyo did not exist in some faraway foreign land, but in that same country of Japan, was what Miyadai says lay behind Aomori's irritation (1997, pp. 36–7).
16 One example of the common ground between such primary industries as agriculture, forestry and fisheries, and religious behaviour such as rituals, is their prolific incorporation of elements not relativised by 'society,' such as physical immediacy or religious extraordinariness. It was once quite a matter of course in provincial life that these 'elements not relativised by "society,' which were ubiquitous in people's lifestyles, became the foundation for 'the affluence of reality.' In regard to the point that religion essentially cannot be separated from the formation of both 'society' and 'the individual,' see, for example, Luckmann 1967.

12 What is at question in youth labour issues?: the two phases of specialisation, 'manual-based' and 'qualified'

Masahiro Abe

When selecting your future job, many of you readers, I imagine, are vacillating (or have vacillated) between the two options of choosing 'work you would like' and 'stable work.'

The ideal would be a job you would like. You might not be able to support yourself just on that, however. Would it not be better to take a well-paid job, even if that meant suppressing your 'preference' somewhat? Or else, you might want to live richly but fleetingly, consuming yourself in a job you love without a thought to your livelihood, because you only live once, after all? Alternatively, you find your reason for living in your family, because you want to treasure it, and so at least a secure job in which you can be home by seven o'clock in the evening would be preferable, and so on. You might be thinking (or have thought) all manner of things like these.

This chapter deals with such a discussion of 'work.' When I was a *freeter* (freelance casual worker) in my late twenties, I experienced working as a 'dispatch rider' for one year, as I loved motorcycles. Accordingly, I tasted both the pleasure and the risk (for the very reason that it was pleasant) of choosing a job I liked. In the first section, I will discuss that issue. Secondly, I will talk about 'care workers' who would prefer to get a stable job, but find it quite elusive. In comparison with dispatch riders who want to do work they enjoy, unstable though it is, care workers want a stable job, but as their jobs are not stable, their situation is even more serious. In the third section, I will delve further into the previous discussion. The problem of youth labour in Japan has become even more complex due to the question of 'housewives and young people' brought about by 'Japanese-style welfare society.' The problem of youth labour is also a 'cry' from young people who are living through the process of collapse of that Japan-specific welfare society. I will also talk about 'specialisation,' which is the focus of expectations for a solution for these problems. There is a need to divide specialisation into two phases for consideration.

The current issue of youth labour

The number of young people who do not (cannot) become regular employees even after graduating from school, but remain in the condition of *freeters* (freelance casual worker) or NEETs (Not in Education, Employment or Training) is rising. Readers, too, will probably all have learned from media such as television, magazines, newspapers or the Internet that it has become a social problem, which is true, as can be appreciated from statistical data, as well.[1]

In regard to such circumstances, on the one hand there are some who look to young people themselves as the source of the problem, saying: 'Youth these days aren't up to scratch!' By contrast, there are others who take into account the socio-economic situation in which numerous young people spilled from the pipeline that should have conveyed them from school to regular employment during the so-called 'lost decade' in the 1990s, when the regular employee pie was drastically whittled away. Accordingly, they retort: 'The problem lies with society!' While the former focus on youth who '*do not* become regular employees,' the latter have their eye on young people who '*cannot* become regular employees,' resulting in the formation of a picture consisting of 'youth-bashing' versus 'the bashing of youth-bashing.' This, too, is something that many of you will already know from the discourse around Japan's 'stratified society.'

This means, in other words, that there is a mixture both of young people who '*do not* become regular employees' and those who '*cannot* become regular employees,' and, as such, the necessity for meticulously separating them for consideration has been pointed out. To connect this to what I wish to discuss here, it would be impossible to speak about people who settle for unstable employment because they are fixated upon it on the same footing as those who have no alternative but to accept unstable employment, even though they have given up on the idea of 'turning what they love into their job.' In short, these each are separate questions. As such, it will be the objective of this chapter to ponder them as distinct issues.

From here on, in the second half of the first section, I will consider the problematic points in 'turning what one loves into one's job,' by examining dispatch riders. This is not a matter that can be managed simply by telling people not to be so naïve. 'Turning what one loves into one's job' in unstable employment is something more complicated and fearsome.

Subsequently, in the second section, by looking at care workers, I will consider the larger social issue of those people who would like to get stable jobs having their hopes dashed. This constitutes the discourse of fake career-advancement, that is, the problem of 'bait-and-switch.'

In order to extricate themselves from a 'bait-and-switch' situation and turn their jobs as care workers into something stable, they need to raise their level of work specialisation and step onto the path of career advancement. However, the 'housewives and young people' issue which spans the care site have the potential to obstruct them. In the first half of the third section, I will ponder the 'Japanese-style welfare society,' which is one of the causes.

In the latter half of the third section, I will consider the potential of what is called 'specialisation,' which is the focus of expectations for solving the problems that will have become obvious through dispatch riders and care workers. Specialisation needs to be divided into two types for consideration, namely Specialisation 1, for prevention of 'self-actualising workaholics,' and Specialisation 2, which makes career advancement possible. The two need to be considered after careful differentiation.

In the fourth section, I will conclude the chapter by conducting a simulation of the reader's 'job choices,' taking the above discussion into account.

The trap in 'making what one loves into one's job'

First, I wish to talk about 'turning what one loves into one's job,' using dispatch riders as my example. Dispatch riding is a new kind of service-industry job that arose in Tokyo in the 1980s, and 'dispatch rider' refers to a person in the delivery business who uses a motorcycle as his or her means of carriage.

The dispatch rider is a presence that seems to symbolise 'turning what one loves into one's job,' and I have elucidated the workaholic problems it brought about in my book, *Sakushu sareru wakamo-*

notachi: baiku-bin raidā wa mita! (Exploited youth: a motorbike delivery rider saw [them]!) (Abe 2006).

Hobby-like labour ties in with the system of discretion, and triggers overwork. So far, so good. In particular, if it is stable work, then problems will be few. In cases where the work is both unstable and low-paid, however, then, as Zygmunt Bauman argues, 'embracing one's work as a vocation carries enormous risks and may be a recipe for psychological and emotional disaster' (Bauman 1998, p. 35). Moreover, there is also a risk that the desire to 'turn what they like into their job' would weaken such people's awareness of their rights as workers, and make them the target of exploitation by enterprises.

The issue of 'self-actualising workaholics,' as represented by dispatch riders, primarily will link directly to the problem of education. Low-paid service occupations, given the nature of the work, are 'dead-end jobs,' and there is a need to teach children at an early stage that choice of that work carries a very high risk. In that sense, my 2006 book on youth exploitation was one written as a criticism towards the kind of education that excessively encourages 'self-actualisation through work,' as typified by Ryū Murakami's 2003 book, *Jū-san-sai no harō wāku* (The job centre at age thirteen). Such details pertaining to the jobs as average annual income, number of years of continuing employment, and pathways to career advancement need to be added to Murakami's volume.[2]

Moreover, this issue is also a question of workplaces. This point is important. In dispatch riders' workplaces, for example, there are two rules: 'dispatch clerks are former commission-based riders' (Rule One); and 'hourly-waged riders can become commission-based riders, but commission-based riders cannot become hourly-waged riders' (Rule Two).

Commission-based riders work at their own discretion: in other words, they are dispatch riders who work under a commission system by which their income rises according to what they have earned from clients, while hourly-waged riders are dispatch riders who work by the hour, a system which is unrelated to job earnings. It is commission-based riding that becomes a hotbed for 'self-actualising workaholics.' Dispatch riders' workplaces have these two categories of riders.

Due to these rules which prescribe their relationality, commission-based riders become a more respected presence than hourly-waged riders (Rule One); and, what is more, commission-based riders who are 'useless,' having burned out and become unable to earn income, end up being excluded from the workplace (Rule Two). As a result, the awareness spreads in their workplace that the commission-based riders who are more deeply immersed in their job are 'cooler.' This is a 'workplace trick' that leads dispatch riders into becoming 'self-actualising workaholics.' In that sense, this issue is also a workplace problem. In order to prevent the development of 'self-actualising workaholics,' there is a necessity to place certain checks upon discretion in the job. I will consider the path to such a solution in the second half of the third section.

Nonetheless, though becoming immersed in an unstable job with the idea of 'turning what one loves into one's work' is something that involves many problems, it often occurs as the 'end result of youthful exuberance,' and so, if riders later jettison 'making what they love into their work' and, for instance, leave the dispatch riders' workplace and are able to find a stable job, then the problem will not become so great. In that sense, *Exploited youth* is also a story of 'the end of youth.'

Bait-and-switch

The care workers handled in my book, *Hatarakisugiru wakamonotachi: 'jibun-sagashi' no hate ni* (Young people who work too much: at the far reaches of 'self-discovery') (Abe 2007), find themselves in a different situation from dispatch riders who burn themselves out by 'making what they love into their job.'

Among the former, there are some care workers who entered that industry seeking 'stability' from the start. In other words, there are also some people who make a self-investment and obtain qualifications, beginning this work not only from the idea of 'turning what they love into their job,' but also in anticipation of its reputation, namely that 'if they gain a care worker's qualification, their livelihood will be secure.' Their despair when they find out that they are in a 'dead-end job' is so deep and heavy that dispatch riders' frustration would seem trivial by comparison. In that sense, my *Young people who work too much* is a tale of 'unfulfilled regeneration.'

Barbara Ehrenreich coined the term 'bait-and-switch' for fake career-advancement programmes. 'Bait-and-switch' means decoy marketing, luring people (with bait) and then immediately switching to something else. This issue is a larger problem of social structure that individual 'preparedness' alone cannot tackle.

Bait and Switch is a work by Ehrenreich, known for her book *Nickel and Dimed*, which became a best-seller in the United States. In *Nickel and Dimed*, having actually experienced low-paid jobs such as waitressing and cleaning, Ehrenreich points a finger at the severity of the toil. Ehrenreich's next book was *Bait and Switch*, published in 2005, which focused on middle-class white-collar workers.

Bait and Switch is subtitled 'The (Futile) Pursuit of the American Dream.' In short, this book constitutes a denunciation of the various products (programmes) to do with white-collar 'fake career-advancement.'

The people who are the subject of that book are those 'who've done everything right,' in other words, people who have 'gotten college degrees, developed marketable skills, and built up impressive résumés' (Ehrenreich 2005, front flap). Why do these people, who have done everything by the book, fall into poverty? The aim of the volume, doggedly based on Ehrenreich's fieldwork, was to shed light on the path that led them there.

The author, one of 'the people who've done everything right,' herself submits to career coaching, personality testing, and attends a series of self-help seminars. At job fairs and networking events, however, she is scammed and proselytised time and time again, having all kinds of terrible experiences. In short, she continues to be at the mercy of 'fake career-advancement = the American dream.'

The people who are the main characters in *Bait and Switch*, tossed around by the fake career-advancement discourse, overlap with the image of the care workers with whom I dealt in *Young people who work too much*, as I have already mentioned.

According to the April 2004 issue of *AIK Report*, after the beginning of the Heisei era (from 1989), there was a steep increase in enrolees in technical colleges in the 'Other [Training]' category in the fifth division ('Education and Social Welfare') of the Ministry of Education, Culture, Sports, Science and Technology (Monbukagakushō)'s *Gakkō kihon chōsa hōkokusho* (Report on the basic survey of schools). The fifth division contains the three categories of 'Childcare Training,' 'Teacher Training' and 'Other [Training].' The ballooning in enrolees in previously small-scale 'Other [Training]' to 2.5 times the number in the two categories of 'Childcare Training' and 'Teacher Training' in the 2003 fiscal year is attributed to the rush by institutions to newly establish such courses as 'Care Welfare,' which are unrepresented in the code table.

People who become certified care workers by attending a technical college or junior college, or take a correspondence course, are fundamentally different from the 'making what they love into their job'-type of dispatch riders in *Exploited youth*. Many of them anticipate a job that is deemed socially to 'have a future' – in other words, they enter the industry by betting on the 'stability' of the work. The actual job of a care worker, however, is one with such poor working conditions that it is difficult for people to continue doing it after the age of thirty.

When young people who entered the industry with expectations of stability realise that their 'dream' of a welfare occupation was a mistake, this must give rise to much disappointment. The discourse of false career-advancement, namely 'bait-and-switch,' is an extremely cruel one that upsets people's lives.

Though they want to get a qualification and make their livelihood secure, that qualification is not one that leads to a stable income. This situation needs to be considered as an issue pertaining to those young people mentioned at the beginning who *'cannot* become regular employees.' This problem is not one which can be tackled on the level of education. It is a larger issue to do with the social structure.

The potential of specialisation

A housewives' and young people's problem

When it comes down to it, the issue is how to enhance the specialisation of caregiving. In other words, it is a question of how to construct pathways to career advancement in the caring profession which (at the present moment) has low specialisation.

Before getting into this problem, however, we need to think whether the caregivers who work onsite have any intention to climb the career ladder in the first place. If they have no wish to do so, then it will be meaningless to build any pathways to career advancement or the like. Let us take a look back at history. It is an issue relating to the merits and demerits of the Japanese type of welfare society.

The Japanese-style welfare society debate was a way of thinking which lay at the root of the government's social security policy from the 1980s onwards, being something that aimed at enrichment of the foundations of the family vis-à-vis Japan's ageing society, that is, the strengthening of the housewife's role, in response to moves to overhaul welfare in the period of low economic growth that followed the post-war high-growth years. This was underpinned by moves to review welfare in the low-growth period, as I have said.

According to Sumitaka Harada, social security – which had been made the target of 'enhancement and expansion' in the early 1970s – was repositioned as an object of obvious 'control' in the 1980s, after having gone through a period of 'improvement and adjustment' following the oil crises.

In such a Japanese-style welfare society, the position vis-à-vis the family in social security policy also met with a huge change of direction. This was a switch from an understanding of the family 'as the object of social assistance' such as was seen at the beginning of the 1970s, to one that apprehended the family 'as a supporter of control of social security,' and, further, to the family 'as the party shouldering responsibility for social security' (Harada 1988, pp. 367–73).

The discourse on the Japanese-style welfare society, which includes the aspect of restoration of traditional family norms, is often criticised as something that 'went up in smoke' (Harada 1988, p. 391). If one considers that the end-result of the outsourcing of care work is not merely the labour of housewives in the home, but also low-paid caregiving jobs, most of which have been shouldered by housewives working part-time, then the argument for a Japanese-style welfare society cannot necessarily be described as 'a failure,' either.

Of useful reference here is Sakiko Shiota's criticism of 'housewives' feminism.' While positing that the 1980s were an age that encouraged housewife diversification, with working housewives, housewives participating in local activities, and so on, Shiota indicates that most of this was borne by housewives' part-time work, and was premised on the existence of spouses who financially supported those housewives. According to Shiota, seventy percent of housewife part-time workers, whose numbers had increased rapidly from 1975, were from dual-income households where they were dependents. This undeniably was the foundation of the gendered division of labour (Shiota 1992, p. 43).

It was these housewives who also took on caregiving jobs. In light of this, the fact that full-time housewives took responsibility for care work, which was only afforded a low social evaluation, is something that can be amply discussed within the framework of Japanese-style welfare society, with the exception of a slight margin of error consisting of the fact that those undertaking the labour were not 'housewives in the home' but 'local housewives doing part-time work.'

Housewife part-time workers are responsible for low-paid care work. The collapse of Japanese-style welfare society came directly as a disintegration of what Emiko Ochiai (1994) describes as the 'fifty-five-year institution of the family,' consisting of the 'full-time housewife/salaryman.' It is a problem of employment for the so-called 'lost generation.' What was talked about with overblown 'expectations' on those occasions was welfare work. As a result, large numbers of young people surged into the world of welfare.

The biggest issue in having both housewives and young people in the caregiving workplace is that a huge gap arises between the two parties' awareness of working conditions. Many of the former, who work for not much above 'pocket money,' place more importance on whether the job is 'challenging and worthwhile' than on any improvement in working conditions. In other words, they are not interested in career advancement. On the other hand, most of the latter, who wish to make care work their stable, lifelong career, want to see working conditions improve even a little as soon as possible. In short, they are interested in career advancement. The collapse of the Japanese-style welfare society drove a wedge into the care workplace. This is what constitutes the 'housewives' and young people's' problem.

The two specialisations

When we think about specialisation and career advancement in care work, in workplaces plagued with the 'housewives' and young people's' problem that is unique to Japan, we must take care not to confuse the two. In other words, we must separate specialisation in care work into the type which ties to career advancement and that which does not, and place young people and housewives into each. It is necessary, for that reason, to make a clear-cut distinction between the types of specialisation.

Here, my argument will link with the problem of workaholism in dispatch riders, which was discussed in the first section. As work

Figure 12.1: The two phases of specialisation

Specialisation 1

Preventing workaholism   Motorbike delivery rider/'challenge-oriented' worker

Specialisation 2

Setting a course for career advancement   'Turning-professional-oriented' worker

and self-actualisation often overlap in the case of 'challenge-oriented' workers who have financial leeway, they run the risk of becoming 'self-actualising workaholics.' The sort of specialisation they require, therefore, is one that would prevent workaholism.

On the other hand, the specialisation needed by 'professionally-oriented' workers who wish to stabilise their livelihood is one that would put them on the path of career advancement, and 'challenge' seldom becomes a problem in that case (see Figure 12.1).

Let me summarise the discussion as far as eliciting the two functions of such specialisation. In a book entitled *Tagenka suru 'nōryoku' to Nihon shakai* (Diversifying 'skills' and Japanese society), sociologist Yuki Honda uses the term 'hyper-meritocracy' (a meritocracy[3] that has been upgraded and become even more powerful) for the principle controlling people's social position (that is, their status-acquisition) in a 'post-modern society'; and the term 'post-modern skills' for the various skills that a hyper-meritocracy demands of people ('all the skills that are flexible, and rooted deeply in an individual's personality and emotional makeup, including ambition, originality, interpersonal skills, networking ability and problem-solving skills'). Honda proposes that people's individually equipping themselves with a specialisation in itself 'will become effective "armour" for resisting calls for the relentlessly slippery "post-modern skills" that a hyper-meritocracy thrusts at them' (Honda 2005, p. 261).

In concert with changes in the industrial structure, there is an advancing shift away from manufacturing to an information-and service-based economy. In that environment, workers' discretionary scope also broadens. In cases where excessive overwork is the result, it is effective to build a breakwater in terms of specialisation in order to prevent it. Its effectiveness does not extend beyond that, however.

Honda's assertion that specialisation can become a worker's 'armour' is correct. At the same time, though, one must be aware that there are also cases in which that very specialisation holds a worker back.

In fact, for many people, equipping themselves with a specialisation is also something that constitutes a 'big gamble' in their lives. Attending a technical college for training in care-giving and becoming a certified care worker; going to law school and becoming a lawyer; enrolling in a technical college that issues qualifications and becoming a real-estate appraiser; attending a catering college and becoming a cook – people spend both time and money, and take on the challenge of the barrier called 'qualifications' with determination. For that reason, the 'armour' called specialisation is not the sort of thing that could promptly be discarded and replaced with some other 'armour.' That 'armour' is imbued with its owner's feelings. It is not something that would be taken off and thrown away immediately just because the work had disappeared.

In other words, in a highly fluid labour market, acquisition of a specialisation can sometimes be a disadvantage in that it removes workers' ability to be mobile, though under normal circumstances they would have to be ready to move, and it makes them stay in a workplace with no future prospects. This will be easy to understand if you think of care workers who, because of their qualification as 'certified care workers,' cannot abandon their pride in that qualification, and so find it very difficult to change occupations. It would be preferable for a 'specialisation without a future' to be something that could be sloughed off at any time.

Let me sum up. Specialisation is something that is necessary in the sense of placing a check on unlimited labour in workplaces where a 'hyper-meritocracy' is demanded. This constitutes the first stage of the discussion. There are two types of specialisation, however, these being 'specialisation that enables career advancement' and 'specialisation that offers no hope of career advancement.' As mistaking one for the other leads to falling into a 'bait-and-switch' situation, it is an important distinction to make. Moreover, the choice of specialisation should be one that can be made in conjunction with the worker's socio-economic conditions. This comprises the second stage in the discussion.

To rephrase this in familiar language, Specialisation 1 could also be said to mean 'manual-based' and Specialisation 2 to 'qualified.' As talking about 'manual-based' in the same terms as 'qualified' will induce a 'bait-and-switch' situation, and the two are heading in different directions to begin with, it is necessary to make a clear-cut distinction when considering them.

'Job-selection' simulation

Finally, taking the above discussion into account, let us try a simulation of 'job selection' involving you, the reader. This will also constitute a 'summary' of this chapter.

Firstly, I would have you think about the job you would prefer. If it is stable work (lawyer or doctor, for example), that would be most fortunate for you. You would merely need to aim for it and give it your best efforts. Problems will arise in the case where your preferred occupation is unstable (such as dispatch rider or animator). As there is greater risk of becoming a 'self-actualising workaholic' in that case, there is a need to take care not to become one, if possible. In other words, it would be better to choose a workplace where Specialisation 1 is established, one that is solidly manual-based.

If you were aware of Specialisation 1, and evaded burnout, you could probably have a life that consisted of hopping from one preferred job to another. If, however, you also grew tired of such a lifestyle and wanted to extricate yourself from a condition of unstable employment – in short, to abandon a job you liked for one that was secure – there would be such an alternative, as well. In that case, Specialisation 2 would become an issue. On that occasion, it would be necessary to note the extent to which that specialisation opened up career pathways.

As a result, if you were able to equip yourself with Specialisation 2, which had a future, then you would finish there. If, though, it turned out to be 'bait-and-switch,' then you would have to go back one step and try once again.

A summary of the simulation can be found in Figure 12.2, illustrating the following conditions: 'Continue a preferred, stable job' (A); 'Burn out in a preferred though unstable job' (B); 'Continue preferred though unstable (multiple) jobs without burning out' (C); 'Continue a job that is neither preferred nor stable' (D); and 'Continue a non-preferred but stable job' (E).

The (B) and (D) conditions are the problematic ones into which 'young people who *do not* become regular employees' and 'young people who *cannot* become regular employees' fall, respectively. Specialisation 1 is that which would enable a transition from (B) to

What is at question in youth labour issues?

Figure 12.2: 'Job choice' simulation

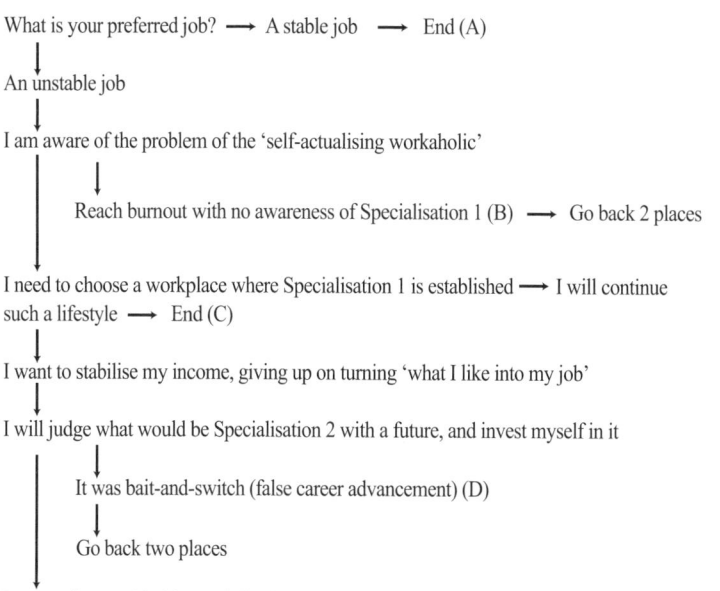

(C), while Specialisation 2 is the one that would enable a transition from (D) to (E).

There is probably a need to think in future of what ways there are of establishing specialisations, while ascertaining the differences between the two.

Notes

1 See, for example, the 2005 research survey relating to youth employment (*Heisei 17-nen seishōnen no shūrō ni kansuru kenkyū chōsa*) conducted by the Naikakufu Seisaku Tōkatsu Kan (Director-General for Policy, Cabinet Office).
2 Useful for reference here is *The Big Book of Jobs*, which perhaps should be called the American version of Murakami's *The job centre at age thirteen*. All sorts of occupations, from medical doctor to dispatch rider, are exhaustively introduced in that occupational guidebook, a thick tome like a telephone directory, with a total of over 700 pages. The 'Couriers and Messengers' section, which corresponds to dispatch riders, notes that the job does not require a post-secondary education, that hiring is on a downward trend due to the spread of such technology as emails and faxing, and that the average annual income is about US$200,000.
3 This refers to a performance-based or ability-based system.

13 What does it mean to be a 'Japanese'?: the current state of 'national identity' in Japan, based on ISSP 2003

Shunsuke Tanabe

What does it mean to be a 'Japanese'?

The 'comfort women' issue, the 'Yasukuni Shrine' question and the like are often taken up in the news as 'troubling' problems that are hard to resolve. Readers have probably heard that critical opinions have also been raised by China, South Korea, the United States (Congress) and so on, over the deletion of description of comfort women from history textbooks, or the official visits by the prime minister to the Yasukuni Shrine in Tokyo, where the war dead are venerated.

Some people in Japan might feel some measure of resistance to such criticism from other countries. Alternatively, though they might not think anything of it themselves, they might see the flood of posts saying: 'I hate China/I hate Korea' on Internet bulletin boards, and get the idea that a lot of people are feeling anger at what China and Korea were claiming. Furthermore, there are probably also people who have read newspaper articles with such headlines as: 'China-hating and Korea-hating, spreading in the Net age,' by reporters who have seen those bulletin boards, or texts composed by 'intellectuals' who lament the 'dangers of nationalism.'

Why, though, do people 'feel resistance' to assertions from other countries which criticise prime-ministerial visits to the Yasukuni Shrine, and suchlike? It is not that they themselves have been directly censured, nor is the reason for their anger 'simple and obvious.' Even so, it is unlikely to mean that their resistance and anger are a complete lie and fabrication, either.

To express the wellspring of that kind of emotion in a word, it would probably be that each thinks: 'I am Japanese.' Being 'Japanese' (or any other '-ese,' for that matter) is something of which people are seldom aware in their daily lives. Being '-ese,' which for the great majority is felt to be a matter of course that leaves no room for doubt, is actually neither inevitable nor obvious. Even if they are born to the same parents, if they happen to have been born while their mother was travelling in the United States, they can become 'American' (in terms of citizenship). Alternatively, even though they were born and raised in Japan, can speak nothing but Japanese, and have never been to Korea, there are also third-generation Korean residents of Japan who are treated as 'Koreans' (at least in terms of citizenship).With this in mind, such a question as who is '-ese' might be a product of coincidence, after all, because nobody can choose their country of birth, or their birth parents. Paradoxically, that might have exerted a strong influence upon people's consciousness and behaviour for the very reason that they believe they became '-ese' naturally, without choosing for themselves.

Then again, is there not a gap, or feeling of discomfort, somewhere between one's directly-perceived idea that one 'is Japanese' and the topics taken up by the mass media, and the like? The mass media only report 'issues' that are topical. For that reason, it might be more natural for there to be a gap between one's own 'regular' consciousness and that of the people in one's vicinity.

Is there no way, perhaps, for the consciousness of the vast majority of people who are not featured in the mass media or who do not post on the Internet to get to know this? Not necessarily. What shines a light onto that darkness is the quantitative approach in social surveys. As such, in this chapter, after having made a summary of prior studies and their methods of analysis in regard to the concept of 'national identity' which ordinary people harbour as '-ese consciousness,' I will elucidate its reality by statistically analysing social survey data.

Ways of apprehending 'national identity'

'Modernism' and 'ethno-symbolism': what is a 'nation'?

Simply speaking, national identity is an emotion that unifies the self in regard to 'national things.' What, though, is that 'nation' which constitutes the basis of those 'national things' in the first place? Theoretical research on that subject has been prolifically conducted since the 1980s.

Firstly, what is important among these studies is Ernest Gellner and Benedict Anderson's claims about 'modernism.' They assert that nations, which are conceived as having a history since time immemorial, and 'nation states,' as well, which are born with those nations as their parent body, are actually 'modern creations' generated as the result of modernisation and industrialisation. Gellner (1983), for instance, had the idea that nations were born in order to re-unify, by linguistic and cultural means, people who had been cut off by industrialisation from such fundamental connections as territorial or blood relationships. Furthermore, in a work with the stimulating title of *Imagined Communities* (1991), Anderson argued that the space and time in which newspapers and novels in a specific vernacular spread widely along with the expansion of print-capitalism, and which people came to imagine as the domain where they could communicate in that language, was a nation as an 'imagined community.'

In counter to those modernist theories, it is Anthony D. Smith's *Nationalism and Modernism* (1998) which asserts that, in order for a nation to be established, there needs to be an ethnic community (*ethnie*) from which it derives its history and origins. Even while acknowledging elements that arose through modernisation, he argues that ethnic communities have existed since pre-modern times in many nations, and that one cannot ignore the fact that their cultural/historical continuity has become the core of their present-day nation. His assertion, which champions historical continuity with the pre-modern in that way, has come to be called 'ethno-symbolism' (Smith 1986, and others).

In the abovementioned research, the genesis of nations and their historical formation process on a macro level (group level) was focused upon. For that reason, those studies were ones conducted from the 'productionist/state-centric' perspective which, to borrow the words of Kōsaku Yoshino, sees 'the cultural/political elite "produce" ideology (knowledge, ways of thinking) relating to the identity of an ethnic group and unilaterally transmit it from above by means of school education and textbooks which the state controls' (Yoshino 1997, p. 230). In consequence, as Yoshino points out, the perspective of what kind of people accept and consume the nation is missing. In other words, those studies have not elucidated the national identity held by 'ordinary' (not elite) people of the 'here' (not in some distant other country) and 'now' (not in the historical past).

Postmodernist research: the quest for multi-faceted national identity

Though modernist and ethno-symbolist arguments depicted a nation-state as a monolithic presence in many cases, the various studies given the name of 'postmodernism' by Anthony D. Smith (1998) focus, by contrast, upon individuals or groups within a nation, and pay attention to such things as the pluralism and diversity of their national identity. In concrete terms, these are studies that discuss the impact of multiculturalism, feminism and globalisation, as well as their connection with national identity, and there are also many which have been influenced by cultural studies, and so on.

Michael Billig, for one, has pointed out that 'flagging the homeland' in 'prosaic, routine words' (1995, p. 93) and media reporting (for instance, the remark often aired in Japan at the time of a plane crash in another country: 'There were no Japanese among the passengers,' et cetera) makes national identity in advanced countries a banal and unforgettable presence. In contrast to the macro (group) perspective of modernism and ethno-symbolism, such research has conducted its discussion from a micro level (individual level), and could be called research into the national identity of the 'here' and 'now' (in counter to modernism and ethno-symbolism's 'past').

Just as the representative advocate of cultural studies, Stuart Hall, regards identities as 'increasingly fragmented and fractured' (1996, p. 4), many postmodern studies restrict their discussion to the connection between their respective issues of research interest (mass media, globalisation, and the like) and national identity, and deftly explain its pluralism and dynamic fluctuation. Conversely, however, because advocates each target a diverse 'national identity' based on their individual interests, its definition and semantic content is correspondingly varied, and theories which seem at a glance to produce quite the opposite conclusion exist concurrently. Much of postmodern research certainly has elucidated some part of the 'here' and 'now,' but it is also a fact that it *only* depicts one part of it (and a 'special' one, at that), with the national identity of 'ordinary' people remaining invisible.

The quantitative approach: the national identity of 'ordinary' people

In the kind of research mentioned above, the object of discussion has been the history of national identity, or else its relationship to other individual phenomena. By contrast, in this chapter, I will outline the 'here' and 'now,' and the national identity of 'ordinary' people, based on data obtained from social surveys. To that end, in this chapter I will not use a hypothesis-verification type of method generally employed in quantitative analysis, which tests a theory by means of data, but will conduct an 'empirical investigation' (Kanomata 2001) which interprets empirical data by theoretical means. By doing so, I will elucidate the national identity held by contemporary, ordinary people through analysis of quantitative data.

Quantitative research, which integrates the multifarious and varied opinions of many people in a questionnaire full of options, is not suited to the detailed delineation of the complexity of individual national identity. Rather, it can only apprehend it in a 'cursory' manner, one might say; yet conversely, its interest lies in its very ability to draw a rough overall picture. It is a fact that (the national identity of) each different individual is different, and is an irreplaceable, unique presence. By collecting those individual responses and scrutinising them through the filter of statistics, however, fundamentally shared commonalities among people and the connections between their mutual consciousnesses, which would not become visible simply by gazing at people one by one, will come into view. That very 'discovery' is one of the joys of quantitative sociological research.

The actual state of 'national identity,' seen from data analysis

In this section, I will conduct analysis using the 2003 data from the International Social Survey Programme (hereafter, 'ISSP'), in order to examine national identity in Japan by means of the quantitative approach shown in the previous section.[1]

ISSP is an international collaborative research programme which began in 1984, involving the four countries of the United Kingdom, West Germany, the United States and Australia, with the aim of obtaining quantitative data that would enable international comparison. Since the initial survey in 1985, surveys based on specific themes have been carried out annually in the ISSP member countries. Those themes are truly broad-ranging, including the role of government, social networks, social inequality, the family and gender roles, religion, and so on. As of 2011, the number of member countries, also, had increased to forty-eight.

The national identity survey employed in the current study was one conducted in 2003, and its target countries totalled a whole thirty-five. The Japanese data within it used in the current analysis was obtained by selecting 'nationals'[2] aged sixteen and above by nationwide stratified random two-stage sampling from the Basic Resident Register. The sample size ultimately obtained by the individual interview method was 1102 (a response rate of 61.2 percent).

Who is 'Japanese'?: conditions for membership of the nation

For many people, it would surely be far from a common experience to be asked: 'Are you Japanese?' Even so, it does not follow that the answer will be easy for everyone. Moreover, it is difficult to suggest that the conditions underlying that question, namely, 'You will be Japanese, if you are such-and-such,' are so self-evident.

Let us think, for example, about the conditions under which a person of Japanese descent (*Nikkeijin*), and a naturalised citizen, respectively, can each be called 'Japanese.' *Nikkeijin* might be regarded as 'Japanese' in the aspect of 'blood (bloodline),' but under the condition of 'citizenship,' they would be 'foreigners.' On the other hand, in the case of a naturalised citizen, by 'citizenship' they would be treated as 'Japanese,' but from the aspect of 'bloodline,' it cannot be denied that they could possibly be seen as 'non-Japanese.'

In this way, the issue of what conditions to use to define a person as '-ese' is quite a difficult problem. Rogers Brubaker (1992), who pursued the question theoretically, discusses methods of defining nationals, or, in other words, the 'bounds of belonging,' that is, whom to regard as 'citizens,' from the differences between France and Germany in the concept of 'nationality (citizenship).' France, which makes 'being born in that country' (*jus soli*) its major criterion, effects an assimilationist understanding of the nation, while in Germany, which established a descent-based (*jus sanguinis*) nationality, namely, 'being born to a (Germanic) ethnic group,' 'immigrants' continued to be 'foreigners' to the bitter end, even if they were born in Germany and had continued to reside there (Brubaker 1992, p. 33).[3]

Present-day Japan has adopted a policy of *jus sanguinis* (like Germany), not a *jus soli* (like France). It has been pointed out in various studies, however, that the pre-war bounds of belonging in Japan related not to a 'mono-ethnic state,' but a 'multi-ethnic empire' (see Oguma 1995, 1998, et cetera, for detail). Nevertheless, that kind of historical and institutional boundary is not one that necessarily matches the boundary in people's minds. So, what might be the 'image of the real Japanese person' that ordinary people of today conceive? The question that was posed in order to find out their 'conditions for membership of the nation' was one akin to the following.

> Question: Some people say that the following things are important in order for a person to be truly Japanese. Others say they are not important. How important do you think each of the following is?
> a. to have been born in Japan (place of birth)*
> b. to have Japanese citizenship (citizenship)
> c. to have lived most of their adult life in Japan (years of residence)
> d. to be able to speak Japanese (language)
> e. to be a believer in Buddhism or Shintoism (religion)
> f. to respect the Japanese political system and laws (observance of laws and institutions)
> g. to feel themselves as being Japanese (self-definition)
> h. to have Japanese ancestry (bloodline)
> * The words in brackets at the end of each line were inserted by the author. From here one, I will use the abbreviations in the brackets to refer to each item.
> Options: 1 Very important; 2 Fairly important; 3 Fairly unimportant; 4 Not important at all

The above responses were summarised into the 'emphasisers' (the 'very important' and 'fairly important' responses) and the 'non-emphasisers' (the 'fairly unimportant' and 'not important at all' responses), with no response, such as 'I don't know,' recorded as 'missing.' The observed response distribution is as in Figure 13.1.

The condition reported by the greatest number of people was 'self-definition.' Moreover, the standard deviation[4] which shows

What does it mean to be a 'Japanese'? 267

Figure 13.1: Distribution of opinions on conditions for membership of the nation (N = 1,102)

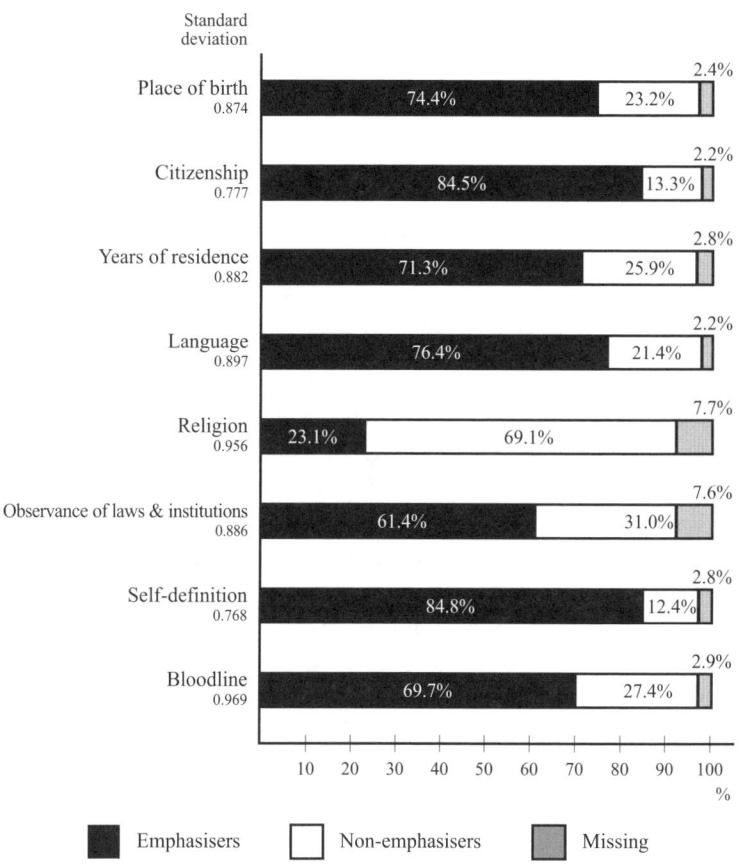

the response dispersion in relation to 'self-definition' is also small, so it is arguably an item that carries a certain measure of popular agreement. Next, the condition called 'citizenship' is emphasised, and it may be seen that there are many people who cite the acquired conditions of citizenship and self-definition as important conditions. On the other hand, 'religion' is the sole condition which only a minority of people thought to be of importance. This is probably a result that reflects the fact that for the majority in contemporary Japan, there is no connection between specific religions (Buddhism or Shintoism) and 'being Japanese,' unlike in the pre-war age of 'state Shinto.' Even now, to be sure, there is still the question of

Table 13.1: Results of factor analysis of conditions for membership of the nation

Eigenvalue	3.95
Place of birth	0.724
Citizenship	0.729
Years of residence	0.690
Language	0.713
Religion	0.543
Observance of laws & institutions	0.451
Self-definition	0.576
Bloodline	0.726

'official visits to Yasukuni Shrine' by the prime minister, and so on. Nevertheless, this is not thought to mean that even people who desire those visits want their head of government to go there 'because it is a religious act in accordance with Shintoism.'

Further, in order to grasp the connections among those items in a structural manner, the outcome of conducting factor analysis[5] vis-à-vis those items has been set out in Table 13.1.

Theoretically speaking, it is also possible to divide the conditions into those which individuals can later acquire (such as self-definition), and those attributive conditions which are determined merely by birth (such as bloodline). In terms of the results of analysis, however, it would be more faithful to the data to regard them as unified. This could be said to be an outcome which indicates that most Japanese people do not differentiate between those two factors – in other words, for many Japanese, being a Japanese national (= an acquired condition, and a civic factor) and having Japanese ethnicity (= an attributive condition, and an ethnic factor) blend together into one whole, and the distinction is seldom made.

What makes you feel 'pride'? National pride

Some people in Japan assert that it is 'masochistic' to teach about such things as the wartime comfort women, or the barbarity of the Japanese army; or they insist that the kind of education which teaches 'pride towards the country' be implemented. Even if their views are not as extreme as the above, more than a few people would like to feel 'pride' in their country, or desire it to have 'dignity.' The feeling called pride in one's country is an emotion that also links with a certain kind of 'patriotism,' and in some people, it can be considered also to constitute the wellspring that generates a sense of self-affirmation.

To feel 'pride' in one's country still might mean that the object of that pride differs according to the individual, however. For some people, the aspect that deserves pride might be the strength of Japan's economy in the world; while for others, it might be the achievements of Japanese athletes. What is more, it would not be strange even for there to be some who felt no pride whatsoever in things relating to Japan. Asking 'what aspect' of their country makes people feel proud is not a simple question, either.

Here, let us call that kind of pride in one's country 'national pride.' Respondents have been asked the following ten question items about this concept.

> Question: How proud are you of Japan in each of the following?
> a. The current situation of democracy in Japan (democracy)
> b. Japan's political influence in the world (world influence)
> c. Japan's economic achievements (economic development)
> d. Japan's social security system (social security)
> e. Achievements made by Japanese in the fields of science and technology (science and technology)
> f. Achievements made by Japanese in the sporting field (sports)
> g. Achievements made by Japanese in the fields of literature and the arts (arts)
> h. Japan's Self Defense Forces (military strength)
> i. Japan's history (history)
> j. Justice and equality in Japanese society (justice/equality)
> Options: 1 Very proud; 2 Somewhat proud; 3 Not very proud; 4 Not proud at all

In relation to the various items, '1 Very proud' and '2 Somewhat proud' were collapsed into 'Proud.' Similarly, '3 Not very proud' and '4 Not proud at all' were collapsed into 'Not proud,' respectively. The observed response distribution and standard deviation are as in Figure 13.2.

The aspects in which a great many people feel pride relate to cultural fields such as 'science and technology,' 'arts,' or else 'sports,' with more than eighty percent of respondents feeling pride in these.

Figure 13.2: Distribution of opinions on national pride
(N = 1,102)

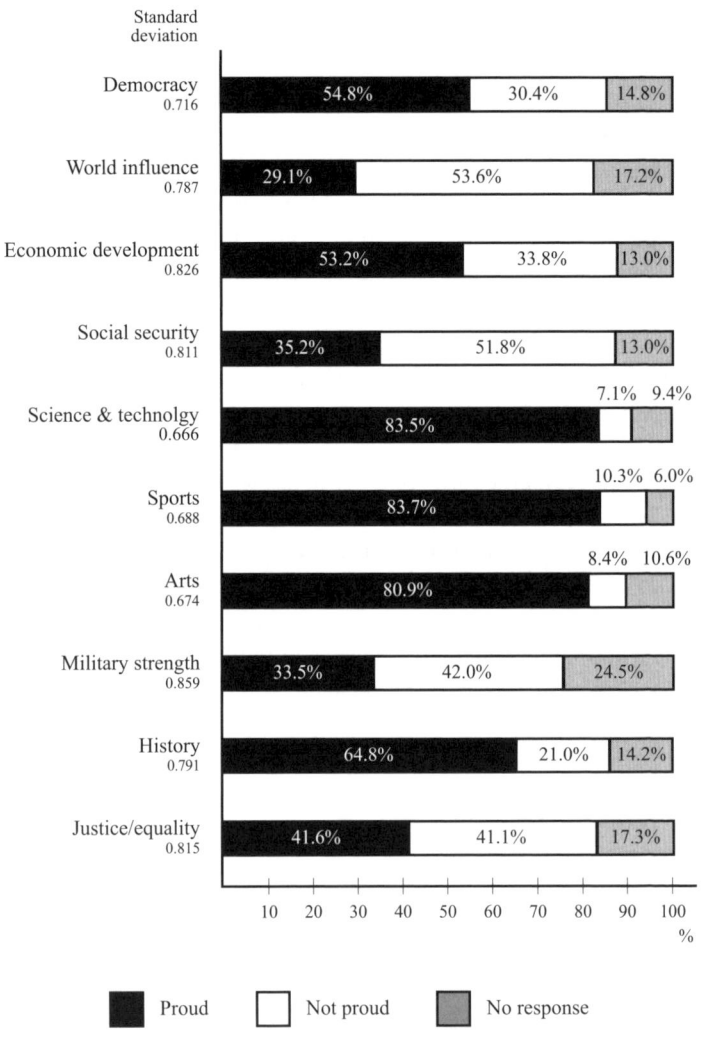

Next come 'history' and 'economic development,' then 'democracy,' these also being items in which more than half of Japanese people have pride. By contrast, 'world influence,' 'social security,' 'military strength' and the like have comparatively low evaluations, with many people *not* feeling proud of these. In Japan, the item about military strength was couched in terms of the 'Self Defense Forces

Table 13.2: Results of factor analysis of national pride
(Bold figures indicate a factor loading of ≥ 0.5)

	Factor 1	Factor 2
Loading (after rotation)	2.78	2.59
Democracy	**0.639**	-0.029
World influence	**0.650**	-0.004
Economic development	**0.579**	-0.032
Social security	**0.651**	-0.066
Science and technology	0.010	**0.782**
Sports	-0.031	**0.863**
Arts	0.010	**0.852**
Military strength	**0.546**	0.119
History	0.350	0.182
Justice/equality	**0.595**	0.002

(SDF),' but, as if to reflect the ambiguous positioning of the SDF in Japan, it is characteristic that the missing data rate due to no response and so on is conspicuously high, at 24.5 percent.

Next, in order to grasp the connectivity between the various items in a structural aspect, I carried out factor analysis. The outcome of extracting two factors from their eigenvalue changes and subjecting these to promax rotation is as in Table 13.2.[10]

In the first factor, the factor loading for items such as 'democracy' (0.639), 'world influence' (0.650), and 'social security' (0.651) is high, so I consider these to indicate pride in the political aspect (political pride). On the other hand, the second factor has a high loading for 'sports' (0.863), 'arts' (0.852), and 'science and technology' (0.782). I interpreted pride in the cultural side of the nation (cultural pride) among those items as a factor. The extraction of two types as a result of factor analysis in this way indicates that people understand pride and self-respect towards the nation in terms of two disparate factors: one political, one cultural.

Moreover, the factor loading for the 'history' item was on the low side in comparison with other items. Usually, 'history' is deemed an important factor in cultural national pride, from its links with such cultural aspects as national creation myths and traditions of all kinds (Smith 1986, p. 35). In Japan's case, however, the interpretation changes completely according to whether people imagine traditional cultural things such as Noh drama or *ukiyoe* wood-block prints from the word 'history,' or, alternatively, political claims relating to a history stating that the pre-war 'Great East Asia Co-Prosperity Sphere' was 'just.' In other words, when an appraisal of 'history' is requested in Japan, there is considerable possibility that the word's interpretation will have diverged greatly among respondents. In consequence, given the higher factor loading on political aspects (0.350), even while indeed having a constant factor loading (0.182) on the second cultural factor, this seems to have been an item that is neither one nor the other.

Various aspects of hatred for foreigners: anti-foreignism

Anti-foreignism is a consciousness which views those who do not belong to one's own nation as dangerous, and ostracises such people. Such a consciousness is something which is also linked to the fear of foreigners that is called xenophobia, and also comprises the 'outgroup hostility' part of the proposition formularised by Georg Simmel ([1908] 2009) as 'ingroup amity and outgroup hostility.' In addition, such a thing as 'hostility and prejudice towards the outgroup,' which is also a topic in social-psychological discussions that consider social identity, is also an argument that shares elements of this anti-foreignism (see Brown 1995, for one, on racism and prejudice).

It was the following series of questions that may be considered to have measured this concept of anti-foreign sentiment.

> Question: How important do you think are the following views regarding foreigners who come to Japan with the idea of settling here?
> a. If such foreigners increase in number, the crime rate will rise. (crime-rate escalation)
> b. Such foreigners are generally good for the Japanese economy.* (economic effects)
> c. Such foreigners take jobs away from Japanese people. (job-stealing)
> d. Such foreigners bring new ideas and culture, and are making Japanese society better.* (cultural diversification)
> e. The government spends too much money on helping such foreigners. (excessive aid)

What does it mean to be a 'Japanese'?   273

   Question: What do you think of the following opinions?[7]
   c. Foreigners who have legally migrated to Japan should have the
      same rights as any Japanese person.* (legal rights)
   d. The Japanese government should more severely crack down upon
      foreigners who are residing illegally, in order to deport them.
      (illegal residency crackdown)[8]
   Options: 1. Agree strongly; 2. Agree; 3. Neither agree nor disagree;
   4. Disagree; 5. Disagree strongly.

   Question: Do you think the number of foreigners who come to Japan
   with the idea of settling here should …? (Increase in foreigners)*
   Options: 1. increase a lot; 2. increase a little; 3. remain the same as it
   is; 4. reduce a little; 5. reduce a lot.

With the thought that items marked with an asterisk (*) are 'non-anti-foreign' as far as content goes, I have reversed the direction of the numerical value of the options.

Firstly, in relation to these eight items, I grouped them into anti-foreign opinions, moderate opinions ('neither agree nor disagree' and 'remain the same as it is'), and non-anti-foreign opinions. The observed distribution and response dispersion are as in Figure 13.3.

Those responding affirmatively to 'illegal residency crackdown' and 'crime-rate escalation' are extremely numerous, which implies that the foreigner issue in Japan is recognised as being a problem of 'public order.'[9] The item 'job-stealing,' on the other hand, had an approval rate that was comparatively low, at 25.3 percent. Many of the 'foreigner issues' in Western developed countries are considered as questions of migrant labour. In Japan, conversely, foreigners' work is officially limited to 'professional jobs,' and even supposing they work as irregular stayers, most are restricted to the 'so-called "3K jobs" (*kitsui* = difficult; *kitanai* = dirty; and *kiken* = dangerous)' in which Japanese people are loath to participate, with the result that occupational 'segregation' between Japanese and foreigners is being conducted. For that reason, the respondents can be considered comparatively non-anti-foreign in regard to 'jobs.' As for 'excessive aid,' perhaps because they do not know if the current government is 'aiding' foreigners, in the first place, about one-third of people made no response. Discussion over 'donor fatigue' relating to aid for foreigners is continuing in Europe and elsewhere, but in Japan, this is probably a result that reflects the dimension of whether 'aid' had existed from the start.

Figure 13.3: Distribution of anti-foreign views (N = 1,102)

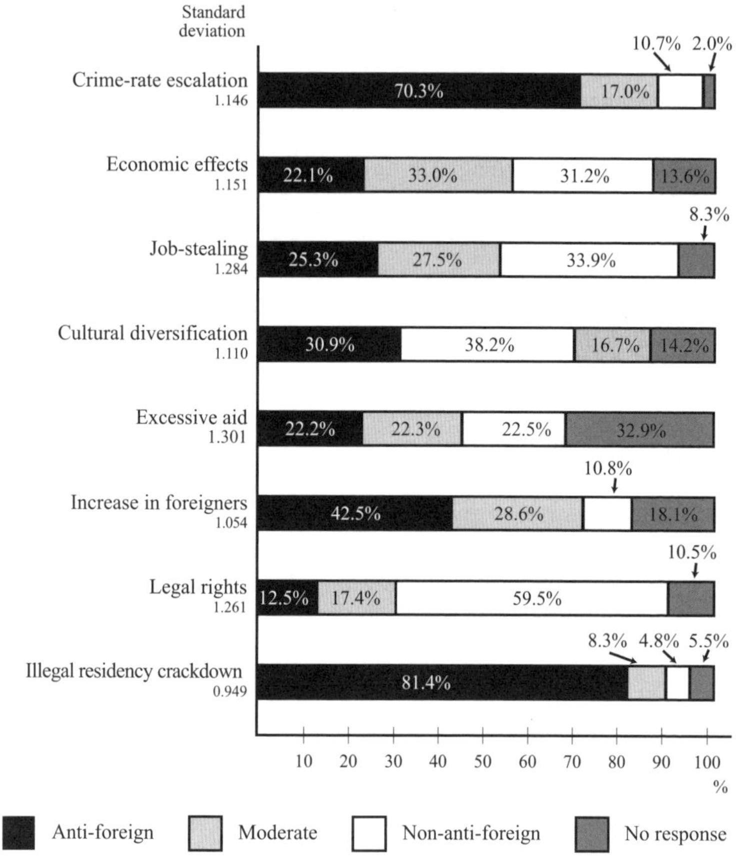

The outcome of factor analysis to examine further connections between the items is as in Table 13.3.[10]

The item with the highest loading (0.706) is 'increase in foreigners.' By contrast, those with low loadings include 'illegal residency crackdown' (0.358), 'legal rights' (0.377), and 'job-stealing' (0.495). Perhaps because responses to 'illegal residency crackdown' and 'legal rights' include people who responded to these as legal issues of illegality or legality, their link to anti-foreignism is thought to have weakened. As for the 'job-stealing' item, this would be a result indicating that, in terms of anti-foreign sentiment in Japan, the importance of the 'jobs' factor is comparatively low, as might be expected.

Table 13.3: Results of factor analysis of anti-foreign sentiment
(Bold figures indicate a factor loading of ≥ 0.5)

Eigen value	2.94
Crime-rate escalation	**0.599**
Economic effects	**0.534**
Job-stealing	0.495
Cultural diversification	0.499
Excessive aid	**0.595**
Increase in foreigners	**0.706**
Legal rights	0.377
Illegal residency crackdown	0.358

The typification of national identity: are Japan's 'patriots' exclusionist?

The analysis thus far has been one that explored the common structure among people in regard to national identity in Japan. By contrast, here I will attempt to discover patterns of national identity characteristic to contemporary Japan. For that purpose, this time I have used a statistical method called cluster analysis.[11]

Table 13.4, is a list of the mean values of subordinate concept scores for each of the four clusters (groups) derived as a result of cluster analysis, and the features of the people belonging to those respective clusters.

In the first cluster, membership conditions, political pride, and anti-foreign sentiment display negative values, and cultural pride is also somewhat low in comparison with the overall mean. Even though its constituents feel a certain amount of pride in Japan's cultural aspects, their boundaries of being a 'real Japanese person' are broad, meaning it is a non-anti-foreign pattern of national identity. Characteristic of people belonging to this cluster is that their average age is the youngest, and their ratio of constituents aged less than thirty is also high. Furthermore, it is also characteristic of them that, in terms of academic background, also, their average number of years of education is 13.3 years, and their university graduation ratio is the highest, as well, at 24.4 percent. Moreover, LDP supporters account for a mere ten percent or so, comprising about one third of the total. If we were to give this pattern a name, with the additional

Table 13.4: Mean values of subordinate concept scores and respective properties in each cluster

	Cluster number				All
	1	2	3	4	
Membership conditions	-0.40	1.66	1.32	0.29	0.88
Political pride	-1.08	0.94	-0.42	-0.05	0.01
Cultural pride	0.43	1.98	0.72	1.72	1.35
Anti-foreign sentiment	-0.42	0.81	1.19	-0.20	0.43
Affiliated sample numbers	168	347	277	310	1,102
Mean age	41.0	57.6	57.4	42.6	50.8
Proportion of <30 yrs	27.4%	9.2%	7.2%	24.2%	15.7%
Mean years of education	13.3	11.2	11.2	13.1	12.0
Proportion of university graduates	24.4%	7.8%	7.9%	19.7%	13.7%
Ratio of support for Liberal-Democratic Party	10.7%	46.7%	35.0%	22.9%	31.6%

consideration that political pride, especially, was low, then it would be something like an 'anti-nationalist national identity.'

As for people in the second cluster, all of their subordinate concept scores are higher in comparison with other clusters, their membership conditions are strict and they are xenophobic, as well, making them people with the kind of national identity that means having strong pride in Japan. In strong terms, this can be considered to be the type of national identity held by 'ultra-nationalistic' people. Characteristic of their attributes is that their average age is the highest (57.6 years), and their average number of years of education and university graduation ratio are low, also. On the other hand, their LDP approval rating is nearly fifty percent, which suggests they comprise a typical conservative stratum. This is a pattern such as can generally be called an 'ultra-nationalistic national identity.'

The third cluster is thought to be composed of people who, while having high membership conditions and anti-foreign sentiment, have comparatively weak political and cultural pride, and could be called something like 'exclusionists without patriotism.' Their characteristics of age and academic background are similar to the people belonging to the second cluster, except that their LDP ap-

What does it mean to be a 'Japanese'? 277

proval rating is slightly lower. On this point, it may be because they cannot feel 'pride in the country' in its current situation that they cannot meekly support the LDP, which typifies current conservative politics. In sum, this could be called an 'exclusionist national identity.'

People who belong in the fourth cluster, while having lower scores for membership conditions and xenophobia than the whole, score highly on cultural pride. In other words, these are people who, though perhaps 'patriots' in cultural terms, are not particularly exclusionist. Looking at their attributes, their university graduation ratio is somewhat lower in comparison with the first cluster, but their other features resemble those of the first cluster, their mean years of education being long, their average age being young, and their ratio aged less than thirty also being high. Their LDP approval rating is higher than the first cluster, however, and the height of their cultural pride can be considered to be linked to a certain extent to their affirmative sentiment vis-à-vis conservative politics. If we were to assign a name to this based on all of these characteristics, we could even call it a 'culturalistic national identity.'

When patterns of national identity were divided into four, as above, people with a national identity of the exclusionist or ultra-nationalist type were overwhelmingly numerous among the elderly. On the other hand, the majority of the young is not so xenophobic, and supposing there were to be pattern divisions within young people, this could be said to have resulted from demonstration that the level of pride (especially cultural pride) is the key.

Discussion: the 'conservative swing in young people' read from the data

There is now lively discussion as to 'young people's swing to conservatism.' For example, 'alarm bells' were rung (Kayama 2002) at the idea that young people who wildly enthused over the soccer World Cup were an ultra-nationalist reserve army (akin to those belonging to the second cluster), as a '*petit*-nationalism syndrome.' Yet if that kind of young people comprised those such as belonged to the fourth cluster in the analysis in the previous section, then, even if their cultural pride were high, their anti-foreign and national membership conditions scores could be anticipated to be comparatively low. In other words, there is a high likelihood that the alarm bells sounded by Kayama and her ilk were nothing more than impressionistic criticism not based on data, after all.

As a result of data analysis, the patterns of national identity in Japan differ enormously by generation (age), with the elderly age-group, in particular, having by far a national identity type that could be called 'nationalistic.' In consideration of this, the oft-mentioned phenomenon of 'young people's conservative swing' might merely be mistakenly seen – in view of those young people with strong 'cultural pride' such as in the fourth cluster – to be an extension of an ultra-nationalistic national identity just like that of people in the second cluster, or the exclusionist national identity held by people belonging to the third cluster. In actuality, it is overwhelmingly the elderly that harbour an ultra-nationalistic or exclusionist national identity. If Japan's current 'conservative swing' is a problem, then the national identity of comparatively older people ought to be made the issue.

If one looks only at bulletin boards on the Web, one could get the impression that the majority of young people have feelings of 'dislike for China' or 'dislike for Korea,' and are championing ultra-nationalism or exclusionism. Of course, some young people with an ultra-nationalist or exclusionist national identity do exist, but their ratio is comparatively small, and they can by no means be said to represent 'young people' in general. It is both the forte and the joy of quantitative sociological research that things such as the above are understood. It does not follow that those who stand out necessarily constitute 'the majority' or are directly 'representative.' What is more, I would be pleased if, from the analysis in this chapter, readers would emulate the perspective which, in counter to the oft-mentioned public assertion that 'young people lately do such-and-such,' tries to relativise it by asking: 'By young people, don't you mean one small portion of the young?'

Acknowledgments

The data utilised in this chapter were documented and made available by the Zentralarchiv für Empirische Sozialforschung, Köln. The data for the 'ISSP' were collected by independent institutions in each country (see principal investigators in the study-description schemes for each participating country). Neither the original data collectors nor the Zentralarchiv bear any responsibility for the analyses or conclusions presented here.

Notes

1 ISSP data are obtainable through the German data archive (GESIS). The analytical method which uses existing data in this way, rather than carrying out a survey of its own, is called secondary analysis. In Japan, also, the consolidation of data archives such as the SSJ data archive (http://ssjda.iss.u-tokyo.ac.jp/en/) run by the Institute of Social Science, the University of Tokyo, has progressed, and the secondary analysis of Japanese data is now available.
2 As will also be discussed later, the question of 'whom' to regard as 'nationals' is in itself a controversial issue. As target selection in the current survey has been carried out based on the Basic Resident Register, in which only people with Japanese citizenship are recorded, 'possession/ non-possession of Japanese nationality' can be thought to have been made a criterion. Thus, the question of 'from where the targets (also called "the sample") have been chosen' becomes extremely important in quantitative social surveys. For example, if this survey had solely targeted university students, would it really be permissible for it to be named '– in Japan'? If readers are interested in such issues, I recommend they read various books on social surveys and sampling methodology.
3 In Germany, however, a law acknowledging the acquisition of citizenship by birth in some instances came into existence in 1999, and it could also be said that the method of defining 'Germans' in Germany is in the process of transition. It is one of the difficulties of sociological research that the very object of study sometimes changes in this manner. At the same time, however, observing those developments and exploring the reason for them are also among its pleasures.
4 The standard deviation is a statistic which shows the extent to which responses are scattered. This case, in other words, illustrates how large the differences of opinion are among people. I recommend a book such as Takahashi and Trend-pro Co., Ltd (2008) *The Manga Guide to Statistics* as an introduction for people who wish to study such fundamentals of statistics. A good volume for those who want to study in more detail is Bohrnstedt and Knoke (1982) *Statistics for Social Data Analysis*.
5 Factor analysis is a statistical method which, assuming that there are latent factors (commonalities) among multiple variables, estimates their parts in common. This time, the maximum-likelihood approach was used as a factor extraction method. Moreover, the value called the eigenvalue, referenced in order to determine the number of factors, was 3.95 for the first factor, 0.87 for the second, and 0.75 for the third; and, in accordance with the Kaiser criterion, that is, choosing a factor with an eigenvalue of ≥ 1, it was judged most appropriate to explain it by means of one factor.
6 The eigenvalues were 3.78 for the first factor, 1.70 for the second, 0.86 for the third, and 0.70 for the fourth. Moreover, when two or more factors

are selected in factor analysis, the axis is 'rotated' in order to facilitate explanation; and out of the options for rotation, oblique rotation (promax rotation), which recognises that there is a connection among the chosen factors, was utilised in this instance. This was because it is hard to think that political pride and cultural pride have 'no connection whatsoever.' For comparison, as varimax rotation, which is often used as a method of rotation, is an orthogonal rotation which calculates on the assumption that there is 'no connection whatsoever' between the extracted factors, it would be inappropriate to use it in this case. Statistics are thus a useful tool, but if they are used wrongly, there is potential for distortion in the results that emerge, so care is needed.

7 The analysis has not included items such as: 'Children born in Japan should be able to have Japanese citizenship even if their parents are not Japanese nationals.' The reason for this is that, in Japanese, the expression: 'even if their parents are not Japanese nationals' can be interpreted as: 'both parents being foreigners' or 'one of the parents being a foreigner,' and so the meaning of the question was judged to be unclear. To avoid this kind of lack of clarity in the meaning of items, as well, the wording of the questions is extremely important.

8 As the very words 'illegal residency' include criminal and negative nuances, it is considered more appropriate to indicate overstaying foreigners whose visa has expired with the expression 'irregular stay(ers).' Here, however, I have employed the original wording of the item.

9 In the mass media and police announcements, it could be thought that public order is worsening because of foreigners, but in actuality that assertion is fairly doubtful. For details, see such volumes as Gaikokujin Sabetsu Wotchi Nettowāku (2004) *Gaikokujin hōi mō: 'chian akuka' no sukēpugōto* (Foreigners [under] siege: scapegoats of 'worsening public order'), or Kubo (2006), *Chian wa hontō ni akka shiteiru no ka* (Is public order really worsening?).

10 Eigenvalue changes are 2.94 for the first factor, 1.11 for the second, and 0.95 for the third; and, if the Kaiser criterion is followed, this will mean choosing up to the second factor. When two factors are selected, however, as the factors will have divided according to the nature of the item – that is, whether the item represents a positive or negative view – here, in consideration of the theoretical implications, I have selected only one factor.

11 Cluster analysis, in short, is an exploratory statistical method for summing up similar things. In the current case, for each respondent, I first assigned a score to their conditions for membership of the nation, political pride, cultural pride and xenophobia. In concrete terms, this meant making the following changes, for example: 'Very proud' = 2, 'Somewhat proud' = 1, 'Not very proud' = -1, 'Not proud at all' = -2 (with the midway option of 'Neither agree nor disagree' and 'no response' being 0); and, having multiplied the numerical values by the factor loading of each item, obtaining the total. Having done this, I divided each individual score by the standard deviation of its composite variables. In relation to the four scores thus created, I used K-means clustering and brought together the people with similar score profiles. In addition, as for determining the number of clusters in each case, I started the number of clusters from two, increasing them one by one, and, from the changes in mean value of

the individual's distance from the centre of the cluster, I determined the number of clusters to be four. However, there is no 'absolute' method of determining the number of clusters, and so, while understanding that it is a 'method for discovering something from data,' the analyst needs to use it skilfully.

12 Reasons for the elderly being more 'nationalistic' could be couched in terms of the 'age effect,' that is, having lived for many years as a 'Japanese national,' or the 'cohort effect,' that is, having been born in a specific generation, such as that which received a pre-war nationalistic education. It is difficult to distinguish precisely between these two types of effect, but if, for instance, one could conduct a survey called a panel survey, which tracks the same individuals continuously, and find out what manner of changes emerged along with the passing of time, this would be discriminable to a certain extent. As such, there is probably a need for sufficient appreciation that there are certain limitations to the analysis of survey data and the interpretation of its results.

Bibliography

Abe, Masahiro, 2006, *Sakushu sareru wakamonotachi: baiku-bin raidā wa mita!* (Exploited youth: a motorbike delivery rider saw [them]!), Shūeisha.
Abe, Masahiro, 2007, *Hatarakisugiru wakamonotachi: 'jibun-sagashi' no hate ni* (Young people who work too much: at the far reaches of 'self-discovery'), NHK shuppan.
Adorno, Theodor W., 1962, *Introduction to the Sociology of Music*, trans. E. B. Ashton, New York: The Seabury Press.
Aiba, Juichi, 1998, *Chihō bunka no shakaigaku* (The sociology of regional culture), Sekaishisōsha.
AIK Report, 2004, April issue.
Anderson, Benedict, 1991, *Imagined Communities: Reflections on the Origin and Spread of Nationalism*, rev. and extended edition, London; New York: Verso.
Andō, Yoshimi, 2003, *Gendai shakai ni okeru raifu kōsu* (Life courses in contemporary society), Hōsō daigaku kyōiku shinkōkai.
Azuma, Hiroki, 2002, *Dōbutsuka suru posuto modan: otaku kara mita Nihon shakai* (The animalising post-modern: Japanese society seen from the *otaku* viewpoint), Kōdansha.
Azuma, Hiroki, 2007, *'Gēmu-teki riarizumu' no tanjō: dōbutsuka suru posuto modan 2* (The birth of 'game-like realism': the animalising post-modern, 2), Kōdansha.
Azuma, Hiroki and Akihiro Kitada, 2007, *Tōkyō kara kangaeru* (Thinking from Tokyo), Nippon hōsō shuppan kyōkai.
Barthes, Roland, 1966, 'Introduction à l'Analyse Structurale des Récits (Introduction to structural analysis of narratives),' *Communications*, no. 8: 1–27.
Baudrillard, Jean, [1981] 1994, *Simulacra and Simulation*, Ann Arbor: University of Michigan Press.
Bauman, Zygmunt, 1998, *Globalisation: the human consequences*, Cambridge, UK: Polity Press.
Bauman, Zygmunt, 2000, *Liquid Modernity*, Cambridge, UK: Polity Press.
Benjamin, Walter, [1936] 2008, *The Work of Art in the Age of its Technological Reproducibility, and Other Writings on Media*, Michael W. Jennings, Brigid Doherty, and Thomas Y. Levin (eds); trans. Edmund Jephcott, et al., Cambridge, Massachusetts: Belknap Press of Harvard University Press, pp. 133–203.
Bessatsu Takarajima EX, 1995, *Manga no yomikata* (How to read *manga*), Takarajimasha.

Best, Joel, 1987, 'Rhetoric in Claims-Making: Constructing the Missing Children Problem,' *Social Problems*, 34(2), April: 101–21.
Billig, Michael, 1995, *Banal Nationalism*, London: Sage.
Bourdieu, Pierre, [1979] 1984, *Distinction: A Social Critique of the Judgement of Taste*, trans. Richard Nice, Cambridge, MASS: Harvard University Press.
Bourdieu, Pierre, [1992] 1996, *The Rules of Art: Genesis and Structure of the Literary Field*, trans. Susan Emanuel, Cambridge, UK: Polity Press.
Brown, Rupert, 1995, *Prejudice: Its Social Psychology*, Oxford, England: Blackwell.
Brubaker, Rogers, 1992, *Citizenship and Nationhood in France and Germany*, Cambridge, Massachusetts: Harvard University Press.
Burgess, Ernest W., [1925] 1967, 'The Growth of the City: an Introduction to a Research Project,' in Robert E. Park, Ernest W. Burgess and Roderick D. McKenzie, *The City*, Chicago and London: The University of Chicago Press, pp. 47–62.
Burgess, Ernest Watson and Harvey James Locke, 1945, *The Family: from Institution to Companionship*, New York: The American Book Company.
Cantril, Hadley, [1940] 1971, *The Invasion from Mars: a Study in the Psychology of Panic*, Princeton: Princeton University Press.
Caune, Jean, 1997, *Esthétique de la communication* (The aesthetics of communication), Paris: Presses universitaires de France.
Chodorow, Nancy, 1978, *The Reproduction of Mothering: Psychoanalysis and the Sociology of Gender*, Berkeley: University of California Press.
Contents Business Kenkyū Kai, 2005, *Zukai de wakaru kontentsu bijinesu* (Illustrated guide to the contents business), Japan Management Centre.
Coser, Lewis A. (ed.), 1963, *Sociology through Literature: an Introductory Reader*, Englewood Cliffs, NJ: Prentice-Hall.
Crane, Diana, 1994, 'Introduction: The Challenge of the Sociology of Culture to Sociology as a Discipline,' in Diana Crane (ed.), *The Sociology of Culture: Emerging Theoretical Perspectives*, Cambridge, MASS: Blackwell, pp. 1–19.
Culler, Jonathan D., [1997] 2009, *Literary Theory: A Brief Insight*, New York, NY: Sterling Publishing Co.
Derrida, Jacques, [1972] 1981, *Positions*, trans. and annotated by Alan Bass, Chicago: University of Chicago Press.
Doi, Takayoshi, 2003, '*Hikō shōnen' no shōmetsu: kosei shinwa to shōnen hanzai* (The vanishing of the 'delinquent child': the individuality myth and juvenile crime), Shinzansha.
Ehrenreich, Barbara, 2002, *Nickel and Dimed: On (Not) Getting by in America*, Owl Books.
Ehrenreich, Barbara, 2005, *Bait and Switch: The (Futile) Pursuit of the American Dream*, London: Granta Books.
Eliacheff, Caroline, and Nathalie Heinich, 2002, *Mères-filles: une relation à trois*, Paris: Albine Michel.
Fiske, John, 1991, *Reading the Popular*, London: Routledge.
Fitzgerald, Joan, 2006, *Moving Up in the New Economy: Career Ladders for U.S. Workers*, Ithaca, New York: Cornell University Press.
Fujimoto, Yukari, 2001, 'Bunshin: shōjo manga no naka no "mō hitori no watashi" (Alter ego: the "another me" in girls' comics),' in Kojirō Miyahara

and Masahiro Ogino (eds), *Manga no shakaigaku* (Sociology of comics), Sekaishisōsha, pp. 68–131.

Fujiwara, Sumiko, 1981, 'Hahaoya no shūrō ga kodomo no shokugyō-teki seiyakuwari ninshiki no hattatsu ni oyobosu eikyō (The influence that mothers' employment exerts upon the development of children's recognition of occupational sex roles), *Kaseigaku zasshi* (Journal of home economics of Japan), 32(2): 119–25.

Furuya, Minoru, 2005, *Shigatera* (Ciguatera), Kōdansha.

Gaikokujin Sabetsu Wotchi Nettowāku, 2004, *Gaikokujin hōi mō: 'chian akka' no sukēpugōto* (Foreigners [under] siege: scapegoats of 'worsening public order'), GENJIN bukkuretto 44, Gendai jinbunsha.

Gans, Herbert J., 1974, *Popular culture and high culture: an analysis and evaluation of taste*, New York: Basic Books.

Gellner, Ernest, 1983, *Nations and Nationalism*, Oxford, England: Blackwell.

Giddens, Anthony, 1992, *The Transformation of Intimacy: Sexuality, Love and Eroticism in Modern Societies*, Cambridge: Polity Press.

Gijinka Tanpakusho Seisaku Iinkai (ed.), 2006, *Gijinka tanpakusho* (Anthropomorphised protein/whitepaper), Asupekuto.

Glaser, Barney G., and Anselm L. Strauss, 1967, *The Discovery of Grounded Theory: Strategies for Qualitative Research*, Chicago: Aldine.

Goffman, Erving, [1974] 1986, *Frame Analysis: An Essay on the Organisation of Experience*, Boston: Northeastern University Press.

Griswold, Wendy, 2008, *Cultures and Societies in a Changing World*, 3rd edition, Los Angeles: Pine Forge Press.

Hall, Stuart, 1980, 'Encoding/Decoding,' in Stuart Hall et al. (eds), *Culture, Media, Language: Working Papers in Cultural Studies*, London: Hutchinson, pp. 128–38.

Hall, Stuart, 1996, 'Introduction: Who Needs Identity?' in Stuart Hall and Paul du Gay (eds), *Questions of Cultural Identity*, London; Thousand Oaks, California: Sage, pp. 3–17.

Harada, Sumitaka, 1988, 'Nihon-gata fukushi-shakai'-ron no kazoku-zō (The family image in 'Japanese-style welfare society' discourse), in Institute of Social Science, Tokyo University (ed.), *Tenkanki no fukushi kokka* (The welfare state in a period of transition), Tōkyō daigaku shuppan kai, pp. 366–78.

Haruno, Nanae, 1995, *Papa Told Me*, no. 14, 77, Shūeisha.

Hase, Masato, 2006, 'Bun'ya-betsu kenkyū dōkō (bunka): "posutomodan no shakaigaku" kara "sekinin to seigi no shakaigaku" e ('Research trends by field (culture): from a "sociology of the post-modern" to a "sociology of responsibility and justice"),' *Shakaigaku hyōron* (Japanese sociological review), 57(3): 615–33.

Hayami, Yukiko, 1999, *Kazoku sotsugyō* (Family graduation), Kinokuniya shoten.

Hebdige, Dick, 1979, *Subculture: the Meaning of Style*, London: Methuen.

Hidaka, Masahiro, 2003, *Yaru ka* (Will you do it?) *FUJI ROCK 1997–2003*), Hankyū komyunikēshonzu.

Hills, Matt, 2002, *Fan Cultures*, London: Routledge.

Hoggart, Richard, 1957, *The Uses of Literacy: Aspects of Working-Class*

Life, with Special Reference to Publications and Entertainments, London: Chatto and Windus.
Holstein, James A., and Jaber F. Gubrium, 1995, *The Active Interview*, Newbury Park, CA: Sage.
Honda, Tōru, 2005, *Denpa otoko* (Electric-wave man), Sansai bukkusu.
Honda, Yuki, 2005, *Tagenka suru 'nōryoku' to Nihon shakai: haipā merito-kurashī-ka no naka de* (Diversifying 'skills' and Japanese society: in the midst of hyper-meritocratisation), NTT shuppan.
Horkheimer, Max and Theodor W. Adorno, [1947] 1979, *Dialectic of Enlightenment*, trans. John Cumming, London: Verso Editions.
Imada, Takatoshi (ed.), 2000, *Shakaigaku kenkyū hō: riariti no toraekata* (Research methods in sociology: how to grasp reality), Yūhikaku.
Inaba, Shin'ichirō, 2006, *Modan no kūrudaun* (The cooling-down of the modern), NTT shuppan.
Inamasu, Tatsuo, 1989, *Aidoru kōgaku* (Idol engineering), Chikuma shobō.
Inamasu, Tatsuo, [1989] 1993, *Zōho aidoru kōgaku* (Idol engineering, enlarged [edition]), Chikuma shobō.
Inamasu, Tatsuo, 1991, *Furippāzu terebi* (Flippers' television), Chikuma shobō.
Inamasu, Tatsuo, 2003, *Pandora no media: terebi wa jidai o dō kaeta ka* (Pandora's media: how did television change the times?), Chikuma shobō.
Inoue, Masahito, 2006, 'Fasshon dezain (Fashion design),' in Hiroshi Kashiwagi (ed.), *Kindai dezain shi* (A history of modern design), Musashino bijutsu daigaku shuppan kyoku.
Inoue, Shun, 2000, *Supōtsu to geijutsu no shakaigaku* (Sociology of sports and the arts), Sekaishisōsha.
Iser, Wolfgang, [1976] 1978, *The Act of Reading: a Theory of Aesthetic Response*, Baltimore and London: The Johns Hopkins University Press.
Ishikawa, Atsushi, Kenji Satō and Kazunari Yamada (eds), 1998, *Mienai mono o miru chikara* (The power to see the invisible), Yachiyo shuppan.
Itō, Gō, 2005, *Tezuka izu deddo: hirakareta manga hyōgenron e* (Tezuka is dead: towards an open theory of expression in comics), NTT shuppan.
Iwakami, Mami, 2003, *Raifu kōsu to jendā de yomu kazoku* (The family, read in terms of life-course and gender), Yūhikaku konpakuto.
Iwasawa, Miho, 1999, 'Dare ga "ryōritsu" o dannen shite iru no ka?: mikon josei ni yoru raifu kōsu yosoku no bunseki (Who has given up on "balancing" [work and family]?: analysis of unmarried women's life-course projections),' *Jinkō mondai kenkyū* (Journal of population problems), 55(4): 16–37.
Kakei Keizai Kenkyūjo (Institute for research on household economics), 2005, *Jakunen sedai no genzai to mirai* (The younger generation's present and future).
Kamada, Daisuke, 1997, '"Shakai kairyō" no "shakaigaku"? (A "sociology" of "social reform"?),' in Makoto Hōgetsu and Masataka Nakano (eds), *Shikago shakaigaku no kenkyū: shoki monogurafu o yomu* (A study on the Chicago school of sociology: reading early monographs), Kōseisha kōseikaku, pp. 320–53.
Kanomata, Nobuo, 2001, *Kikai no byōdō to kekka no fubyōdō: sedaikan idō to shotoku/shisan kakusa* (Equality of opportunity and inequality of outcome: intergenerational mobility and income/asset disparity), Minerva shobō.

Kasai, Hirosuke, 2005, *Intabyū chōsa e no shōtai* (Invitation to interview surveys), Sekaishisōsha.

Kasesniemi, Eija-Liisa and Pirjo Rautianinen, 2002, 'Mobile culture of children and teenagers in Finland,' in James E. Katz and Mark Aakhus (eds), *Perpetual Contact: Mobile Communication, Private Talk, Public Performance*, Cambridge: Cambridge University Press, pp. 170–92.

Kashiwagi, Hiroshi, 1998, *Fasshon no nijusseiki: toshi, shōhi, sei* (Fashion's twentieth century: cities, consumption, sex), Nippon hōsō kyōkai.

Kawakami, Shiori, 2006–07, 'Naze mikon no wakamonotachi ga hidari kusuri-yubi ni yubiwa o suru no ka (Why do unmarried young people wear a ring on their left-hand ring finger?)' ([Unpublished] graduation report, Daisuke Tsuji Seminar, Faculty of Sociology, Kansai University).

Kayama, Rika, 2002, *Puchi nashonarizumu shōkōgun: wakamonotachi no Nippon shugi* (The *petit*-nationalism syndrome: young people's Japanism), Chūkō shinsho.

Keishichō (Metropolitan Police Agency), 2004, *Seishōnen no ishiki/kōdō to keitai denwa ni kansuru chōsa kenkyū* (Survey study on youth awareness/ behaviour and mobile telephones).

Kihara, Yoshihiko, 2006, *UFO to posutomodan* (UFOs and the post-modern), Heibonsha shinsho.

Kindaichi, Kyōsuke (chief ed.), 1997, *Shinmeikai kokugo jiten, dai-5 han* (New clearly-understandable Japanese dictionary, fifth edition), Sanseidō.

Kinoshita, Eiji, 1996, 'Oyako kankei kenkyū no hatten to kadai (Development and challenges in parent-child relationship research),' in Hisaya Nonoyama, Takako Sodei and Masami Shinozaki (eds), *Ima kazoku ni nani ga okotte iru no ka* (What is happening in the family now?), Minerva shobō, pp. 136–58.

Kitada, Akihiro, 2005, *Warau Nihon no 'nashonarizumu'* (Laughing Japan's 'nationalism'), Nippon hōsō shuppan kyōkai.

Kitayama, Seiichi, 1991, *Oshare no shakai shi* (A social history of style), Asahi shinbunsha.

Kobayashi, Naoki, 2003, '"Tennō no iku kuni" no terebi to ōdiensu (Television and audience in the "land of the dying emperor"),' in Naoki Kobayashi and Yoshitaka Mōri (eds), *Terebi wa dō mirarete kita no ka* (How has television been viewed?), Serika shobō, pp. 153–79.

Kokuritsu Shakai Hoshō/Jinkō Mondai Kenkyūjo (National institute of population and social security research), 2004, *Heisei jūyonen waga kuni dokushin seinensō no kekkon-kan to kazoku-kan: dai-jūnikai shusshō dōkō kihon chōsa* (Twelfth basic survey of birth trends: Our country's young singles' view of marriage and the family, 2002).

Kristeva, Julia, [1967] 1986, 'Word, dialogue, and the novel,' in Tolil Moi (ed.), *The Kristeva Reader*, New York: Columbia University Press, pp. 35–61.

Kubo, Hiroshi, 2006, *Chian wa hontō ni akka shiteiru no ka* (Is public order really worsening?), Kōjinsha.

Kuramochi, Fusako, 2001, *Tennen kokekkō* (Natural cock-a-doodle-doo), Shūeisha.

Lazarsfeld, Paul. F., Bernard Berelson and Hazel Gaudet, [1944] 1948, *The People's Choice: How the Voter Makes up His Mind in a Presidential Campaign*, second edition, New York: Columbia University Press.

Le Bon, Gustave, [1895] 1968, *The Crowd: A Study of the Popular Mind*, second edition, Dunwoody, GA: Norman S. Berg.
Lévi-Strauss, Claude, 1958, *Anthropologie Structurale* (*Structural anthropology*), Paris: Librarie Plon.
Lewis, Lisa A. (ed.), 1992, *The Adoring Audience: Fan Culture and Popular Media*, New York; Routledge.
Ling, Richard and Birgitte Yttri, 2002, 'Hyper-coordination via mobile phones in Norway,' in James E. Katz and Mark Aakhus (eds), *Perpetual Contact: Mobile Communication, Private Talk, Public Performance*, Cambridge: Cambridge University Press, pp. 139–69.
Luckmann, Thomas, 1967, *The Invisible Religion: the Problem of Religion in Modern Society*, New York: Macmillan.
Mabuchi, Kōsuke, 1989, *'Zoku'-tachi no sengo shi* (A post-war history of 'tribes'), Sanseidō.
Makimura, Satoru, 2002, *imagine*, comic version, vol. 1, Shūeisha bunko.
Mannheim, Karl, [1922] 1982, *Structures of Thinking* (*Strukturen des denkens*), trans. Jeremy J. Shapiro and Shierry Weber Nicholsen, London: Routledge and Kegan Paul.
Marx, Karl H., [1859] 1912, *Capital: A Critical Analysis of Capitalist Production* (*Das Kapital 1. Kritik der politischen Öekonomie*), trans. Samuel Moore and Edward Aveling, London: William Glaisher Ltd.
Masaoka, Kanji, 1993, 'Raifu kōsu ni okeru oyako kankei no hattatsuteki henka (Developmental changes in parent-child relationships over the lifecourse),' in Kunio Ishihara and Masami Morioka (eds), *Kazoku shakaigaku no tenkai* (The evolution of family sociology), Baifūkan, pp. 65–79.
Matsubara, Ryūichirō, 2002, *Ushinawareta keikan: sengo Nihon ga kizuita mono* (Lost views: things that post-war Japan built), PHP kenkyūjo.
Matsui, Yutaka (ed.), 1994, *Fan to būmu no shakai shinri* (The social psychology of fans and booms), Saiensusha.
Matsutani, Sōichirō, 2004a, 'Ureru zasshi no tsukurikata (How to make magazines that sell),' *Nikkei entateinmento!* (Nikkei entertainment!), September, Nikkei BP.
Matsutani, Sōichirō, 2004b, 'Wakamono no "jibunrashisa" shikō wa honmono ka? (2): zōshoku suru kamayatsu onna: gaitō ankēto chōsa kekka (Is young people's aim to "be themselves" the real thing? (2): the increasing women [who prefer] cheap-and-cheerful [clothing]: results of a streetside questionnaire survey),' *Psiko*, May, Tōjusha.
McCloud, Scott, 1993, *Understanding Comics: the Invisible Art*, Northampton, MA: Tundra Publishers.
McQuail, Denis (ed.), 1972, *Sociology of Mass Communications: Selected Readings*, Harmondsworth: Penguin.
Mead, George Herbert, 1934, *Mind, Self, and Society: From the Standpoint of a Social Behaviourist*, Chicago and London: University of Chicago Press.
Merton, Robert King, 1946, *Mass Persuasion: the Social Psychology of a War Bond Drive*, New York: Harper and Brothers.
Minamida, Katsuya, 2001, *Rokku myūjikku no shakaigaku* (Sociology of rock music), Seikyūsha.
Minamida, Katsuya, 2005, 'Enkōdingu/dekōdingu (Encoding/decoding),' in Eishō Ōmura, Kōjirō Miyahara and Keiichi Nabe (eds), *Shakai bunka riron*

gaidobukku (Socio-cultural theory guidebook), Nakanishiya shuppan, pp. 147–50.

Minamida, Katsuya, 2006, 'Media bunka no mirai (The future of media culture),' in Hidenori Tomita, Katsuya Minamida and Izumi Tsuji (eds), *Dejitaru media torēningu* (Digital media training), Yūhikaku, pp. 227–49.

Minamitani, Eriko and Akari Ii, 2004, *Fasshon toshi ron: Tōkyō, Pari, Nyū Yōku* (On fashion cities: Tokyo, Paris, New York), Heibonsha shinsho.

Mita, Munesuke, 1978, *Gendai Nihon no shinjō no rekishi* (History of sentiment in contemporary Japan), Kōdansha.

Miura, Atsushi, 2004, *Fasuto fūdoka suru Nihon: kōgaika to sono byōri* (Japan attuning to a 'fast-food-like' culture: suburbanisation and its pathology), Yōsensha.

Miura, Atsushi, 2005a, *Karyū shakai: aratana kaisō shūdan no shutsugen* (Low society: the emergence of a new stratum group), Kōbunsha shinsho.

Miura, Atsushi, 2005b, '*Kamayatsu onna*' *no jidai: josei kakusa shakai no tōrai* (The age of women [who prefer] 'cheap-and-cheerful' fashion: the advent of a society [with a] female income gap),' Makino shuppan.

Miyadai, Shinji, [1996] 1997, 'Kōgaika to kindai no seijuku (Suburbanisation and the maturation of modernity),' in *Maboroshi no kōgai: seijuku shakai o ikiru wakamonotachi no yukue* (The illusionary suburbs: the path of youth living in a mature society), Asahi bunko.

Miyadai, Shinji, 1997, *Maboroshi no kōgai: seijuku shakai o ikiru wakamonotachi no yukue* (The illusionary suburbs: the path of youth living in a mature society), Asahi shinbunsha.

Miyadai, Shinji, [1999] 2002, '"Kamigata jiyū zoku" ga karada o ijiru wake (The reason why the "freestyle hair tribe" fiddle with their bodies),' in *Enkō kara tennō e* (From compensated dating to the emperor), COMMENTARIES: 1995–2002, Asahi bunko.

Miyadai, Shinji, Hideki Ishihara and Meiko Ōtsuka (eds), 1993, *Sabukaruchā shinwa kaitai* (Deconstructing subculture myths), Parco shuppan.

Miyadai, Shinji, Hideki Ishihara and Meiko Ōtsuka (eds), [1992/1993] 2007, *Zōho sabukaruchā shinwa kaitai: shōjo, ongaku, manga, sei no hen'yō to genzai* (Enlarged edition: Deconstructing subculture myths: the changing appearance of girls, music, comics and sex, and their present form), Chikuma shobō.

Miyahara, Kōjirō, 2001, 'Chiteki shokubai toshite no manga (Comics as intellectual catalysts),' in Kōjirō Miyahara and Masahiro Ogino (eds), *Manga no shakaigaku* (Sociology of comics), Sekaishisōsha, pp. 4–31.

Miyahara, Kōjirō and Masahiro Ogino (eds), 2001, *Manga no shakaigaku* (The sociology of *manga*) Sekaishisōsha.

Miyajima, Takashi, 2000, 'Sōron, gendai no bunka-kenkyū no kadai (Introduction, Subject of present-day cultural studies),' in Takashi Miyajima (ed.), *Kōza shakaigaku 7. Bunka* (A series of lectures on sociology, 7. Culture), Tokyo daigaku shuppan kai, pp. 1–19.

Miyamoto, Michiko, 2004, *Posuto seinenki to oyako senryaku: otona ni naru imi to katachi no hen'yō* (Post-adolescence and parent-child strategies: transformations in the meaning and shape of becoming adult), Keisō shobō.

Miyamoto, Michiko, Mami Iwakami and Masahiro Yamada, 1997, *Mikon-ka shakai no oyako kankei: okane to aijō ni miru kazoku no yukue* (Parent-child relationships in an increasingly unmarried society: the direction of the family seen in money and love), Yūhikaku.

Miyasaka, Yasuko, 2000, 'Oya imēji no hensen to oyako kankei no yukue (Transitions in parental image and the direction of parent-child relationships),' in Hiroko Fujisaki (ed.), *Oya to ko: kōsaku suru raifu kōsu* (Parents and children: entangled life-courses), Minerva shobō, pp. 19–41.

Miyoshi, Haruki, 2005, *Kaigo no senmonsei to wa nani ka* (What does specialisation in care mean?), Kirara shobō.

Mizuta, Noriko, 1996, '"Haha to musume" o meguru feminizumu no genzai (The present [state] of feminism regarding "mothers and daughters"),' in Noriko Mizuta, Sachie Kitada and Kei Hasegawa (eds), *Haha to musume no feminizumu: kindai kazoku o koete* (The feminism of mothers and daughters: transcending the modern family), Tabata shoten, pp. 7–20.

Mobile Contents Forum (sup. ed.), Impress R & D Internet Media Sōgō Kenkyūjo (ed.), 2006, *Keitai hakusho 2006* (White paper on mobile telephones 2006), Impress.

Morioka, Kiyoshi, 2007, *Gaidobukku shakai chōsa dai-2 han* (Guidebook [on] social surveys, second edition), Nihon hyōronsha.

Morley, David, 1980, *The 'Nationwide' Audience: Structure and Decoding*, London: British Film Institute.

Muggleton, David and Rupert Weinzierl (eds), 2003, *The Post-Subcultures Reader*, Oxford; New York: Berg.

Murakami, Ryū, 2003, *Jū-san-sai no harō wāku* (The job centre at age thirteen), Gentōsha.

Nagae, Akira, 2002, *Intabyū-jutsu!* (Interview technique!), Kōdansha gendai shinsho.

Nagai, Hitoshi, 2000, *Manga wa tetsugaku suru* (*Manga* do philosophy), Kōdansha.

Nagai, Jun'ichi, 2007, '"Sanka" suru chōshū: Fuji rokku fesutibaru ni okeru kēsu sutadi (The "participating" audience: a case study of the Fuji Rock Festival),' in Nihon popyurā ongaku gakkai (Japanese association for the study of popular music), *Popyurā ongaku kenkyū* (Popular music studies), October: 96–111.

Naikakufu Seisaku Tōkatsu Kan (Director-General for Policy, Cabinet Office), 2005, *Heisei 17 seishōnen no shūrō ni kansuru kenkyū chōsa* (2005 research survey relating to youth employment).

Nakahara, Masaya, Yoshiki Takahashi, Melon Uminekozawa, and Shūichirō Sarashina, 2006, *Ken otaku ryū* (Hating the *otaku* wave), Ōta shuppan.

Nakamura, Isao, 2003, 'Keitai mēru to kodoku (Mobile phone email and loneliness),' in Matsuyama Daigaku Gakujutsu Kenkyūkai (ed.), *Matsuyama daigaku ronshū* (Matsuyama university collected papers), 14(6).

Nakanishi, Yasuko, 2004, 'Tomodachi oyako no nani ga warui?: "kazoku no naka no wakamono" to iu shiten (What is wrong with mother/daughter friendships?: the perspective of "young people within families"),' in Shinji Miyadai and Hiroki Suzuki (eds), *Nijūisseiki no genjitsu* (The realities of the twenty-first century), Minerva shobō, pp. 53–73.

Nanba, Kōji, 2007, *Zoku no keifugaku: yūsu sabukaruchāzu no sengo shi* (The genealogy of tribes: the post-war history of youth subcultures), Seikyūsha.

Nanbei@ Kōichi Suzuki, 2006, *Fesutibaru raifu: boku ga mita Nihon no yagai fesu jū-nen no subete* (Festival life: ten years of Japan's outdoor fests I saw, in their entirety), Marbletron.

Narumi, Hiroshi, 2007, 'Fasshon: ryūkō no seisan to shōhi (Fashion: the production and consumption of vogue),' in Kenji Satō and Shun'ya Yoshimi (eds.), *Bunka no shakaigaku* (Sociology of culture), Yūhikaku.

Natsume, Fusanosuke, 1997, *Manga wa naze omoshiroi no ka* (Why are *manga* entertaining?), Nippon hōsō shuppan kyōkai.

Natsume, Sachiko, 2005, 'Nihon no haha to musume (Japanese mothers and daughters),' in Caroline Eliacheff and Nathalie Heinich, *Dakara haha to musume wa muzukashii* (That's why mothers and daughters are difficult = *Mères-filles: une relation à trois*), trans. Sachiko Natsume, Hakusuisha, pp. 337–46.

Negus, Keith, 1996, *Popular Music in Theory: an Introduction*, Oxford: Polity Press.

NHK Hōsō Bunka Kenkyūjo (Broadcasting culture research institute) (ed.), 2003, *Terebi shichō no gojūnen* (Fifty years of television viewing), Nippon hōsō shuppan kyōkai.

NHK Hōsō Bunka Kenkyūjo (Broadcasting culture research institute) (ed.), 2004, *Gendai Nihonjin no ishiki kōzō, dai-6-ppan* (Attitude structure of contemporary Japanese people, sixth edition), Nippon hōsō shuppan kyōkai.

NHK Hōsō Yoron Kenkyūjo, 1983, *Terebi shichō no sanjūnen* (Thirty years of television viewing), Nippon hōsō shuppan kyōkai.

Nishida, Hiroshi, 2007, *Rokku fesutibaru* (Rock festivals), Shinchōsha.

Nishimura, Masanori, Tomoaki Ishibashi, Yukari Yamada and Wataru Koyano, 2000, 'Kōreiki ni okeru shitashii kankei (Intimate relationships in old age),' *Rōnen shakai kagaku* (Japanese journal of gerontology), 22(3): 367–74.

Nobuta, Sayoko, 1997, *Ichiransei oyako na kankei* (Monozygotic mother–daughter relationships), Shufunotomosha.

Ochiai, Emiko, 1994, *Nijūisseiki kazoku e* (Towards a twenty-first-century family), Yūhikaku.

Ochiai, Emiko, 2004, *Nijūisseiki kazoku e: kazoku no sengo taisei no mikata/ koekata* (Towards the twenty-first-century family: ways of looking at [and] transcending the post-war family system), Yūhikaku sensho.

Ochiai, Shinji, 2007, *Ongaku wa shinanai! Ongaku gyōkai no uragawa* (Music does not die! The reverse side of the music industry), Seikyūsha.

Ogawa, Hiroshi, 1988, *Ongaku suru shakai* (Societies that do music), Keisō shobō.

Oguma, Eiji, 1995, *Tan'itsu minzoku shinwa no kigen: 'Nihonjin' no jigazō no keifu* (The origin of the single ethnicity myth: the genealogy of the self-portrait of 'the Japanese'), Shin'yōsha. English version: *A Genealogy of 'Japanese' Self-images*, Melbourne: Trans Pacific Press, 2002.

Oguma, Eiji, 1998, *'Nihonjin' no kyōkai: Okinawa, Ainu, Taiwan, Chōsen. Shokuminchi shihai kara fukki undō made* (The boundaries of 'the Japanese': Okinawa, Ainu, Taiwan, Korea. From colonial control to reversion movements), Shin'yōsha.

Okada, Kōsuke, 2003, 'Ibento no seiritsu, popyurā bunka no seisan (The establishment of events, [and] the production of popular culture),' in Mamoru Tōya (ed.), *Popyurā ongaku e no manazashi: uru, yomu, tanoshimu* (Looking at popular music: selling, reading, enjoying), Keisō shobō.

Okada, Kōsuke, 2007, 'Ongaku: "yōgaku shijō shugi" no kōzō to kōyō (Music: the structure and utility of "Western-music-supremism"), in Kenji Satō and Shun'ya Yoshimi (eds), *Bunka no shakaigaku* (The sociology of culture), Yūhikaku, pp. 111–135.

Okada, Tomoyuki, 2002, 'Media henyō e no apurōchi: pokeberu kara keitai e (Approaches to media transformation: from pocket bells to mobile phones)' in Tomoyuki Okada and Misa Matsuda (eds), *Keitaigaku nyūmon: media komyunikēshon kara yomitoku gendai shakai* (Introduction to mobile phone studies: contemporary society deciphered from media communication), Yūhikaku sensho.

Onojima, Dai, 2002, 'Fuji rokku fesutibaru wa bokutachi ni nani o motarashita no ka (What did the Fuji Rock Festival provide us?),' *Myūjikku magajin* (Music magazine), September: 22–28.

Ōsawa, Masachi, 1996, *Kyokō no jidai no hate: Ōmu to sekai saishū sensō* (The ends of the age of fiction: Aum and Armageddon), Chikuma shobō.

Ōta, Shōichi, 2002, *Shakai wa warau: boke to tsukkomi no ningen kankei* (Society laughs: the human relationship between the funny man and straight man). Seikyūsha.

Ōtsuka, Eiji, [1989] 2001, *Teihon monogatari shōhi ron* (Authentic book on story-consumption), Kadokawa shoten.

Ōtsuka, Eiji, 2003, *Kyarakutā shōsetsu no tsukurikata* (How to make a character[-based] novel), Kōdansha.

Ozawa, Masako [1985] 1989, *Shin, kaisō shōhi no jidai: shotoku kakusa no kakudai to sono eikyō* (New [edition], The age of stratified consumption: the expansion of income disparity and its impact), Asahi bunko.

OZmagazine, 2007, no. 419: 22.

Parsons, Talcott, 1961, 'Introduction to Part Four,' in Talcott Parsons, Edward Shils, Kaspar D. Naegele and Jesse R. Pitts (eds), *Theories of Society: Foundations of Modern Sociological Theory*, New York: The Free Press of Glencoe, pp. 963–93.

Pia, 2007, Kansai Edition, no. 623, 14 June.

Rheingold, Howard, 1994, *The Virtual Community: Homesteading on the Electronic Frontier*, New York, NY: HarperPerennial.

Rheingold, Howard, 2003, *Smart Mobs: The Next Social Revolution*, Cambridge, MA: Basic Books.

Ryūkō kansoku (Trend watching), 1997, October, ACROSS Books.

Sakaguchi, Hiroko, 1997, 'Fushigi shōjo no yūwaku (The allure of the mysterious girl),' *Bart*, 27 January, Shūeisha.

Sakuta, Keiichi, 1981, *Kojin shugi no unmei: kindai shōsetsu to shakaigaku* (The destiny of individualism: the modern novel and sociology), Iwanami shoten.

Sakuta, Keiichi and Shigeki Tominaga (eds), 1984, *Jison to kaigi: bungei shakaigaku o mezashite* (Self-esteem and skepticism: aiming for literary sociology), Chikuma shobō.

Sasakibara, Gō, 2004, *'Bishōjo' no gendaishi: 'moe' to kyarakutā* (The contemporary history of 'beautiful girls': the euphoric response to fantasy characters, and [those] characters), Kōdansha.

Satō, Takeshi, 1990, *Masukomi no juyō riron: gensetsu no ika-baikaiteki henkan* (Mass communications reception theory: the differentiation-mediating transformation of discourse), Hōsei daigaku shuppan kyoku.

Shinjō, Kazuma, 2006, *Raito noberu 'chō' nyūmon* (A 'super' introduction to the light novel), Softbank creative.

Shiota, Sakiko, 1992, 'Gendai feminizumu to Nihon no shakai seisaku (Contemporary feminism and Japanese social policy),' *Joseigaku to seiji jissen: Joseigaku kenkyū, dai-2-gō* (Women's studies and political practice: Research in women's studies, no. 2), Keisō shobō, pp. 29–52.

Shiraishi, Nobuko, Miwako Hara and Daisuke Terui, 2005, 'Nihonjin to terebi. 2005: terebi shichō no genzai (The Japanese and television. 2005: the present age of television viewing,' *Hōsō kenkyū to chōsa* (Broadcasting research and surveys), 55(8): 2–35.

Shōji, Yōko, 1997, 'Kōgakureki shakai to tomodachi oyako (High-academic-achievement society and parent-child friendships),' *Kikan kodomogaku* (Child science quarterly), 14: 119–124.

Simmel, Georg, [1908] 2009, *Sociology: Inquiries into the Construction of Social Forms* (2 vols) (*Soziologie: Untersuchungen über die Formen der Vergesellschaftung*, Leipzig: Duncker and Humblot), trans. and ed. Anthony J. Blasi, Anton K. Jacobs and Mathew Kanjirathinkal, with an intro. by Horst J. Helle, Boston: Brill Academic Publishers.

Simmel, Georg, [1911] 1976, 'Fashion,' *American Journal of Sociology*, 62,(6): 541–58, in Shūhei Maruko and Kenji Ōkubo (trans), *Jinmeru chosaku shū* (Collected works of Simmel), Hakusuisha.

Smith, Anthony D., 1986, *The Ethnic Origins of Nations*, Oxford, England: Blackwell.

Smith, Anthony D., 1998, *Nationalism and Modernism: a Critical Survey of Recent Theories of Nations and Nationalism*, London: Routledge.

Stone, Allucquére Rosanne, 1995, *The War of Desire and Technology at the Close of the Mechanical Age*, Cambridge, MASS: MIT Press.

Suzuki, Kensuke, 2003, 'Dōshite koi o suru dake de wa shiawase ni narenai no ka: Yazawa Ai ni okeru inosento (Why can one not become happy merely by being in love? The innocent in Ai Yazawa),' *Yurīka* (Eureka), November, Seidosha.

Suzuki, Kensuke, 2005, *Kānibaruka suru shakai* (A society that turns into a carnival), Kōdansha.

Tagg, Philip, 1982, *Kojak – 50 Seconds of Television Music: toward the Analysis of Affect in Popular Music*, Göteborg: Musikvetenskapliga Institutionen (Studies from the Dept of Musicology, Göteborg, 2).

Takahashi, Shin, 2004, *Manga de wakaru tōkeigaku* (Statistics understood through comics), Ohmsha.

Takahashi, Shin, 2005, *Manga de wakaru tōkeigaku: kaiki bunseki hen* (Statistics understood through comics: regression analysis edition), Ohmsha.

Takahashi, Shin, 2006, *Manga de wakaru tōkeigaku: inshi bunseki hen* (Statistics understood through comics: factor analysis edition), Ohmsha.

Takahashi, Shin, and Trend-pro Co., Ltd, 2008, *The Manga Guide to Statistics*, San Francisco: No Starch Press.

Takarajimasha, 2008, 'Takarajima channeru: media gaido (Takarajima channel: media guide),' Takarajimasha, http://tkj.jp/press/media/*CUTiE*.html.

Takeda, Seiji, 2001, *Gengoteki shikō e: datsukōchiku to genshōgaku* (Towards linguistic though: deconstruction and phenomenology), Komichi shobō.

Takeshita, Toshio, 1998, 'Masu media no riyō to kōka (The use and effectiveness of mass media),' in Ikuo Takeuchi, Kazuto Kojima and Yoshiaki Hashimoto (eds), *Media komyunikēshon ron* (On media communication), Hokuju shuppan, pp. 159–75.

Takeshita, Toshio, Makoto Nakada, Keiko Kodama and Ryō Makita, 1978, 'Seikatsu fasshon-shi no "riyō to manzoku" kenkyū ("Uses and gratifications studies" of lifestyle fashion magazines),' *Shinbun kenkyū* (Newspaper studies), Nihon shinbun kyōkai, no. 322: 82–91.

Takeuchi, Ikuo, 1990, *Masu komyunikēshon no shakai riron* (Social theory of mass communication), Tōkyō daigaku shuppan kai.

Tani, Tomio (ed.), 1996, *Raifu hisutorī o manabu hito no tame ni* (For people who learn [about] life histories), Sekaishisōsha.

Tanimoto, Naho, 2006, 'Monogatari no yokubō ni kōshite (Resisting the desire in a narrative: with a focus on 'growth' in popular culture),' in Kazuma Yoshimura and Yoshiaki Fukuma (eds), *"Hadashi no Gen" ga ita fūkei* (The scene where *Barefoot Gen* was), Azusa shuppan, pp. 87–118.

Tarde, Gabriel de, [1901] 1989, *L'opinion et la foule*, Paris: Presses universitaires de France.

Thompson, John B., 1995, *The Media and Modernity*, Cambridge: Polity Press.

Tsuji, Izumi, 2003, 'Keitai denwa o moto ni shita kakudai pāsonaru nettowāku chōsa no kokoromi: wakamono no yūjin kankei o chūshin ni (A study on growing personal networks on the memory bank of a mobile phone: from a viewpoint of friendship relations of contemporary youth),' *Shakai jōhōgaku kenkyū* (Journal of Socio-Information Studies), vol. 7: 97–111.

Tsuji, Izumi, 2004, 'Popyurā bunka no kiki: Janīzu fan wa "asobete iru no ka" (The crisis in popular culture: are Johnny's fans "able to have fun"?),' in Shinji Miyadai and Hiroki Suzuki (eds), *Nijūisseiki no genjitsu: shakaigaku no chōsen* (The reality of the twenty-first century: the challenge of sociology), Minerva shobō, pp. 2–52.

Tsuji, Izumi, 2007, 'Kankeisei no rakuen/jigoku: Janīzi-kei aidoru o meguru fantachi no komyunikēshon (The paradise/hell of relationship: fans' communication over Johnny's-type idols),' in Hiroaki Tamagawa, Takako Nafuji, Yoshihiro Kobayashi, Takayuki Okai, Sonoko Azuma and Izumi Tsuji, *Sorezore no fan kenkyū* (Various fan studies): *I am a fan*, Fūjinsha, pp. 243–89.

Tsuruta, Sachie and Tomone Komiya, 2007, 'Hitobito no jinsei o kijutsu suru (Describing people's lives),' *Soshioroji* (Sociology), 52(1): 21–36.

Turkle, Sherry, 1995, *Life on the Screen: Identity in the Age of the Internet*, New York: Simon and Schuster.

Ueno, Chizuko, [1982] 1992, 'Shōhin: sabetsuka no akumu (Commodities: the nightmare of differentiation),' in *Zōho 'watashi'-sagashi gēmu* (Expanded [edition], the search-for-'me' game), Chikuma gakugei bunko.

Ueno, Toshiya, 2005, *Āban toraibaru sutadīzu: pāti, kurabu bunka no shakaigaku* (Urban tribal studies: the sociology of party and club culture), Getsuyōsha.

Veblen, Thorstein, B., [1889] 1973, *The Theory of the Leisure Class: An*

Economic Study of Institutions, introd. John Kenneth Galbraith, Boston: Houghton Mifflin.

Wakabayashi, Mikio, 2003, *Toshi e no/kara no shisen* (The gaze towards/from the city), Seikyūsha.

Wakabayashi, Mikio, 2007, *Kōgai no shakaigaku: gendai o ikiru katachi* (Sociology of the suburbs: forms of living in the present), Chikuma shobō.

Wallace, Patricia, 2001, *The Psychology of the Internet*, Cambridge, UK; New York: Cambridge University Press.

Watanabe, Hiroshi, 1989, *Chōshū no tanjō: posuto-modan jidai no ongaku bunka* (The birth of the audience: music culture in the post-modern age), Shunjūsha.

Watanabe, Kazuhiro and Tarako Productions, 1984, *Kinkonkan: gendai ninki shokugyō sanjūichi no kanemochi binbōnin no hyōsō to chikara to kōzō* (Kinkonkan: the surface layer, power and structure of the wealthy [and] paupers in thirty-one contemporary popular occupations), Shufuno-tomosha.

Weber, Max, [1922] 1962, *Basic Concepts in Sociology*, trans. H.P. Secher, New York: The Citadel Press.

Williams, Raymond, 1958, *Culture and Society: 1780–1950*, London: Chatto and Windus.

Willis, Paul E., 1977, *Learning to Labour: How Working Class Kids Get Working Class Jobs*, Farnborough, England: Saxon House.

Yamada, Masahiro, 1997, 'Tomodachi oyako ga katarareru haikei (The background to discussion of parent-child friendship),' *Kikan kodomogaku* (Child science quarterly), 14: 16–21.

Yamada, Masahiro, 1999, 'Aijō sōchi toshite no kazoku: kazoku dakara aijō ga waku no ka, aijō ga waku kara kazoku na no ka (The family as an affectional mechanism: does love grow because it is a family, [or] is it a family because love grows?),' in Yoriko Meguro and Hideki Watanabe (eds), *Kōza shakaigaku 2: kazoku* (Course [in] sociology: the family), Tōkyō daigaku shuppan kai, pp. 119–51.

Yamamoto, Naoki, [1992] 1997, *YOUNG & FINE: umibe no machi de bokura wa nakayoshi datta ka* (Were we pals in the seaside town?), Futabasha.

Yamamoto, Naoki, 1995, *Arigatō* (Thanks), Shōgakukan.

Yamamoto, Naoki, 1997, *Furagumentsu I* (*Fragments I*), Shōgakukan.

Yamamoto, Naoki, 2000, *Birībāzu* (Believers), Shōgakukan.

Yamamoto, Naoki, 2007–, *Reddo* (Red), Kōdansha.

Yanabu, Akira, 1995, *Bunka: ichigo no jiten* (Culture: a single-word dictionary), Sanseidō.

Yazawa, Ai, 2000–2003, *Paradise Kiss*, 5 vols, Shōdensha.

Yoshimi, Shun'ya, 1998, 'Karuchuraru sutadīzu no media komyunikēshon kenkyū (Media communication research in cultural studies),' in Ikuo Takeuchi, Kazuto Kojima and Yoshiaki Hashimoto (eds), *Media komyunikēshon ron* (On media communication), Hokuju shuppan, pp. 176–94.

Yoshimi, Shun'ya and Mikio Wakabayashi (eds), 2005, *Tōkyō sutadīzu* (Tokyo studies), Kinokuniya shoten.

Yoshino, Kōsaku, 1997, *Bunka nashonarizumu no shakaigaku* (The sociology of cultural nationalism), Nagoya daigaku shuppan kai.

Yuyama, Reiko, 2005, *Kurabu karuchā* (Club culture), Mainichi shinbunsha.
Zenkoku Shuppan Kyōkai Shuppan Kagaku Kenkyūjo (ed.), 2007, *2007 shuppan shihyō*[,] *nenpō* (2007 publishing index[,] annual report), Zenkoku shuppan kyōkai shuppan kagaku kenkyūjo.
Žižek, Slavoj, 2002, 'The Interpassive Subject,' http://www.lacan.com/interpassf.htm.

Note. With Yamamoto (1995), Yamamoto (2000), Kuramochi (2001) and Furutani (2005), the list indicates the year of publication of the final instalment.

Index

active receiver 105, 111, 115, 118
active television viewing 119–21
addiction 93–4, 102
Adorno, Theodore W. 18, 176, 191
AGIL paradigm 5
alienation 236, 238, 242
anime/animation 11, 37, 46, 55, 60, 150, 153–4, 156–9, 161–4, 168–9
analyses of favourite things 38
Anderson, Benedict 262
audience 9, 23–4, 26, 37, 105–8, 111–12, 114–21, 152, 173–9, 183, 183–4, 191
Azuma, Hiroki 156–8, 164, 167, 244

baby boomer 205
bait-and-switch 249, 251, 253, 257–9
Barthes, Ronald 45
Baudrillard, Jean 156
Bauman, Zygmunt 190, 250
Best, Joel 131
Billig, Michael 263
bishōjo (beautiful girl) 149–51, 153–5, 160–1, 163–6, 170
Bourdieu, Pierre 55–7, 60
Brubaker, Rogers 265–6
Burgess, Ernest W. 49–50, 60, 215

Cantril, Hadley 18, 110
career advancement 249–50, 253, 255–7, 259
carnival communities 190
character 8, 10–12, 190–22, 24, 26–7, 29–32, 35, 38, 42, 48, 53–4, 75, 85, 88–9, 101–2, 108–10, 113, 115, 118, 126, 128–30, 134, 136, 149–55, 157–65, 170, 175, 178, 183, 200–1, 204, 225–8, 231–2, 244, 252, 271, 275–7
cloakroom communities 190
cluster analysis 275, 280
communication 9–10, 15, 17, 19, 22, 27, 35, 37–40, 47, 52–3, 83–4, 86, 88–92, 94–6, 102, 108–12, 119, 121–23, 127–8, 140, 144, 146–8, 165, 167, 171, 173–4, 183, 188–9, 191, 206, 222, 244
connectibility 88, 90, 101–2
conspicuous consumption 124
Coser, Lewis A. 46
Crane, Diana 6–7
critical school 14, 17–19, 23, 27–9, 33
cross-tabulation table 75
cultural capital 55
cultural diamond 7
cultural mediator 184
cultural objects 7

cultural studies 7, 17, 23–4, 26–9, 54–5, 263
cultural tastes 53, 55, 127

data-base consumption 159
dead-end job 250–1
death of the author 45
decoding 24, 112, 115, 118
deconstructivist 46
Derrida, Jacques 45
differentiation 10, 122, 124–8, 131, 134, 137, 139, 142–8, 249

Ehrenreich, Barbara 251–2
empirical school 14, 17–19, 22–3, 27–8, 33–4
encoding 24, 112, 115, 118
ethno-symbolism 261–3
existence 15–6, 18, 24, 34, 60, 122, 137, 139, 144, 148, 155, 166, 171, 173, 176, 180, 218–19, 221, 223–5, 227, 232, 241–5, 254, 279

factor analysis 34, 268, 271, 274–5, 279–80
fan 8, 15–16, 19–27, 29–35, 52–3, 114, 116, 133, 150, 152–3, 156–7, 171–3, 175, 181–2, 190–2
fantasy 152, 157, 159, 162, 222, 224, 228, 244
faza-kon (father complex) 201
Fiske, John 24–5
freeter (freelance casual worker) 247–8
friend-like parent and child 203
friend-like parent/child dyad 195

Fuji Rock Festival 171, 174, 177, 180, 186–7, 191–2, *see also* rock

Galapagosisation of Japan 86
Gans, Herbert 53
Gellner, Ernest 262
general education 48
generalised others 144
Giddens, Anthony 196, 201
globalisation 8, 12, 104, 263
Goffman, Erving 115
goth/goth-loli 133
Griswold, Wendy 7

habitus 56
Hall, Stuart 24, 35, 112, 263
Hebdige, Dick 54
Hoggart, Richard 23, 54
hypothesis-confirmatory survey 66

idol 10, 15, 29–32, 35, 52, 114, 116, 151–3, 155
Inaba Shin'ichirō 158–9, 164
Inamasu Tatsuo 115–16, 151
informant 44, 64, 67–70, 72–3, 76–80, 179, 186, 188, 190
Inoue Shun 46, 58, 124, 245
interactive television viewing 119–20
International Social Survey Programme *see* ISSP
interpassive subjects 121
intertexuality 45
interview survey 9, 55, 61–2, 66–8, 71–2, 76–7, 79, 160, 174, 191, 216
Iser, Wolfgang 45
ISSP 260, 264–5, 278–9

Japanese-style welfare society 12, 247, 249, 253–5

Kashiwagi Hiroshi 126–7
Kihara Yoshihiko 166–7
ko-gyaru 122, 128, 131, 133–4, 136–7, 139–45
Kristeva, Julia 45

Lazarsfeld, Paul F. 110–11
Lévi-Strauss, Claude 48–9, 60
literary criticism 41, 46
lost decade 248

Madonna 24–6, 35
manga 11, 74, 129, 138, 157, 161–4, 169–70, 198–9, 202, 218, 225–7, 240, 245, 279
Mannheim, Karl 5
Maruyama Masao 7
Marx, Karl H. 4–5, 17
mass communication 108–12, 121, 123
mass media 16–17, 54, 58, 106–7, 109–12, 117, 132, 167, 170, 184, 261, 263, 280
maza-kon (mother complex) 201
Mead, G. H. 137
media-and-group culture 8, 14–19, 22–3, 26–35
minimal effects model 110–11
Miura Atsushi 146–8, 220–1, 223–4
Miyadai Shinji 11, 34, 38, 43, 128, 139, 222–4, 243–4, 246
mobile phones 9, 15–16, 35, 83–7, 96, 102–3, 123

modernism 261–3
moe 10–11, 123, 129, 149–50, 155, 157, 159–60, 163–5, 168, 170
multi-method approach 14, 27–30, 33–4

Nanba Kōji 128, 148
Narumi Hiroshi 133
nation 12, 37, 54, 261–3, 265–7, 271–2, 280
national identity 260–1, 263–5, 275–8
nationalism 260, 262, 277–8
Negus, Keith 184, 191
new type 3
nori (being 'into it') 177, 182, 190

observers 115–16, 118–20
Oda Kazumasa 20–2, 27, 34
Ogawa Hiroshi 152, 177, 181
onlooker 115
opinion leaders 111
otaku 10, 15–16, 34, 128, 149–51, 155–7, 159–61, 164–6, 168—70
Ōta Shōichi 118, 121
Ōtsuka Eiji 157–8

parent/child friendship 195, 200, 214 *see also* friend-like parent/child dyad; friend-like parent and child
Parsons, Talcott 5
patriotism 12, 269, 276
post-structuralist 46
powerful effects model 18, 110–11

proper name 39–40, 48–50, 53
pure relationship 196, 202, 213–14

questionnaire survey 9–10, 31, 34, 55, 61–3, 65, 67, 71–5, 79, 96, 204

random sampling 76–7
receiver 7, 10, 19–20, 22–4, 26–7, 29, 41–2, 45, 57, 105, 108–12, 114–16, 118–21, 158
recorded culture 6–7
region 6, 11, 161, 184, 218–28, 234–5, 240–2, 244–6
Rheingold, Howard 16, 94
rhetorical analysis 10, 131
rock 11, 29–33, 35, 42, 49, 50–2, 60, 125–6, 171–2, 174–8, 180, 182–3, 185–7, 189, 191–2
  Arabaki Rock Festival 180, 182–3, 185
  Fuji Rock Festival 171, 174, 177, 180, 186–7, 191–2
  Rising Sun Rock Festival 171, 174–5, 189, 191

Sakuta Kei'ichi 46, 227, 245
self-enclosed individuality 141, 143, 146, 148
semi-structured interview 68
sender 10, 19, 24, 27, 29, 57, 108–12, 115–16, 118–21
Simmel, Georg 125, 272
Smith, Anthony D. 262–3, 271
SNS 84, 188, 190–1
social individuality 143, 146
social reality 78–9

social strata 43–4, 54–5, 125–6, 1128, 131, 143, 47
socialisation 58–9
sociology of knowledge 6
specialisation 12, 247–9, 253, 255–9
spectatorly-appreciative television viewing 119
spectators 113, 119–20
Stone, Allucquére Rosanne 92
story consumption 157, 160
street fashion 122, 125, 133
structural hearing 176–7
structured interview 67–8, 80
suburb 11, 205, 220–3, 227, 241
subversive riposte 10, 105, 114–18, 120–1

Thompson, John H. 108–10
Tominaga Shigeki 46, 245
trickle-down theory 124
Tsurumi Shunsuke 7
Turkle, Sherry 91–2

unstructured interview 67
uses and gratifications studies 23

value-free 44
Veblen, H. B. 124–5

Wallace, Patricia 90–1
Watanabe Hiroshi 147, 175
Weber, Max 43–4
Worth, C. F. 124

Yamamoto Naoki 11, 60, 218, 225–44, 246
Yoshino Kōsaku 262
youth labour 11, 247–8